TRIBAL DEVELOPMENT AND ITS ADMINISTRATION

About the Editor

Lalita Prasad Vidyarthi (*b*. 1931) received his doctorate from the University of Chicago and is now Professor and Chairman of the Department of Anthropology at the University of Ranchi, India. Currently (1974-1978) he is the President of the International Union of Anthropological and Ethnological Sciences and of the 10th International Congress of Anthropological and Ethnological Sciences to be held in India in 1978. Dr. Vidyarthi is the President of the Indian Anthropological Association, a Founder-Member of the Indian Council of Social Sciences Research, Chairman of the Task Force on Development of Tribal Areas of the Planning Commission, and a Member of the Central Council on Tribal Research Institute of the Ministry of Home Affairs, Government of India. He is Founder-Editor of The Journal of Social Research, The Indian Anthropologist, and The Research Journal of Ranchi University. His major fields of research are the Tribal Culture of India including the Andaman and Nicobar Islands; Urban-Industrial political, and action Anthropology; Indian Civilization, the History of Indian Culture, Folklore, village studies and History of Anthropological Theories. He has to his credit several internationally popular books.

TRIBAL DEVELOPMENT AND ITS ADMINISTRATION

Edited by

L.P. VIDYARTHI

CONCEPT PUBLISHING COMPANY PVT. LTD.
NEW DELHI-110059

ISBN: 978-93-5594-619-5

Edition 2023

Published and Printed by

Concept
Since 1974

Concept Publishing Company Pvt. Ltd.
A/15-16, Commercial Block, Mohan Garden,
New Delhi-110059 (India)
T: 91-11-41101460
E: publishing@conceptpub.com, *W*: www.conceptpub.com

INTRODUCTION

AMONG the myriad problems that this country is beset with perhaps none is more urgent and knotty than that of tribal development. Missionaries belonging to more than one denomination, voluntary agencies, governmental or quasi-governmental bodies both at Central and State levels, and individual crusaders in the cause of the tribals, have all entered the fray during the past three decades or more. Divergent views have been aired; schemes have been formulated and the motions of implementing them have been gone through. Yet today we still face the problem of under-development of our tribals in as acute if not a worse form than ever. Perhaps the reason can be attributed to several causes. Wherein lies the remedy ? This is the question that has been baffling the country's planners and policy-makers and those deeply involved in the welfare of the nation and the amelioration of the weak and defenceless millions of our countrymen many of whom live in the most appalling conditions of poverty—often below subsistence level—and ignorance. The problem seems to defy all solution particularly when extraneous forces have unwittingly or otherwise sought to influence these simple denizens of our forests and hills in the interior and the mountain fastnesses along our frontiers.

A great deal has doubtless been done to alleviate the condition of the tribals who are dotted all over this vast country. There are, however, pockets of tribal concentration which have latterly developed into hotbeds of uprising and insurgency. There has been a general disenchantment with the steps taken towards bringing these peoples into the mainstream of national life. Now is the time to take stock of the whole situation and plan more effectively for tribal development. Vital to such planning and its implementation is its administration and feed-back mechanism so that evaluation and assessment can be made almost simultaneously. The management of administration is an all-important factor in bringing this vexing problem of tribal under-development nearer solution or even in localizing and containing it until further ameliorative measures can be taken.

A gradual consensus of opinion has developed on the lines along which such development can be undertaken. What is noteworthy is the fact that the cooperation of anthropologists and specialists in the field has been sought by governmental agencies seized with the problems of administering for the tribals. Training programmes have been initiated involving anthropologists, administrators and planners so that concerted efforts can be made in the right direction and the benefits of development can percolate more evenly to the recipients thus paving the way for a speedier attainment of the goal of development.

What is important in any programme or planning for development is to take a holistic view of the problem and not merely to add up the sum of its various parts. Solutions must be sought with a view to ensuring the "health and happiness" of the population as a whole. Ad hocism in such volatile and at times inflammable situations would perhaps aggravate matters all the more.

Against this background we have put together several papers, most of them presented at a training and reorientation programme organized jointly by the Department of Personnel and Administrative Reforms, Ministry of Home Affairs, Government of India and the Department of Anthropology, Ranchi University in collaboration with the J.P. Institute of Social and Industrial Studies and the Administrative Training Institute, both at Ranchi. Several more have been added to present a fuller picture of the problem and the programmes along with their implementation. In so doing what has emerged is a fairly clear evaluation and assessment of what has been achieved or remains to be achieved during the past three decades and a reshaping of our programmes to suit the targets.

This volume has been divided into four parts and papers assigned to each part according to whether they deal with general issues, strategies, training programmes and institutions, implementation and case studies. The focus of the volume as a whole is necessarily on Tribal Development and its Administration.

Part I deals with General Issues, Anthropology, Administration and Development. The field here is held, as it were, by anthropologists. Professor Vidyarthi's main thrust in his paper "The Cultural Factors in Development Process" is the overwhelming need for planners and administrators to bear in mind the cultural background and life-styles of such tradition-bound societies. The concept of Nature-Man-Spirit complex epitomizes the life-styles of tribal communities and this can be ignored only at the risk of making planning programmes go off the rails with disastrous results.

Ajit K. Danda's article concerns the statutory provisions which have been made for safeguarding the interests of Scheduled Tribes and Scheduled Castes. It deals with each Article of the Constitution which incorporates such provisions and also mentions other safeguards made through certain Acts and Orders which are protective, ameliorative, and concessional in nature.

Forests and forest policy are very much a part of tribal development. To many tribal communities the forests provide shelter and food and the means to a livelihood. P.K. Bhowmick in his article on forests and forest policy pleads for an integrated approach to the development of forests as well as for meeting the needs of the tribal people.

V.S. Upadhyay's paper enumerates some of the special problems of minor tribes which emerged from his numerous field trips and which deserve the careful attention of planners. He discusses the anthropological considerations, mainly of a demographic character, which enable a tribal group to be considered as a minor group.

P.K. Bhowmick, in a second article, makes a survey of various reports on Scheduled Tribes and offers a critical appraisal along with strategies for development.

S.P. Sinha's paper gives an historical overview of tribal development administration from the days of British rule in India. He winds up by giving a grim warning against complacency in dealing with such problems. S.N. Ratha makes an appraisal of the problems of tribals and enunciates the anthropologist's and the sociologists's views on tribal development. K.B. Srivastava's paper is again a historical account though it mainly concentrates on the administrative aspects. Well-researched and documented, it concerns the stages through which the tribals of the Chotanagpur region have been administered.

Part II discusses the strategies of development. Bhupinder Singh deals in a competent manner and quite comprehensively with the problems of development among the major tribes and the strategy evolved to deal with them. Extensive notes and a select reading list should prove useful to both researcher and administrator.

B.K. Roy Burman, brings to bear his academic and analytical mind in suggesting strategies of tribal development.

K.K. Srivastava's paper focuses on the planning aspects of tribal development and the strategies that could be formulated based on earlier experiences during the Plan periods.

Hari Mohan Mathur presents a very strong case for strengthening administrative capability for the development of tribal regions which could be ignored at the cost of the very administration itself.

Part III contains four excellent papers by K.K. Srivastava, G.S. Grewal, S.M. Shah and S. Patankar on training programmes for the functionaries and personnel involved in tribal administration. Evaluation techniques have also been discussed and scientific management principles have been brought to bear on the subject of development administration. The right note is struck by S. Patankar in his paper where he says "The tribals themselves should be allowed to decide change and the development administration should only help the tribals to develop the ability to grasp the implication of change".

Part IV gives a wider perspective to tribal development. Beginning with S.K. Sharma's article which looks at the administrative issues involved in the problem of tribal underdevelopment, we pass on to L.M. Prasad's comprehensive survey of administration in tribal areas with special reference to Bihar. Extremely well-documented, the paper ends on the note : "Let the tribals feel that the administration is for them, of them and by them."

The significance of political, economic and social institutions have been analyzed in the various papers by A.C. Sinha,

A.R.N. Srivastava, S.P. Sinha, B.N. Sahay and A.P. Sinha thus providing a suitable background for the implementation of development projects.

Narayan Mishra and K.N. Sahay have given detailed and practical accounts of the methods, and techniques and tools of working with the tribals based on experiences during field work. The all-important aspect of education for tribals has been dealt with by S.N. Ratha and S.M. Shah. Shah's paper is an evaluation of the post-Matric scholarship scheme for Scheduled Tribes and Scheduled Castes. R. Gupta and A. N. Sandhwar brings up the rear with their case studies : one on Bidisha and the other on tribal Bihar. These studies serve to bring out the practical difficulties and shortcomings of project implementation and the need for an anthropological approach to development.

Taken together, the entire volume should help clear the cobwebs and impart a fresh outlook to planners and administrators who are actively involved in tribal development in this country.

The Editor wishes to thank the following for their cooperation and participation in the training programme as well as for contributing articles to this volume : The Union Ministry of Home Affairs, and in particular, Sri K. A. Chandrasekharan, Dr. Bhupinder Singh and Sri Hari Mohan Mathur; the faculty members and others who participated in the Training Programme organized by the Department of Personnel and Administrative Reforms; the participants of the programme from the Government of India and from the State governments of Bihar, West Bengal, Madhya Pradesh, Kerala, Tamilnadu, Maharashtra, Manipur and Karnataka who were instrumental in initiating discussion and feed-back; the staff members of the Department of Anthropology, Ranchi University, the J.P. Institute of Social and Industrial Studies, and the Administrative Training Institute, Ranchi.

The Editor would also like to take the opportunity to express his gratitude to Dr. S.P. Sinha, Visiting Professor and Dr. V. S. Upadhyay of the Department of Anthropology, University of Ranchi for their valuable assistance both in organizing the Training Programme and in editing the papers in a presentable form for the volume. To Mr. Naurang Rai and

Mrs. S. Ramaswamy thanks are due for their special efforts to make these papers available to a wider reading public within the shortest possible time.

The Training Programme out of which the idea of this volume in its present form grew, was organized by the Training Division, Department of Personnel and Administrative Reforms, Government of India under the Plan Scheme of Training and Personnel for Development Administration. Their cooperation is gratefully acknowledged here. The Editor would also like to express gratitude to them for making provision for the publication of this volume.

Finally, the individual authors alone are responsible for the opinions expressed in their respective articles. This volume has merely provided a forum for the free discussion and dissemination of views and ideas on tribal development administration.

RANCHI
10 December 1980

L. P. VIDYARTHI
Director of the Course

CONTENTS

PART II
STRATEGIES OF TRIBAL DEVELOPMENT

PART III
TRAINING PROGRAMMES

PART IV
INSTITUTIONS, IMPLEMENTATION AND CASE STUDIES

LIST OF CONTRIBUTORS

P. K. Bhowmick
Professor of Anthropology, Calcutta University, Calcutta

B. K. Roy Burman
Professor of Anthropology, Viswa Bharati, Shantiniketan, West Bengal

Ajit K. Danda
Deputy Director, Anthropological Survey of India, Eastern Region, 27 Jawaharlal Nehru Road, Calcutta

G. S. Grewal
Joint Secretary, Ministry of Home Affairs, Government of India, New Delhi

R. Gupta
Ex-Inspector General of Police, Bihar, and President, Institute of Social Anthropology, Calcutta

Hari Mohan Mathur
Joint Secretary, Ministry of Home Affairs, Government of India, New Delhi

Narayan Mishra
Professor in Anthropology, Ranchi University, Ranchi

S. Patankar
Director, Administrative Training Institute, Ranchi

L. M. Prasad
U. G. C. Teacher Fellow, Department of Anthropology, Ranchi University, Ranchi

S. N. Ratha
Professor of Anthropology and Sociology, Sambalpur University, Sambalpur

B. N. Sahay
Joint Director, P. E. O., Planning Commission, Yojana Bhawan, New Delhi

K. N. Sahay
University Professor, Department of Anthropology, Ranchi University, Ranchi

Abnindra Narayan Sandhwar
Postgraduate Department, of Anthropology, Ranchi University, Ranchi

S. M. Shah
Joint Secretary, Programme Evaluation Organisation, Planning Commission, New Delhi

Sudesh Kumar Sharma
Reader, Department of Public Administration, Punjab University, Chandigarh

Bhupinder Singh
Joint Secretary, Government of India, Ministry of Home Affairs, New Delhi

A. C. Sinha
Department of Sociology and Anthropology, North Eastern Hill University, Shillong

Anand Prasad Sinha
Judicial Commissioner, Chotanagpur, District Ranchi

S. P. Sinha
Visiting Professor, U. G. C. Centre of Special Assistance in Anthropology, Ranchi University, Ranchi

A. R. N. Srivastava
Reader in Anthropology, Ravishanker University, Raipur, Madhya Pradesh

K. B. Srivastava
Director, Akhil Memorial Institute, Rathu Road, Ranchi

K. K. Srivastava
Adviser, Planning Commission, Yojana Bhawan, New Delhi, D. G. of Tourism

K. K. Srivastava
Adviser, Planning Commission of India, Yojana Bhawan, New Delhi

V. S. Upadhyay
Department of Anthropology, Ranchi University, Ranchi

L. P. Vidyarthi
Professor and Head, Department of Anthropology, Ranchi University, Ranchi

PART I

GENERAL ISSUES

Anthropology, Administration and Development

ONE

L. P. Vidyarthi

THE CULTURAL FACTORS IN DEVELOPMENT PROCESS
Case Studies from Tribal Bihar

WHILE WRITING the introduction to the book, *Cultural Factors in Technological Change*, Spicer rightly observes that changing people's customs is an even more delicate responsibility than surgery. When a surgeon takes up his instruments he assumes the responsibility for a human life. On his skill and judgment during each moment of an operation depends the future of the individual. The administrator of a programme engaged in a development programme carries a heavier responsibility. When he seeks to alter a people's way of life, he is dealing not with one individual, but with the well-being and happiness of generations of men and women (Spicer, E.H. : 1952). As a "social" doctor, he has to diagnose the disease, prescribe the medicine, and follow up the treatment with utmost caution in such a way that "health and happiness" are ensured to the community as a whole.

In their zeal to "better the lives" of others, planners and administrators overlook the cultural background of the community and make desperate efforts to alter the way of life by introducing modern technology and methods even in tradition-bound societies. Such desperate efforts to interfere with the life styles of the people sometimes by a team or by sponsors of cross-cultural missions is bound to meet with "resistance".

Our researches among the various dimensions of Indian society go to establish that people resist such changes that go to interfere with their respective core culture or their basic cultural adjustments. They also resist the proposed changes they either do not understand or interpret differently in their respective cultural background. In some cases, the resistance is of an emotional nature too, as a plan or project is imposed on them without taking them into confidence.

The operations of such cultural factors in the development processes, can be better illustrated from my study of the tribal belt of Bihar.

II

If we examine the tribes of Bihar in terms of their cultural types considering their ecological and economic adaptations, they may be classified into five categories : (1) Forest hunting type, (2) Hill-cultivation type, (3) Settled agriculture type, (4) Simple artisan type, and (5) Industrial and non-industrial labour type (Vidyarthi : 1958).

Cultural Ecology and Nomadic Hunters

The first set of tribes is typically represented by the Birhor (3464) who are in the stage of hunting and food gathering, and only a few of them have a rather tenuous attachment to the agricultural practises as casual labourers. The efforts of the Government to introduce agriculture in a section of the nomadic Birhor in Ranchi district have almost failed and the traditional adjustment of the Birhor with the ecology and related economy could not be modified very much. It is rather exclusively a cultural problem to rehabilitate the Birhor or similar marginal and pre-farming tribes through agricultural practices.

Considering the ecological, ethnological, demographic and cultural settings of the Birhor, I initiated the study of four Birhor villages (locally known as *Tandas*) as early as 1955 and the ethnographic details were reported in a paper presented at the Fifth International Congress of Anthropological and Ethnological Sciences held at Philadelphia in 1956 (Vidyarthi : 1960). The demographic details of these four temporary migratory villages in that year were as follows:

Demography of the Birhor (1955)

Name of village	No. of families	No. of migratory groups	No. of huts	No. of persons	Distance from Bishunpur Police Station
Manjira	3	2	9	27	3 M.S.E.
Sorka	2	1	3	9	2 M.S.E.
Chatakpur	7	3	10	23	10 M.N.W.
Narma	3	3	5	10	8 M.N.W.
	15	9	27	74	

From the table it is clear that the four villages in the year 1955 were located in the two regions of Bishunpur P.S., each in a group of two. In each region the two *Tandas* were in close proximity, while the two regions south-east and north-west were far apart. Economically the location of these Birhor *Tanda* was mainly determined by three factors : (a) close proximity to the forest, (b) accessibility to the weekly market and some neighbouring villages, (c) a reasonable distance from other such Birhor *Tanda* to avoid the sharing of the same forest or market.

The first factor was chosen from the point of view of the availability of food resources and other forest products. Unlike most other nomadic tribes of the world, Birhor economy of these villages does not revolve round cattle or horses but round the forests. Their very name indicates that they are the "people of the forest" (*Bir*-forest, *hor*-man). Wherever they go they make fairly water-proof huts from the materials collected in abundance from the forest. The daily routine of these villagers consisted in going to the forest for hunting and food gathering, particularly, for monkey-hunting for which they were famous. Other notable games were rabbits, wild goats, and squirrels. Next to hunting, their second economic occupation was rope-making. From the forest, they extracted chop-strings from suitable trees andused to make ropes out of them. Both the male and female Birhor were expert in rope-making, and this craft found increased emphasis owing to a growing local demand. These Birhor also made certain wooden objects like the frames of drums, bowls, pestle and mortars. A particular area was occupied by these Birhor families till either the resources of the forests were exhausted on the one hand or the demand of the products made by them fell off. On these resources depended the size and number of *Tandas* as also the duration of their stay in a particular area. .

The second important factor, the proximity to the market and nearness to agriculturists' villages, helped them in disposing of jungle products, the home-made ropes, and wooden objects. While these *Tandas* were located on the one hand in the forested foot-hill zone, they were on the other hand, near the two markets. The Birhor of Manjira and Serka *Tandas* used to go to Bishunpur weekly market on every Thursday, while the Birhor of Chatakpur and Narma *Tandas* used to go to Banari weekly market on Monday. From the respective groups of villages Bishunpur market would be at a distance of about two or three miles while Benari would fall within four miles from the other group of villages. On market day each Birhor family used to sell things worth Rs. 5 The Birhor also used to go to the neighbouring villages with their goods and exchange them for grain (Sinha, D.P. : 1968).

These migratory groups of the Birhor stayed at a particular place till the raw materials and food stuff in the forest were exhausted. They also saw to it that the needs of the local people for ropes and wooden articles were adequately met for some time. The study of the nature and extent of migration also brought out an interesting point that in some cases a migratory group wandered from place to place in quest of food and market in a cyclical order.

The major change in the Birhor culture of these four *Tandas* was marked with the implementation of the "Birhor Resettlement Scheme" of the Government of Bihar according to which two colonies Jehangutua and Beti were formed to accommodate the Birhor of the above mentioned four *Tandas*. This scheme was planned firstly to put an end to the nomadic life of the Birhor, and secondly to convert the forest economy of the Birhor to an agricultural economy.

Under this scheme each family was persuaded to resettle in these two colonies and each family was usually given 5 acres of wasteland, a mud-hut, a pair of bullocks, a cow, agricultural implements, seeds, and then an initial subsistence allowance for seven months till the land, was reclaimed and crops raised. In addition, a common provision of a school, rope-making-cum-production centre, community hall and minor irrigation schemes were initiated at an initial cost of Rs. 1,30,000 in the year 1957-58. As a result fifteen mud dwellings at Jehengutua and thirty of them at Beti were constructed.

With the adoption of a sedentary life and agricultural occupation the Birhor economy has undergone a major change. The two colonies have been exhaustively studied by the members of this department at frequent intervals, the last being in February, 1980. From all these reports it is clear that while the Birhor have not been able to develop an agricultural economy, their traditional forest economy has been greatly disorganised. The Birhor could not develop an agricultural economy owing to several reasons, mention among them may be made of the following :

Firstly, some portion of the land allotted to the Birhor was claimed by the local villagers. They did not feel happy that their land was given to the nomadic Birhor families for their settlement in their neighbourhood. Some of the Birhor were frightened by these persons and were asked not to plough the land. Buddanam was threatened to be killed if he would cultivate the land, and he preferred to leave the colony instead of losing his life. The leader of the colony, Manjira Birhor was similarly frightened. As the Government officials were at the back of the Birhor, they could cultivate the disputed land but it aggravated the tension and a Birhor does not dare go into the nearby villages in the night lest he be killed.

Secondly, the allotment of the wasteland (upland) to the non-agricultural Birhor with almost no knowledge about cultivation has proved to be an impediment. Even after two decades of settlement they do not feel attracted to cultivation and prefer to go to the forest in quest of game and raw materials.

Thirdly, the inadequate and irregular supply of agricultural implements, bullocks, seeds, proved further impediments in the exploitation of the wasteland.

Owing to the above factors, the Birhor feel discouraged to undertake cultivation seriously and they still look to the forest as the major source of subsistence.

The processes of sedentarisation, again, was adversely affected because of the poor housing scheme adopted by the Government without caring for their cultural background. The Birhor traditionally living in leaf thatched huts have failed to live, and maintain mud-houses with big windows and tiled roofs, and most of the houses were reduced to ruins within a year or two. Some of the Birhor families abandoned the houses and reverted to the migratory life again. Passing through all these hazards of socio-ecological adjustments presently, there are only 17 families of the Birhor in Beti and 8 families of Birhor at Jahangutua. Some of them again have reverted to their traditional huts, which they have constructed on the respective sites of resettlement.

The forest again has become unsuitable and inadequate to support these twenty five families on a permanent footing. Their market for their finished articles has also become limited and constant. This has brought about competition among the Birhor sellers themselves. The demand curve owing to constant and large supply has gone down in the market. Malhotra (1968) reported in the mid sixties, that the price of wooden articles and ropes had gone down by 20 per cent to 30 per cent. As regards, the price of monkeys, it has also gone down owing to the entry of middle men, between the actual purchasers and sellers. The local officials of the Forest Department also come in the picture now, who force the Birhor to sell the monkeys through them. But owing to their constant visits and that also in large numbers, the monkey has fallen short in supply and has become quite rare in the forest.

In view of all these, while the income of the Birhor from their traditional occupation has gone down, the newly adopted occupation has not yet contributed materially. Moreover, the items of expenditure have also increased owing to the changes in the housing condition. Originally, the Birhor used to live in the leaf thatched huts which protected them adequately from cold in the winter, and from water in the rainy season. But this poorly constructed mud-structures with country tiles, and more than necessary ventilation and accommodation have created the need for blankets for the Birhor in the winter and adequate repairs of the house during the rainy season.

As this area falls in the Multi-purpose tribal block, and

as it is a much talked of scheme of the Government of Bihar, this scheme has been followed up to see how the phase of transition has in due course led to the process of disintegration among the nomadic Birhor in the course of a quarter century.

The Cultural Ethos of the Shifting Cultivators

The second type of tribes which are unfortunately very few in Bihar, but numerous in other States of middle and north eastern India, practise slash and burn a type of rotational cultivation popularly known as shifting or *Jhum* cultivation. In my study of the Maler tribe of Rajmahal hills in Santhal Parganas, it has been established that they have developed a style of life suited to the particular natural surroundings that has been termed as Nature-Man-Spirit Complex (Vidyarthi : 1963). Their entire economy and socio-cultural relationship have been adjusted to *Kurwa* style of shifting cultivation. For them the forest is not non-agricultural land but it provides the main economic base for the shifting cultivation. The problem of rational used of terrace cultivation as well as of *Bari* (horticulture) and *Dhani* (paddy) cultivation are again socio-cultural problems. The mere efforts to provide them with an alternative agricultural economy on the plains attempted by the Bihar Government during the sixties have failed and finally the Dhebar Commission has recommended a complete discontinuation of re-settlement schemes among the hill tribes of Bihar (Report Dhebar Commission).

A reference about that scheme, however, provides a lesson for the planners and administrators to take cultural factors into consideration in the implementation of development programmes.

According to this scheme, the Paharia families were to be brought down in the plains and were given facilities to resettle there in colonies built by Government. The Paharia families, were given some two acres of land with bullocks, pigs, goats, hens and a cow. Grain and stipends for their maintenance were also given for the interim period till the crops were ready. The resettlement schemes were chalked out by Government, as far as I have been able to understand, in view of (protection or presentation of the forests which are in a state of devastation because of the slash and burn cultivation by the Maler Paharia and (2) effective implementation of uplift programmes, such as education, water supply, health and sanitation schemes which cannot be effectively operated if the Paharias remain on the hill tops.

With these purposes in view the administration undertook the first resettlement scheme of Parerkal in 1954, which was followed by Munda Pahar (1959), Dunarchir (1959) and Murgabani (1959) colonies. Among these colonies the first two colonies were thoroughly studied by me and the results have been published (Vidyarthi : 1968). In general, it has been noted that the Maler Paharia of high hilly villages showed a great deal of resistance against this type of geographical rehabilitation. They have developed a great love for the hill way of life. Their economy revolves round the forest and the efforts of the administration to better their economic lot and save the forest from their devastation by transferring the hill population to the plains do not appeal to them in the least.

The Factors of Cultural Resistance

From the "insiders' view" i.e. the natives, living on the hillsides is not a problem at all ; on the contrary, settling down on the plains is not as easy to them. The administrators' object and that of the social workers (both "outsiders") is to make modern amenities easily available to these hill-people on the plains and thus save the forest from destruction and denudation.

This "insiders' view" has developed owing to their unique cultural experiences. They eat all types of roots, leaves, fruit and game available in their forests. They have seen the ravage of famines down on the plains while they have escaped them on the hills owing to varieties of jungle products.

Secondly, their major economy revolves round the slash-and-burn cultivation, and in raising of maize. For them the maize is life itself. Their ritual calendar revolves round the *Khallu* or shifting cultivation and the maize. Their values and moral standards are determined by them. The woodman, the moral man is he who grows maize by the *Khallu* method.

Thirdly, their spirits and Gossainyans are settled in and

around the village on the hills which need to be worshipped in response to the tradition of the hill culture. They receive sacrifices on various *Khallu* operations. They are non-vegetarian to the extent that some of them accept sacrifices of calves, cows, buffaloes, which the plain dwelling tribes and castes may not allow.

Fourthly, the Paharia have developed a pattern of sexual life and a set of social customs, which they think can be maintained only in their forest habitat.

Fifthly, the hills, cut off from the plains, provide for them a safe place for brewing "mahua" which again, owing to the forest setting is found in abundance.

Sixthly, owing to their historical experiences the Maler do not like to live near the Santhal villages on the plains. Their mutual relations, usually, are of animosity, enmity and aggression.

Lastly, the Maler look at any scheme of the Government with suspicion. This is because of many factors exploitation of the Paharia during the British rule, the prevalence of and the recent increase in bribery and corruption among the local officials, the imposition of schemes without the consultation and co-operation of the Maler. They look at every scheme of the Government with suspicion and try to avoid them as far as possible. Some of them have their own ways of looking at these schemes. They believe that schools have been opened to take the young ones in the war; the grain golas have been started to entrap the Maler; the Maler are being taken down to the Plains as the Government want to acquire their property on the hills etc. etc. These are some of the stereotype attitudes of the Paharias which reflect as to how they have been interpreting the schemes of the Government.

To conclude then, the Maler villagers in view of their ecological setting and many historical experiences have developed a style of life, a type of "Nature-Man-Spirit Complex" which they are not prepared to abandon under any circumstances.

In view of these cultural considerations, in spite of all assurances and coercion, very few Maler families have come down to occupy these colonies. The efforts of the Government to resettle even typical Paharia families have proved an utter failure. The colonies constructed by them on the foot-hills, remained unoccupied for several years and finally were reduced to ruins.

Agricultural Tribes and Cultural Factors

The third type of tribes living on the undulating plains or plateaux are relatively more exposed to cultural transformation. These agricultural tribes live in the mixed villages of the tribal and non-tribal population. They have, in general, two types of lands, the low land (Don) and upland (Tanr) and they raise paddy in the first kind of land, and millets, maize, oil-seeds, etc. in the second. In several areas, the non-tribals have got possession of the fertile land by giving money on loans to the indigenous cultivators or by exploiting them in several other ways. The fragmentation of land has continued to occur, despite the fact that several brothers though living separately at home continue to cultivate jointly. The increase in population in the village has also taken place at the rate of 10-20 per cent during the last two censuses.

In other words, the areas of agricultural tribes are characterised by (1) fragmentation of lands, (2) land alienation, and (3) excessive pressure of population. These negative factors get a further fillip and produce negative results owing to poor agricultural technology and traditions, lack of irrigational facilities and poor and impoverished agricultural workers. In addition, the level of aspiration of the tribal villagers is at the lowest, they seldom aspire for a surplus economy, and any effort on their part to raise the standard of living is almost nil. They are under the spell of a traditional and religious orientation which put a great check on any type of departure from the existing agricultural traditions and in spite of community development programmes etc., they almost continue to maintain their traditional adjustments and style of life.

There are, however, some cultural values which may be directed to improve the agricultural conditions of Chotanagpur. The tribals by tradition are co-operative. Co-operation at various levels, and on various occasions is reflected differently among different tribals. In general, at the family level both the male and the female and children play almost equal roles in the various agricultural operations as well as in the construction of houses or in food gathering and food collection. However, it is taboo for the women to touch a plough, as such an action they believe, will result in the failure of crops etc.

Above the family level, we notice co-operation at the kin-level among the agricultural and non-agricultural tribes. The frequent exchange of labour in any economic pursuit, specially in the construction of houses, major agricultural operations and hunting etc. is practised. Such a co-operation is recorded at the clan and village levels. A tribal group or an individual in the village helps in the construction of a house or in other major agricultural operations. Such a spirit of co-operation is reflected in collective ownership at the village level of the pasture and grazing land, the religious shrines, youth-dormitory, village and regional councils and so on. This value of co-operation still persisting among the tribal communities may be directed in improving the agricultural conditions among the tribal areas.

It is unfortunate that the tribals because of their tradition-orientation and closed-group norms have not been able to introduce many new crops, new implements, new fertilisers and other new areas in agriculture. Community development, in general though broken the stagnation in the agricultural practices among the tribal communities, the need to bring about certain significant changes still remains to be done and an integrated plan to introduce reclamation of culturable wasteland, and the introduction of new agricultural ideas suited to Chotanagpur still remains. The sporadic experiments to introduce vegetable crops, cash-crops, fruits and new food crops if intensified and made acceptable to the people are likely to yield good results. It is time enough to examine all these questions of agricultural development in Chotanagpur Plateau in the light of their traditions. For this, a study team of experts drawn from the various fields will go a long way in evolving as integrated scheme of regional agricultural development (Vidyarthi: 1972).

Artisan and Cultural Values

Among the fourth type are those tribals like Mahali (the basket makers), the Asur and the Agaria (the iron smelters), the Lohra (the blacksmiths), the Chik Baraik (traditional weavers) and such others whose economy and culture revolve round a specific craft in which they specialise. Verrier Elwin, writing about the Agaria, for example, establishes as to how the entire style of life of the Agaria revolves round iron-smelting. The selection and collection of iron ore, the process of smelting, their related social interactions and religious beliefs and practices, all revolve round the iron complex (Elwin : 1970).

It is unfortunate that owing to the introduction of the mill-made iron the entire life style of the Agaria of Madhya Pradesh and the Asur of Netharhat plateau have undergone drastic disorganisation, and they are being threatened with economic crisis and cultural stagnation. The other artisan specialists, as well, are also facing a worse situation as their traditional crafts of weaving, basket-making, iron-smelting etc. have sustained a similar setback.

Among the several craftsmen belonging to the caste groups, mention may be made of the Kumhar (the potters) whose entire economy and life style revolve a round the traditional crafts of pottery (Behura, N.K. : 1978, Chakravarty, B. : 1972 and 1980), which is under the process of transformation in different parts of India.

In terms of correct developmental processes, it would have been more desirable to modernise their traditional crafts and allow them to produce similar materials with improved technology which can be easily marketed and will enable them to earn a livelihood. The complete negation of cultural factors and traditional background have resulted in the loss of confidence of these tribals as they have not been able so far to re-adjust themselves with the changed economy, and for that matter with new ways of life.

From Folk-Culture to Industrial Culture

Of late, the tribal belt of middle India which is originally characterised by folk culture, has been undergoing a large scale industrialisation specially during the last four decades. The present affluent industrial society which thrives on the ashes of the indigenous villages has brought about large-scale socio-cultural disintegration of pre-existing cultures. The detailed results of our longitudinal study of the industrial complexes of Ranchi have been published elsewhere (Vidyarthi: 1970). It has been established that this large scale industrialisation, though operating in the folk tribal area is geared to the economic development without much conscious efforts to benefit the local tribal and semi-tribal communities. Such an approach has obviously led to unexpected consequences of social disruption among the folk and tribal communities, and by and large, instead of being benefited by these developments their economy and culture, have been adversely affected. The net result of the uprooted tribals in due course is loss of traditional occupation, land, house, traditional way of life, exhaustion of cash received by way of compensation, unemployment, keen and unfair competition with the migrants in the labour market, high aspirations and great frustration. All these find reflection in different types of unrest and agitation in tribal areas and are of great socio-political significance.

The cultural factors, again, are closely linked with the acceptability or rejection of the different types of manual jobs. The land holders of high and middle castes are averse to the acceptability of manual jobs. For example, when such families were uprooted in the wake of industrialisation in the Bokaro Industrial Complex, they preferred to sell their ornaments, utensils, and even face starvation rather than accept the work of manual labour which was supposed to be the work of the male and female of low castes (Sarkar, J.K. : 1970).

The value attached to manual work with the tribals, however, were different. As they have been used to work on the land and in the forest, they took up the challenge of industrialisation somewhat differently. Not only the male but even the tribal women are found engaged in a greater proportion in the varied labour force (Vidyarthi : 1969). A large number of tribal women from the neighbouring villages migrate daily in quest in unskilled type of labour which Ranchi and other towns offer them in abundance.

A study of tribal labour force in the Hatia Industrial Complex is quite fascinating. In this industrial complex which has witnessed the uprooting of 25 villages inhabited by 12,990 souls, the situation arising out of it is quite challenging. While the elderly members of the families preferred to migrate to the other villages to purchase land from the compensation money and continue their traditional occupations, the young and the adult ones faced the challenge of industrialisation by settling down in the rehabilitation colonies and the slums, and to press the management through the trade unions to procure unskilled or semi-skilled job (Vidyarthi : 1970).

There was a time when almost no industrial workers, skilled or unskilled, were found in any tribal villages, and a simple type of agriculture and/or agricultural labour provided the exclusive means of their livelihood. With the first wave of industrialisation several villagers took up unskilled jobs in the industrial complexes and started commuting by bicycle and other means of communication. With their same values of work, many of the tribal labourers left for Andaman and Nicobar Islands (Vidyarthi : 1971) and the tea gardens of North-Eastern India (Kar, R.K. : 1976), and more recently, to several other parts of India. The tribal labourers working in the forests in Chotanagpur did not find it very difficult to work in the forests of the Andamans and they may be safely termed as the modern builders of Andamans as they have been working since several decades with the forests department, P.W.D., the bush police and *jettys* (Vidyarthi : 1971).

To conclude, then, it must be emphasised that development means "growth" plus "change". It involves both the material and the human factors. The school of thought which subscribes almost wholly to what has come to be known as "growthmanship" is not acceptable to us.

They believe that a given number of material inputs, when assembled in certain proportions, yields the desired output measurable in quantified indicators such as rate of growth, national income, per capita income etc. They seem to be under the impression that growth, as assessed in terms of such gross indicators, is a value in itself. The non-material factors constitute for them but a context; social service, a more infrastructure; and social change, a by-product of such growth. To an anthropologist such a mechanical concept of growth is not acceptable, and he has consistently emphasised that socio-cultural factors are an integral part of the dynamics of growth and that social change is not simply a non functional or a dis-functional side effect of development planning.

In this context the concept of development has to be defined and operated in terms of the cultural background of the community concerned. While striving for the development of a group or an area, due emphasis has to be given to their traditional values and historical experiences. Among the communities of Asia, for example, religion continues to play a dominant role and any attempt to overlook it, in the long run, will not deliver the desired results.

Among the Hindus, for example, there is a deep-rooted belief in *Purushartha,* which sets four-fold integrated goals for the development of man and his societies. These are : *Dharma* (religion), *Artha* (wealth), *Kama* (sex) and *Moksha* (salvation). An average Indian aims to work for *Unnayan* (an integrated development of self in the society), and any plan or programme either of technological or economic change has to take into consideration the traditional concepts of development, which continue to influence the Indian mind.

Every cultural group, in view of its respective ecological setting and many cultural experiences has developed a style of life, a type of Nature-Man-Spirit complex which persists through the ages. As it is evident, such a complex or a system of penetrating network of mutual interactions and an intimate interrelation of Nature-Man-Spirit remains almost undisturbed among the simplest pre-farming and marginal tribal groups.

As one goes deep into the analysis of the Maler forest economy, for example, the cycle of slash and burn cultivation, and the various dimensions of the man-to-man interactions, the functions of the "spirit" (Gossainyas) in regulating nature-man-relationship and in the overall moulding of their culture, becomes clearer still. It appeared that by and large the Maler represented a style of life in which maize, man and "God" have definite mutual roles to play (Vidyarthi, 1963 : 173).

The situation, however, with the agricultural tribes who live with the non-tribals or are relatively more exposed to industrial and other modern experiences are somewhat different, though the concept of Nature-Man-Spirit complex stands valid and needs to be taken into consideration in matters concerning their development.

SUGGESTED READINGS

Behura, N.K., *Peasant Potters of Orissa : A Sociological Study*, New Deihi, Sterling Publishers Pvt. Ltd., 1978.

Chakravarty, B., "Vanishing Crafts of Artisans of Chotanagpur", *Bulletin of the Cultural Research Institute*, Vol. IX, Nos. 1 & 2, 1972.

Chakravarty, B., "Traditional Industry and Artisans of Chotanagpur : An urgent need in anthropological research" *Bulletin of the Cultural Research Institute* Vol. 14, Nos. 1 and 2. 1980.

Elwin, V., *The Agaria*, London, Oxford University Press, 1970.

Kar, R.K., "A Tribe in the Context of a Tea Industry in India : Some Preliminary Observations", *Anthropos*, Vol. 71, 1976, pp. 868-877.

Malhotra, S.P., "The Birhor Resettlement Scheme", In *Applied Anthropology in India* (ed.) L.P. Vidyarthi, Allahabad, Kitab Mahal, 1968.

Sarkar, J.K., "The Uprooted Families in Bokaro Industrial Complex", Ph.D. Thesis submitted to Ranchi University, Ranchi, 1970 (Unpublished).

Spicer, E.H., *Human Problems in Technological Change : A Case Book*, New York, Russell Sage Foundation, 1952.

Sinha, D.P. *Culture Change in an Inter-Tribal Market*, Calcutta, Asia Publishing House, 1968.

Vidyarthi, L.P., "Cultural Types in Tribal Bihar : A Methodological Appraisal", *Journal of Social Research*, Vol. 1, No. 1, 1958.

Vidyarthi, L.P., "The Birhor: A Study in Ecology, Economy and Wandering", *In Men and Culture* (ed) Anthony Wallace, Philadelphia, 1960.

Vidyarthi, L.P., *The Maler : A Study in Nature-Man-Spirit Complex in a Hill Tribe of Bihar*, Calcutta Bookland, Pvt. Ltd., 1963.

Vidyarthi, L.P., "Anthropology and the Tribal Policy : A Case Study among the Maler", In *Applied Anthropology in India* (ed) L.P. Vidyarthi, Allahabad, Kitab Mahal, 1968.

Vidyarthi, L.P., "Aspects of Tribal Labour Force in Chotanagpur", *Tribe*, Vol. VI, No. 3. 1969, pp. 1-9.

Vidyarthi, L.P., "Urbanisation, Industrialisation and Social Change *Research Journal of Ranchi University*, Vol. VI and VII, 1969-70.

Vidyarthi, L.P., *Socio-Cultural Implications of Industrialisation in India : Tribal Bihar : A Case Study*, New Delhi, Planning Commission, Govt. of India, Distributor : Council of Social and Cultural Research, Bihar, 1970.

Vidyarthi, L.P., "The Ranchi Tribals in Andaman and Nicobar Islands", *Journal of Social Research*, Vol. XIV, No. 2, 1971, pp. 50-59.

Vidyarthi, L.P., "Socio-Cultural Implications of Reclamation of Wasteland in the tribal belt of Bihar", *Bulletin of the Indian National Science Academy* (New Delhi), Vol. 44, 1972, pp. 117-125.

TWO

Ajit K. Danda

STATUTORY PROVISIONS SAFEGUARDING INTERESTS OF SCHEDULED TRIBES AND SCHEDULED CASTES

A NUMBER of special provisions have been made in the Constitution of India for sefeguarding rights and interests of Scheduled Castes and Scheduled Tribes who constitute about 22 per cent of the total population of India, as well as for their accelerated rate of development so as to bring them up to the level of the general population of the society at large as early as possible. Provisions for safeguard can be traced back from the very first session of the Constituent Assembly in which, in December 1946, Jawaharlal Nehru had moved the principal resolution on the declaration of objectives which, along with other matters had outlined :

> Wherein adequate safeguards shall be provided for minorities, backward and tribal areas, and depressed and other backward classes.

The resolution was adopted in the second session of the Constituent Assembly that held in January 1947. This, of course, found adequate expression in Article 46 under the Directive Principles of State Policies in Part IV of the Constitution which reads as follows :

> The State shall promote with special care the educational and economic interests of the weaker sections of the people, and, in particular, of the Scheduled Castes and the Scheduled Tribes, and shall protect them from social injustice and all forms of exploitation.

All the safeguards have, apparently, been provided to facilitate the implementation of the Directive Principles contained in this Article of the Constitution.

Over the years a number of modifications have come about in the provisions of the Constitution and the special provisions for the Scheduled Castes and Scheduled Tribes are not exceptions in this respect. The present discussion takes into account modifications of Articles and clauses as amended up to 1968. Since statutory provisions have been made more or less conjointly for the Scheduled Castes and Scheduled Tribes, they have been dealt with accordingly in this paper.

Special safeguards for the Scheduled Castes and Scheduled Tribes provided in the Constitution of India have been spelt out in 24 Articles including Article 46 as referred to above and in two Schedules, namely the Fifth and the Sixth Schedules which, in fact, elaborate provisions outlined under Articles 244 and 275.

Eight of the 24 Articles come within the purview of the Fundamental Rights under Part III of the Constitution. This implies that any provision made in these Articles are enforceable through courts of law and even any law inconsistent with the spirit of these Articles is liable to be declared void. The eight Articles under reference are 15, 16, 17, 19, 23, 25, 29 and 35.

Article 15 deals with prohibition of discrimination on grounds of religion, race, caste, sex, or place of birth and emphasizes that no citizen shall be subject to any disability, liability or restriction on this count with particular reference to (a) access to shops, public restaurants, hotels and places of public entertainment or (b) the use of wells, tanks, bathing ghats, roads, and places of public resort maintained wholely or partly out of State funds or dedicated to the use of the general public.

Through a later amendment it has been added that nothing in this Article shall prevent the State from making any special provision for the advancement of any socially or educationally backward classes of citizens for the Scheduled Castes and the Scheduled Tribes. Special provisions as such being somewhat discriminatory in nature the amendment was considered essential to ward off any steps contrary to the spirit of the Constitution.

Equality of opportunity in matters of public employment has been ensured through Article 16, in addition to prohibition of discrimination on grounds of religion, race etc. This, at the same time 'specifies that nothing, however, prevents the State from making any provision for the raservation of appointments or posts in favour of any backward class of citizens which, in the opinion of the State, is not adequately represented in the services under the State.

Article 17 abolishes untouchability in unequivocal terms and declares its practice in any form forbidden. It emphasises that enforcement of any disability arising out of any untouchability shall be an offence punishable in accordance with law.

Protection of certain rights regarding freedom of speech, movement throughout the territory of India, right to reside and settle in any part of the territory of India, and to acquire, hold, and dispose of property etc, have been outlined in Article 19. For the protection of interest of any Scheduled Tribe the Article further specifies that nothing relating to sub-clauses on freedom of movement, residences, and acquiring property shall affect the operation of any existing law in so far as it imposes, or prevent the State from making any law imposing restrictions.

Article 23 deals with prohibition of traffic in human beings and forced labour like *begar* and prohibits any discrimination while imposing compulsory service for public purposes only on grounds of religion, race, caste or class. Thus, though in an indirect manner, this ensures equality between citizens.

Article 25 details freedom of conscience and free profession, practice, and propagation of religion. This also in an indirect manner ensures equal entitlement of India's citizens, particularly regarding freedom of conscience.

As part of the cultural and educational rights, protection of interests of minorities have been dealt with in two clauses of Article 29. They are as below :

(1) Any section of the citizens residing in the territory of India or any part thereof having a distinct language, script or culture of its own shall have the right to conserve the same.

(2) No citizen shall be denied admission into any educational institution maintained by the State or

> receiving aid out of State funds on grounds only of religion, race, caste, language or any of them.

Under Right to Constitutional Remedies, legislation to give effect to the provisions of Part III has been dealt with in Article 35.

Two Articles, namely, 38 and 46 belonging to Part IV of the Constitution of India under Directive Principles of State Policies have dealt with special provisions toward promotion of welfare of the people at large and with particular reference to the weaker sections like the Scheduled Castes, Scheduled Tribes and other backward classes. According to Article 38 :

> The State shall strive to promote the welfare of the people by securing and protecting as effectively as it may, a social order, in which justice, social, economic and political, shall inform all institutions of the national life.

And Article 46, as already indicated, dealing with promotion of educational and economic interests of Scheduled Castes, Scheduled Tribes, and other weaker sections outlines the Directive Principles according to which special provisions need to be implemented.

Part VI of the Constitution of India deals with the States in Part A of the First Schedule. Article 164 belonging to this part indicates other provisions as to ministers. According to this Article :

> The Chief Minister shall be appointed by the Governor and the other Ministers shall be appointed by the Governor on the advice of the Chief Minister, and the Ministers shall hold office during the pleasure of the Governor :

Provided that in the States of Bihar, Madhya Pradesh and Orissa, there shall be a Minister in-charge of tribal welfare who may in addition be in-charge of the welfare of Scheduled Castes and backward classes or any other work.

Part X of the Constitution of India pertains to the administration of Scheduled and Tribal Areas and its only Article namely 244 outlines the matter as below :

(1) The provisions of the Fifth Schedule shall apply to the administration and control of the Scheduled Areas and Scheduled Tribes in any State specified in Part A and Part B of the First Schedule other than the State of Assam.

(2) The provisions of the Sixth Schedule shall apply to the administration of the tribal areas in the State of Assam.

The Fifth Schedule makes provision for establishment of Tribes Advisory Council examining applicability of laws to the Scheduled Areas, delineation of boundary of the Scheduled Areas, and making amendment of the Schedule as such.

The Sixth Schedule makes provisions as to the administration of Tribal Areas of Assam by setting up Autonomous Districts and Autonomous Regions and constituting District Councils and Regional Councils. It also specifies powers of the District Councils and Regional Councils to make laws and administration of justice in the Autonomous Districts and Autonomous Regions. The Schedule also makes provisions for delineation of (1) executive powers of the District Council, (2) District and Regional Funds, (3) powers to assess and collect land revenue and to impose taxes, (4) licences or leases for the purpose of prospecting for an extraction of minerals, (5) power of District Council to make regulations for the control of money lending and trading by non-tribals, (6) publication of laws, and regulations made under the Schedule, (7) application of Acts of Parliament and of the Legislature of the State to Autonomous Districts and Autonomous Regions, (8) estimated receipts and expenditure pertaining to Autonomous Districts to be shown separately in the annual financial statement, (9) appointment of commission to inquire into and report on the administration of Autonomous Districts and Autonomous Regions, (10) annulment or suspension of Acts and Resolutions of Districts and Regional Councils, (11) dissolution of a District or a Regional Council, (12) Exclusion of areas from Autonomous District in forming constituencies in such districts, (13) application of the provisions of this Schedule to areas elsewhere like North East Frontier Tract including Balipara Frontier Tract, Tirap Frontier Tract, Abor Hills District, and Misimi

Hills District, (14) transitional provisions until constitution of a District Council and (15) tribal areas of Assam.

Article 275 under Finance, property, contracts, and suits of Part XII of the Constitution of India deals with grants from the Union to certain States. This makes provision for payment from the Consolidated Fund of India as grants-in aid of the revenues of a State such capital and recurring sums as may be necessary to enable the State to meet the costs of such schemes of development as may be undertaken by the State with the approval of the Government of India for the purpose of promoting the welfare of the Scheduled Tribes in the State or raising the level of administration of the Scheduled Areas therein to that of the administration of the rest of the areas of that State :

> Provided further that these shall be paid out of the Consolidated Fund of India as grants-in-aid of the revenues of the State of Assam such capital and recurring, equivalent to the average excess of expenditure over the revenues during the two years immediately preceding the commencement of this Constitution in respect of the administration of the tribal areas . . .

Thus, in a way, Article 275 forms part of the Sixth Schedule of the Constitution of India.

Part XIV of the Constitution deals with Services under the Union and the States. Article 320 belonging to this part details functions of Public Service Commissions ensuring equal treatment for all.

Most of the Articles enlisted in Part XVI of the Constitution under Special Provisions relating to certain clauses pertains to the Scheduled Castes and Scheduled Tribes.

Article 330 makes special provision for reservation of seats for (a) the Scheduled Castes ; (b) the Scheduled Tribes except the Scheduled Tribes in tribal areas of Assam and the Scheduled Tribes in the Autonomous Districts of Assam.

Article 332 makes provision for reservation of seats for the Scheduled Castes and the Scheduled Tribes, except the Scheduled Tribes in the tribal areas of Assam, in the Legislative Assembly of every State specifies in Part A or Part B of the

First Schedule. There is provision for reservation of seats for the Autonomous Districts in the Legislative Assembly of the State of Assam.

Article 334 specifies the tenure of reservation of seats and special representation.

Article 335 deals with claims of Scheduled Castes and Scheduled Tribes to services and posts and indicates that their claims shall be taken into consideration, consistently with the maintenance of efficiency of administration, in the making of appointments to services and posts in connection with the affairs of the Union or of a State.

Articles 338 makes provision for appointment of a special officer for the Scheduled Castes and Scheduled Tribes and specifies his duty as to investigate all matters relating to the safeguards provided for the Scheduled Castes and Scheduled Tribes under the Constitution of India. It is also his responsibility to report upon the working of those safeguards at such intervals as the President may direct. It further outlines that the President shall cause all such reports to be laid before each House of Parliament.

Article 339 outlines control of the Union over the administration of Scheduled Areas and welfare of the Scheduled Tribes. As the Article indicates, the President may at any time and shall at the expiration of ten years from the commencement of this Constitution appoint a commission to report on the administration of the Scheduled Areas and the welfare of the Scheduled Tribes. It further specifies that the executive power of the Union shall extend to the giving of directions to any State as to the drawing up and execution of schemes specified in the direction to be essential for the welfare of the Scheduled Tribes in the State.

The mechanism of scheduling castes by public notification has been dealt with in Article 341. According to the Article, the President after consultation with the Governor of the concerned State may specify castes, races, or tribes etc. which, for the purpose of this Constitution, shall be deemed to be Scheduled Castes in relation to that State. It further specifies that the Parliament, by law, may include in or exclude from the list of Scheduled Castes any caste, race, or tribe.

Article 342 deals with the mechanism of scheduling tribes.

In accordance with the said Article the President, after consultation with the Governor of the concerned State, may by public notification declare the tribes or tribal communities, or parts of or groups within tribes or tribal communities which shall for the purpose of this Constitution be deemed to be Scheduled Tribes in relation to that State. The Article also empowers the Parliament to modify by law the list of Scheduled Tribes.

Part XIX of the Constitution deals with miscellaneous matters. Article 366 under this part specifies meaning of Scheduled Castes and Scheduled Tribes. According to clause 24 of the said Article, 'Scheduled Castes' means such castes, races or tribes or parts or groups within such castes, races or tribes so are deemed to be Scheduled Castes. In accordance with clause 25 of this Article, 'Scheduled Tribes' means such tribes or tribal communities or parts of or groups within such tribes or tribal communities as are deemed to be Scheduled Tribes for the purpose of this Constitution.

Article 371-A, that came into effect through an amendment, details special provisions with respect to the State of Nagaland.

Thus, the safeguards provided in the Constitution make provision for representation in Parliament and the State Legislatures, appointment of Ministers in charge of tribal welfare particularly in Bihar, Madhya Pradesh, and Orissa, appointment of a Minister specially in charge of the welfare of the Autonomous Districts and Autonomous Regions in Assam, representation in the Central and State services, abolition of the practice of untouchability, throwing open of the Hindu religious institutions, admission into educational institution, special provisions for social, educational and economic advancement, banning of traffic in human beings, appointment of special officer to investigate all matters relating to safeguards provided for the Scheduled Castes and Scheduled Tribes and the development and administration of Scheduled and Tribal Areas etc.

In addition to the above, special provisions for the Scheduled Tribes were also made through certain Acts and Orders which are protective, ameliorative, and concessional in nature. Special provisions have been made for family and land rights exempting the Scheduled Tribes from the Hindu succession Act 1956, Hindu Adoption Act 1956, and Hindu Marriage Act 1956. Thus, the customary marriage and succession rules of the Scheduled Tribes have remained largely untouched. Protection of land rights of them has also been made by recognising their traditional rights over it and restricting the alienation of tribal land. Most of the State Governments have also taken executive and legislative measures in order to protect tribal lands.

Legislative and executive measures have also been adopted for the members of the Scheduled Castes and Scheduled Tribes by reserving seats for them in local bodies such as municipalities, Zilla Parishads, Panchayats etc. in different States. Further, in addition to reservation in services, concessions in age, qualifications, and rate of fees have also been granted by various States as well as the Central Government.

The Government of India has also accepted the conventions and recommendations of the International Labour Organization dealing with protection and integration of tribal communities.

SUGGESTED READINGS

Banerjee, A.C., *The Constitution of the Indian Republic*, Calcutta : A. Mukherjee & Co. Ltd., 1950.

Banerjee, H.N., "Statutory Safeguards for Scheduled Tribes and Scheduled Castes", *Bulletin of the Cultural Research Institute*, Vol. 1, No. 1, 1962.

Office of the Commissioner for Scheduled Castes and Scheduled Tribes. *Handbook on Scheduled Castes and Scheduled Tribes*, New Delhi : Office of the Commissioner for Scheduled Castes and Scheduled Tribes, 1968.

THREE

P. K. Bhowmick

FORESTRY, TRIBE AND THE FOREST POLICY IN INDIA

WITH ITS wide range of climatic conditions from torrid to arctic, and its widely differing topography, India has a rich and varied vegetation. The Indian word 'jungle' meaning a large conglomeration of wild trees and shrubs, is sometimes equated with forest, which denotes technically 'any vegetation under a systematic management'. Forest has been defined as* :

(a) (In general) an area set aside for the production for timber and other forest produce, or maintained under woody vegetation for certain indirect benefits which it provides e.g. climatic or protective.
(b) (In ecology) A plant community predominantly of trees and other woody vegetation, usually with a closed canopy; and
(c) (In law) An area of land proclaimed to be forest under a forest law.

India can be divided into eight distinctive floristic regions—(1) Western Himalayas, (2) Eastern Himalayas, (3) Assam, (4) Indus Plain, (5) Ganga Plain, (6) Deccan, (7) Malabar, and (8) Andaman. In India forests account for 22 per cent of the total land surface. The National Forest Policy of 1952 laid down that the area under forests should be increased steadily to 33 per cent of the total area, the proportion to be covered

* Sagreiya, *Forest and Forestry* (1967).

ultimately being 60 per cent in the hilly regions and 20 per cent in the plains.

The forest plays a very vital role in the life of the Indian people. We have historical references of gradual deforestation made by the indigenous communities during their long transition from food-gathering forest economy to agricultural economy. But the life and culture of many so-called indigenous communities i.e. the tribals, have grown and thrived meaningfully in the forest ecology until these communities were beaten by the Aryan invaders and retreated into the forest for safe shelter. The Aryans destroyed many of their agricultural lands by grazing their cattle, and for raising crops and survival, they shifted farther into the interior, into the inhospitable regions from the Gangetic Valley. The other indigenous communities living in the areas where the Aryans did not penetrate during the proto-historical period also depended on the forest.

But there are a good number of tribal communities who still cling to 'shifting cultivation'. In this process, they fell the forest trees indiscriminately, allow these to dry up, then burn them and raise crops on such lands for one to three years before moving on to another forest site and repeating the process there. This cultivation is described as 'slash and burn' or 'Swidden' in the English language, whereas in India, the process of shifting cultivation is differently known in different tribal belts. In the north-east India it is known as *jhum* or *jum*; in Orissa it is *podu, dabi, koman, bringa*; in Bastar it is *deppa*; *kumari* in the Western Ghats, *watra* in south S.E. Rajasthan. The Maria call it *penda, bewar, dahia* in Madhya Pradesh.* It has been estimated that about 26 lakhs of people practise 'shifting cultivation' in various States and Union territories like Arunachal, Manipur, Nagaland, Tripura, Orissa, Bihar, Madhya Pradesh, Andhra Pradesh, Tamilnadu, Maharashtra, Karnataka and Kerala—comprising an area of 14 lakh acres with varying crop-patterns.

This sort of continuous deforestation has been causing a lot of concern to the administration. But shifting cultivation is a way of life of some Indian tribes. Naturally a change in outlook for land reforms and administration is necessary, both for the survival of the tribal people and protection of the forests which are being denuded very fast by them.

* Bhowmick, P.K., *Some Aspects of Indian Anthropology* (1980).

II

Forest plays a vital role not only in the life of the tribals, but other people too. The forests of India provide many kinds of timber with various utility values. Forests are also sources of supply of fire-wood to the urban community, and small timber is required by the rural communities for construction purposes. They provide pasture land, hay and fodder for the cattle. Forests perform the function of protecting the soil on sloping lands from accelerated erosion by rain and flood. They conditions the climate too and keep the wild life alive.

The tribals derive more than the above benefits from the forest. To a large number of them, it is their home. They maintain their livelihood from the forest. Edible roots and tubers, leaves and fruits are collected from the forests and consumed by many tribal people, both as staple and substitute food. They also get honey in plenty from the forest. They not only consume it, but also sell or exchange it with other people for getting other necessary commodities. Wild game are also killed in plenty in these forests and used as an important variant in their monotonous food-menu. House-building materials are also collected from the forest. In the biting winter, they warm themselves by burning faggots and relax under its shade during the hot summer. A good number of clan names of the tribals are associated with the trees, ventilating the nature of their sentimental emotion tinged with religiosity. A good number of virgin forest trees are also found to be kept untouched, as if these were the seats of their gods and goddesses. They also worship these. The *Sarna*, the sacred grove of the Oraon or the Munda, is a patent example of this. The *Jahersthan* of the Santhal is another illustration of such tribal faith.

Generally a big *Sal* or *Mahua* tree in the periphery of the village is considered as the seat of the tutelary village deity Gram or Baram by the Lodhas. 'Tree marriage' is very common among many tribes and communities. Among the Lodha, on the day of the marriage, a mango tree is selected by the chief conductor of marriages for this purpose. The bridegroom is directed to walk round the tree three times and place his right palm with fingers pointing upwards on the tree. The chief conductor then ties a dyed yellow thread round the tree and the palm of the bridegroom together. He then applies three vermillion dots just above the fingers and direct the bridegroom to bow down before the tree. The bridegroom does accordingly. Later the conductor unties the thread. Thus the ceremony of marrying the tree is done and from that day the particular mango tree becomes taboo to the bridegroom. He no longer takes any fruit or plucks leaves or cuts the branches of that tree. In the same fashion the bride has to marry a *Mahua* tree. Here the bride has to place her left palm whereas the bridegroom has to place his right palm. This tree becomes ceremonially taboo to her also. The marriage with the tree has a special meaning. In case death visits the household accidentally, the mango and the *mahua* surrogates are believed as likely to be affected with any possible evil effect in place of the real wife or husbands. It is thus believed to give some kind of magical protection to the newly married couple. Even during burial or cremation, some trees are considered to be very auspicious and hence are worshipped.

Thus forest and the trees are interlaced with their culture and tradition and regulate their socio-economic life. Folk-tales, myths, etc. reflect their close forest association. The booming of the trees in the spring heralds the beginning of the tribal year. The first fruit is offered to the ancestral spirits along with other gods and goddesses. Thus the tribal life and culture are deeply identified with the forest. This clearly indicates that the forest is the real home of the tribals. Tribals are the supreme lords of the forest and enjoy all the resources and benefits it offers and thereby maintain their secluded happy life and tradition. This was the pattern of earlier tribal life.

But later a time came, specially during the earlier historical period when the tribals began to be dislodged due to unrestricted penetration of non-tribals into their secluded domain. Even the meagre lands they owned and made fit for cultivation by deforesting have been gradually acquired by the non-tribals by ruse or purchase from them. This has made them landless creating manifold problems both to the administration and the tribal communities.

III

How and to what extent, displacement from their forest homes has caused some serious problems to this human group can be examined and well-ascertained from the history of the Lodhas—a so-called ex-criminal tribe. The cause of their criminality has been attributed to their territorial displacement from forest moorings. The forest-dewlling Lodhas used to live peacefully in the forests utilising the minor forest products and selling these in the neighbouring villages. They still collect bark, herbal plants, leaves for sewing together to serve as plates for eating and manufacture of hand-made cigars or *bidis*. A good number of Lodhas used to grow *tusser cocoons* from the *Asan* (Terminolia Tomentosa) trees and earne a handsome amount by selling these. But later, due to acquisition of their forest habitat by the government, which deprived them of the use of forest resources, the food-gathering Lodhas could not reorient their style of life with the changed situation and, as such, they had to indulge in anti-social activities to eke out their existence, and in course of time, became inveterate criminals. The peculiar mentality of the tribal folk and the nature of their land proprietorship and full dependence on the forest economy along with their existing value sense should, therefore, be considered on a 'need-based perspective', while planning and initiating any upliftment scheme for them. There are many such examples of tribal disintegration.

IV

The Forest Policy of 1894

A German expert Dr. Voelcker examined the condition of Indian forests vis-a-vis the agricultural condition and made certain suggestions for reform. Accordingly, the Government of India issued a resolution formulating a revised forest policy. It reads :

> The sole object with which State forests are administered is the public benefit . . . the cardinal principle to be observed is that the rights and privileges of individuals must be limited, otherwise than for their own benefit, only in such degree as is absolutely necessary to secure that advantage.

This new conception affected the tribal people very deeply

and was the root cause of the delicate relations between them and the Forest Department which continues up to the present time.

In general, the growth and preservation of a forest involve the regulation of the rights and the restriction of privileges of the users of the forest, as also by the neighbouring population.

National Forest Policy of 1952

After independence, adoption of a new outlook became necessary to reconsider the policy of administration of forests once more to prevent indiscriminate use of the forest by the tribal folk. Accordingly the new policy of 1952 was introduced effecting greater restrictions as below :

> Village communities in the neighbourhood of a forest will naturally make greater use of its products for the satisfaction of their domestic and agricultural needs. Such use, however, should in no event be permitted at the cost of national interest . . . Therefore the needs of the local population must be met to a reasonable extent, national interests should not be sacrificed because they are not directly discernible, nor should the rights and interests of future generations be subordinated to the improvidence of the present generation.

V

The two forest policies are of different nature and as a result these have had adverse impact over the interest of the tribals living near the forest.

(i) The old policy envisaged the release of forest land for cultivation subject to certain safeguards. The new policy withdrew this concession.

(ii) The old policy had left a margin for the supply of the villagers' needs from the outlying areas in the reserved forests. The new policy decided that there should be village forests for this purpose.

(iii) The old policy did not touch the private forests of the tribals. The new policy applied the same controls to them.

(iv) The old policy did not prevent free grazing in the forests. The new policy sought to bring it under control. Fees were introduced and grazing facilities were scaled down to the minimum.

(v) The new policy made one important concession. It admitted that while it was emphatically opposed to shifting cultivation, persuasive and not coercive measures should be used in a sort of missionary, rather than in an authoritarian manner, to attempt to wean the tribals from their traditional methods.*

Thus the tribals who formerly regarded themselves as lords of the forests, were through a deliberate process of law, turned into subjects and brought under the control of the Forest Department. The traditional rights of the tribals were no longer recognised as rights. In 1894 they became 'rights and privileges' and in 1952 they became 'rights and concessions'. Now they are regarded as 'concessions'.

VI

Village forests are intended in the main to serve the needs of the surrounding villages in respect of small timbers for housing and agricultural implements, firewood, leaves for manure and fodder, fencing thorns, grazing and edible forest products.

Regeneration of the forest was emphasised under the new forest policy. Uncontrolled grazing in the forest areas was restricted and minimum wages were introduced for the tribals who served under the Forest Department. The tribals who lived near the forest and had no employment, were directed to be employed by the Forest Department, as far as possible. There were many suggestions for the improvement of the living condition of the tribals and development of the forest by the Dhebar Commission as well as by the Shilu Ao Committee. Forest product collection, processing of minor forest products for the employment of the tribal people were suggested by these Commissions for the employment of the tribals. The recommendations included that the major forest products should be used locally and raw materials marketed by the tribals.

* V., Elwin, *A New Deal for the Tribal India* (1962).

Formation of Forest Labourers' Co-operative Society and Co-operative Finance and Development Corporation were also suggested by the Commissions. Gujarat, Maharashtra and Andhra Pradesh Governments took the initiative to implement these schemes and these are well in progress now. All over the forest areas in the country it is found that the contractors are the greatest enemies of the forests and the tribals. The poor tribals have no trucks to carry the logs home clandestinely or to the market for sale. The contractors however do just this destroying the forests indiscriminately and making the tribals the scapegoats. They poison the whole tribal people in various wavs and by their manipulation and influence, thus making them victims.

There is a gulf of difference between the so-called civilized man's perception of forest and forest regulations and the primitive man's perception of forest and forest regulations. The problem has its links with the concept of property, inheritance and succession. This has substantively been illustrated by A.K. Danda by citing examples from Eastern Madhya Pradesh, particularly from Surguja and Raigarh Districts. He wrote :

> Among the tribal communities living in these districts, the Oraon, Kawar Negesia, Korowa, Kodaku, and Pando are important. Although some sort of territoriality can be established so far as their physical distributions are concerned, in general, they inhabit the same eco-cultural niche; forest, hills, plateaux and undulating plains being important characteristics of them. Among the tribal people of this area in general, in spite of the existing knowledge about the state-ownership of forest, the Korowa are considered the masters and real owners of forests. As a token of recognition of this right of the hunter-gatherer Korowa, the Negesia and the Kawar who form part of the peasantry, pay an annual cess to the Korowa for enjoying the privilege of gathering forest products from the neighbouring jungles.
>
> The Korowa are fully aware and assertive about their customary right over the forests but according to their own perceptions of forest and forest regulations, only the surface materials of forests are generally considered to

belong to them. They do not claim any right over the land on which the forest stands. Their right is upon the trees, shrubs, herbs, roots, tubers, and forest games. The neighbouring tribal peoples pay cess to them for having access to this property of the Korowa. There is, however, an exception so far as our knowledge goes, in this respect. The Mohua trees are not owned by the Korowa although they also grow in forests. They are individually owned by members of forest dwelling tribal communities of the neighbourhood and all peoples living in the neighbourhood honour this individual property right over Mohua trees.

It was observed among the Kodaku, a forest dwelling tribe, that each and everyone of them exactly knew which particular Mohua tree of what forest belonged to whom and there is no incidence of infringement of this right in our record. As a result, we find three different kinds of ownership of forests in North East Madhya Pradesh. At the highest level the state owns all forests that have been declared as the state forests. This right is established more through police force than otherwise. The customary right of the Korowa over the forest is honoured more or less spontaneously by people of the neighbourhood and individual ownership of Mohua trees of forest is also honoured likewise.

The point that I am trying to make out here is that in dealing with forest regulations as we are often guided by the so-called civilized man's perception of forest and property right, we generally ignore the established norm and customary right of the indigenous. As a result, there has been an apparent hiatus in the communication of information between the so-called civilized and primitive people. The problem of criminal activities of ex-criminal tribes has also some bearing upon such communication gap.

Many suggestions have been made by various committees in the past, some of whom wanted to terminate individual and private forest rights. But even their application could not totally prevent pilfering and destruction of forests. Therefore, an integrated approach is necessary for proper development of forests as well as for meeting the needs of the tribal people.

Adoption of "Social forestry" was suggested as a means of development and protection of forests in the 1952 Forest Policy. This includes extension of forestry, reforestation of denuded forests and recreation forestry, i.e. formation of new forests. Provision of recreational benefits for the forest dwelling communities were also suggested in order that in a joyous atmosphere they may learn to love the forest and protect it as their own.

FOUR

V. S. Upadhyay

SPECIAL PROBLEMS OF MINOR TRIBES

IN INDIA millions of aboriginals have remained outside the main stream of Hindu civilization, and as long as Muslims, Christians and Parsis are free to follow their traditional ways of life, it would seem only fair that the social system of aboriginals, however distinct from that of the majority community, should also be respected. No doubt assimilation will occur automatically and inevitably, wherever small tribal groups are enclosed within numerically stronger population. There are 313 tribal communities in India ranging from 19 Great Andamanese to 4 million Gond or 3 million Santhal and Bhil. The minor or small tribal communities have attracted the attention of administrators, sociologists and anthropologists alike, but no specific idea of development appears to have been developed. Apart from the theoretical and applied nature of interests of the social scientists, the administration faces special problems regarding minor tribal groups.

As an anthropologist, one always becomes cautious in using a blanket term like tribe, and controversy still prevails around the question to whom we should call a tribal and also about defining a community as a tribe. Even if we go by the schedule of the President of India, the word tribe represents agriculturists, agricultural and industrial labourers, artisans, nomads, pastoralists, food gatherers and hunters. An agriculturist tribal group like Munda and Oraon can be further subdivided into Christians, animists (Sarana) and Bhagats (Hinduized sections). Furthermore, all these horizontal categories are fast changing, meaning thereby that the artisans are taking up agriculture, nomads have settled down, agriculturists are becoming industrial labour, non-Christians are becoming Christians and so on.

Apart from distinct socio-cultural characteristics and changes therein, the tribal population belongs to various stages of cultural development. The first category is that of the purest of the pure tribal groups comprising about two to three million persons. The highly isolated groups like Sentinalese, Onge, Shompen, Iarwa, Bonda Highlanders, Cholanayakan are examples of this class. The second class has been experiencing 'contact with the plains, and consequently has been undergoing change. The tribes belonging to category three constitute the largest section of the total tribe population, about four-fifths of it, i.e., nearly twenty million members of this class of tribal groups are in a peculiar state of transition. These tribes have been appreciably affected by external contacts. They have been exposed to the influences of economic and socio-cultural forces of Hindu society. They have been also subjected to missionary influences. Specially during the British period, under the impact of new economic and new politico-administrative measures, these tribesmen lost their moorings from their tribal economy, tribal social-organisation, tribal religion and tribal cultural life. The class four tribals consists of a very small population represented by the old aristocracy of the country like great Bhil and Naga Chieftains, the Gond Rajas, a few Binshevar and Bhuyia landlords, Korku noblemen, wealthy Santhal, Oraon leaders and some highly cultural Munda. They are said to have won the battle of culture contacts. Thus we have a further classification as tribal communities, semi-tribal communities, acculturated tribal communities and totally assimilated tribals in the Indian population.

Concept of Development among Tribes

While dismissing economic development of under-developed people and areas, Ragner Nurske (1957) propounded what he aptly called "vicious circle" theory :

> A country is poor because it is poor. With regard to supply, the real income of the population is low, and it has but a small capacity to save and to accumulate capital, hence its productivity is low ; hence, in turn, the low level of real income is maintained. With regard to demand, the country is poor, and it has but a small buying power, thus it cannot attract capital ; hence its productivity is low; therefore, its real income is low, which discourages investment. Each of the links of the circular chain is both the cause and the consequence of the other links.

The explanation of the cause and factors of under-development is perhaps best suited to clarify the overall set-up of the tribal communities in India, The word "development" implies orderly movement of an organism or a social system from a lower level of functioning to a higher level of functioning and integration. The lower-higher continuum in terms of quantitative as well as quantitative changes is reflected in the capacity of a community to respond to the more complex and remote objects of environment with a complex and varying response. Hence it is a product of unconscious maturation as well as that of conscious guidance through education, social controls and participation in organised life. And this brings in the role of outside agencies like administration in development.

As a field worker I have always been puzzled by the question of whose standard we are seeking 'development' from our own or theirs ? To our mind every aspect of their life poses a problem. The location of a tribal village causes inaccessibility. The settlement pattern is so distributed that a village unit covers a large territory. The houses and the sanitation, along with their personal habits and water supply are the source of their low health standards. The larger mass is completely illiterate. And the economy is at a lowest-ever standard of production and consumption. All these are not a matter of concern for the tribals. They seem to a most happy and contented group enjoying a carefree life with songs and dances. To them the problem begins at the supply of two meals a day for the family, passes on to occasional health problems like fever and other diseases and ends with the provision of a roof over their heads. That is why when a development programme is planned, they try to find the fulfilment of these bare necessities, all others including education receive a cold shoulder from the natives of tribal India.

Administration and Development

It becomes difficult for administrators to pinpoint the root-cause of negligence on the part of tribals. The multiplicity of tribal groups and their cultural fabric also defy the blanket development efforts applied for all the tribal groups on a common basis. Hence, many of the efforts either bypass a majority of the tribals or have only an indifferent impact. Really tribal development can be compared with a school system. It has different classes (like tribals), different courses of study at different classes (representing problems), different teachers (personnel engaged in tribal administration), supported by budget and planning as the background. An efficient school shows highly co-ordinated efforts, the administrator engaged in tribal development is to develop such co-ordination among different branches of such planning.

Who are to be Considered as Minor Tribe

As referred to earlier, the 313 tribal communities of India have a population range from 19 Great Andamanese to 4 million Gond. These groups are found in almost all corners of the country including the islands of Andaman and Nicobar, Laccadive-Amindivi and Minicoy. But to call a group minor, there are some anthropological considerations, though mainly of demographic nature:

(a) *Population* : It is the general notion that a tribe which has a population of less than five thousand should be considered minor. And this includes many ethnic groups of India who deserve special attention;

(b) *Concentration of Population*: But if the population is distributed over a middle or large area, the numerical strength is minimised. For example, the Abhujmarias of Bastar number about 13,000, but are distributed in an area of 15,000 sq. miles. Thus one person a mile makes any planning difficult for their problem. Take artisan communities like Chik-Baraik or Lohra or Maler of Bihar. For a better clientage, these tribes are distributed throughout Bihar, two to five families are found in each village supplying these village folk with clothes or agricultural instruments. Such a distribution hinders in deciding about a plan of development for these communities;

(c) *Rate of Growth* : Thus these numerically strong artisans have very low rate of growth of population. The new family has to migrate in search of new pasture of their own. Hence any development work planned in an area has very limited effect.

(d) *Nature-Man Equilibrium* : To consider the levels of development, one tries to analyse the degree of dependence of the community on the nature. The less the dependence, the higher is the stage of development. Therefore, a group which still has to depend on nature for its food, raw material for the products etc. has to be considered minor. For example, the case of Hill Gonda can be cited. They are primarily slash and burn cultivators and hunters. Their abode are deep in the jungle, the area as accessible only by foot-track. To reach from one village to the other or from one tola to the other, one has to cover quite a distance. The Shompen of Great Nicobar, numbering only 92, occupy an island of 400 sq. miles covered with thick tropical forest. This community is completely dependent on the forest for its livelihood. It must be understood that any plan of development changes this equilibrium; and hence due care must be taken in planning the measures that a drastic change is not welcomed and so will not be accepted.

(e) *Economic Level of Production* : There are more than ten thousand Hill Kharia living in Singhbhum district of Bihar. The district has a large industrial and mining base, but still these tribes have to stick to age-old traditions of food gathering or working as agriculture labourers. And one finds their production either at subsistence or below subsistence level. This keeps them under the minor category. Measures like rehabilitation have been tried on them with little success. One cannot think of providing subsidy from outside for years together to make a group of people settle in one place or think of making a settlement scheme for thousands of people.

(f) *Isolation*: This factor of isolation also compels one to think about the question of minorities. The groups of Andaman and Nicobar Islands are the best example. The Negritoes of Andamans Onge, Great Andamanese, Jarwa, Sentinalese—occupy one island each. Furthermore, the degree of isolation varies from the hostile Sentinalese (complete) to the friendly Great Andamanese. Each tribe lives completely apart from the other and each occupies an island. The inacceptability and isolation of the islands forbid any culture contact from outside and hence they continue their traditional life-pattern.

Programmes for their Development

The chief characteristics make it clear that these communities face questions of their total survival (isolated group) and economic survival (for communities living with larger group).

Several anthropologists and others have sought the answer to the question who is to decide about the validity and the course of development for minor groups. Once it has come to light that for total or economic survival, outside help is imperative, a development plan has to be envisaged. These plans are bound to bring about change. The only caution required about very small groups is that they sometimes may lose their identity. Such a conclusion has been drawn from the experiences of the Great Andamanese and Onge of Andaman Islands. The Great Andamanese were the first to come into contact with outsiders and try to change their way of life. The result is that they adopted all the bad habits of the outsiders and have developed acute health problems. This also could not check their fall in population and now what was once a big community covering

10 sub-groups numbers only 19. As regards their cultural identity, nothing traditional is left with them, which can show an inter-connection between old and new. One cannot imagine today what their culture was. At present, the development process is taking its full swing on Onges of little Andaman Island. If caution is not taken as a rule, one will not be surprised that they will go the Andamanese way.

Such experiences even leads one to the validity of the development process. Should there be development at all? The basic assumption is that large groups cannot change suddenly, hence the slow process gives time for adjustment. Even different sections of the population of a large community accept the change according to their own likes and dislikes. But this very process works like mutation on the smaller group and they lose their identity, even in one generation, as in the case of Great Andamanese. Hence the age-old process of "hastening slowly" should be the order with the fight against total survival. Assistance on a smaller scale, just like first aid, should begin the course of development. Gradual addition of new measures could be done as the needs of the community increase. The needs would naturally increase the demands of the native group, then only new items can be introduced. This will also control the imposition of solutions on the part of planners from above.

The second question of economic survival is somewhat different from the first one. The communities involved have varied characteristics, hence no blanket solution for these minor groups can be forwarded. The nomads, shifting cultivators, food gatherers, artisans—all have separate and typical problems. Hence this category too have sub-categories which must be treated differentially.

Take for example nomads. The migratory nature of the group makes it very difficult to plan for their development. There can hardly exist plans of development, which can move according to the pattern of migration of the community. Every process of development needs a permanent ecology to work in. The economy, education, health—all these need that their subjects should be constant.

Shifting cultivation has remained a constant problem in the process of agricultural development. New forest laws have banned the process of slash and burn cultivation. And the hilly tracts do not provide any other economic pursuits for the natives. Hence they have either to disobey the laws or go hungry. Such a situation has been found with the Bonda Highlanders of Orissa, who are facing a great problem of economic survival. The ban has not been associated with any other provision of economic alternatives.

The artisans have been a part and parcel of tribal villages since long. Industrialization has provided better alternatives than what they used to produce and hence they are losing their market. They know nothing except their craft. Their sparse distribution has again posed a problem. The above in a nutshell are some of the factors to be taken into consideration in any plan for tribal development.

APPENDIX

SPECIAL MINOR GROUPS

	Name	Area	Population
1.	Onge	Little Andaman	118
2.	Great Andamanese	Straight Islands	19
3.	Jarwa	S.W. Andamans	300 (Est.)
4.	Santinalese	Sentinal Island	100 (Est.)
5.	Shompen	Great Nicobar	72
6.	Hill Kharia	Bihar	9,423
7.	Birhor	Bihar	3,464
8.	Cholanaya Kans	Kerala	130
9.	Hill Kharia	M.P.	4,000
10.	Hill Juang	Orissa	6,000
11.	Bonda Highlanders	Orissa	5,338
12.	Chenchu	Andhra Pradesh	229
13.	Abhujhmaria	Bastar (M.P)	13,000
14.	Jenu Kurumba	Karnataka	6,656

SUGGESTED READINGS

Bose, N.K., *Cultural Anthropology and Essays*, Calcutta.

Elwin, Verrier, *The Aboriginals*, 2nd Ed., Bombay : OUP, 1944.

Ghurye, G.S., *The Scheduled Tribes*, Bombay : Popular Book Depot, 1959.

Memoria, C.B., *Tribal Demography in India*, Allahabad : Kitab Mahal, 1950.

Ragnar, Nurske, "Problems of Capital Formation in Under-developed Countries", New York : O.U.P., 1957.

FIVE

P. K. Bhowmick

REPORTS ON SCHEDULED TRIBES
An Appraisal

THE ADIVASIS or the aboriginal population of our country are considered as early-settlers. They are generally found to live in unhealthy jungle-covered regions, mostly inaccessible to other people. In the Constitution of India they have been described as 'weaker section' because they are not in a position to compete with their stronger brethren in socio-cultural and economic spheres. Naturally provisions have been made in the Constitution not only to ameliorate the deplorable conditions of the so-called primitive tribes, but also to safeguard their rights and interests in various ways to elevate them to the level of other advanced classes. A Tribe is generally defined as "A social group, usually with a definite area of living, dialect, cultural homogeneity and unifying social organisations. It may include several sub-groups as sibs or villages". Lack of specialisation i.e., least functional interdependence can be considered as a basic criteria to differentiate a tribe from the rest of the people. Tribal community generally cling to a crude economic state or organisation, i.e., they have a primitive technology and this is considered as one of the important criteria. Homogeneity or lack of social stratification is another tribal feature. Group-consciousness or ethnocentrism may be counted as yet another aspect of tribal life. This tribalism is again reinforced by endogamous principles governed by a strong communal organisation reflected in the form of the tribal panchayat even today.

There are three important tribal-concentrated zones in India where most of the tribals inhabit. These are :

(1) North and north-eastern zones of India comprising the sub-Himalayan mountainous region with dominating tribes e.g., Naga groups like Konyak, Rengama, Sengama, Ao, Angama, Dhota, Phom, Chang, Kabui ; Kuki group including Lushai, Lakher, Chins ; Khasi, Garo, Kachari, Lepoha, Bhutia, Rabha, Tharu, Khasa, Cheri etc.

(2) The central or middle zone comprising the States of West Bengal, Bihar, Orissa, southern Uttar Pradesh, northern Maharashtra, Madhya Pradesh, northern Rajasthan in which a good number of tribal communities live. The important tribal communities of these areas are Santhal, Munda, Oraon, Bhumij, Kora, Lodha, Saur, Juang, Khond, Korku, Gond, Bhil, Birhor, Kol, Maler, Asur, Baiga, Pradhan, Birjhia, Agaria, Hill Maria, Bison-horn Maria etc.

(3) The southern zone consisting of Kerala, Tamilnadu, Andhra States where the important tribal communities like Chenchu, Toda, Badaga, Kota, Panian, Irula, Kurumba live.

Tribal communities are also found in some other pockets like Andaman and Nicobar Islands, Laccadive, etc. The hostile Jarawa, Nicobarese Onge, etc. are notable for their primitive style of life.

Due to various factors and impact of historical forces some tribal communities have been pushed back into the interior of the forests, whereas other groups have come into closer interactions with other communities. This interaction process has however brought about unsual changes from tribe to tribe in various spheres of life. Thus it can be said that the tribes have no permanent crystalline structures belonging to a particular stage of historical or social development.

II

The 1971 Census has enumerated the total tribal population as 38,015,162 out of the total population of 547,949,809 of India, constituting roughly 7 percent. Considering their backward condition, the framers of the Constitution have made some special provisions for their economic and educational upliftment and to protect them from social injustice all forms of exploitation by others, as laid down in Article 46 of the Constitution. Article 342 of the Constitution, specifically states that the President may with respect to any State or Union Territory specify the tribes or tribal communities or parts of or groups within tribes or tribal communities which shall be deemed to be *Scheduled Tribe* in relation to the State or Union Territory. In pursuance of this provision, the President made an order in 1950 for the Part 'A' and Part 'B' States called the Constitution (Scheduled Tribes) Order 1950. In the following year a similar order was issued in respect of the then Part 'C' States. But these have been revised from time to time either due to re-organisation of the States or on the recommendation of some or other Commission of Enquiry appointed from time to time to probe into their conditions of living and disabilities. In all the lists or recommendations so made, emphasis was given to a tribe or community on its primitiveness and backwardness. The Advisory Committee constituted in 1956 prepared a report examining the conditions, and in the light of discussions held with the State Ministers, Members of the Parliament belonging to Scheduled Tribes and Castes and leading social scientists to amend the list in 1967.

III

Thus a good number of Reports were published from time to time to highlight the tribal problems. These are :

Annual Reports of the Commissioner of Scheduled Castes and Scheduled Tribes, Report of the Backward Classes Commission, Report of the Study Team on Social Welfare and Welfare of Backward Classes (1959), Report of the Estimate Committee (1959), Report of the Committee on Special Multi-purpose Tribal Blocks (1960) headed by Dr. Verrier Elwin, Report of the Scheduled Areas and Scheduled Tribes (1960-61) headed by U.N. Dhebar, Report of Study Group on Welfare of the Weaker Sections of the Village Community, Study Team on Tribal Development Programme 1966 headed by P. Shilu Ao, and Task Force on Scheduled Tribes by Prof. Vidyarthi.

After independence successive Five Year Plans have been implemented all over the country for the overall development of these tribal people because ours is a Welfare State. The British Administration in India treated the tribal people in different ways, though in the Government of India Act 1935, a reference was made to the "Backward Tribes" and the Thirteenth Schedule to the Government of India (Provincial Legislative

Assemblies) Order 1936 specified certain tribes as backward in the then Provinces of Assam, Bihar, Orissa, Central Provinces and Berar, Madras and Bombay. However, the first serious attempt to list "Primitive tribes" in the country was made during the Census of 1931. The British Administration maintained a policy of isolation which resulted in reducing them to a state of extreme poverty. Many of them were exposed to hostile external situations, which subjected them to exploitations of a different nature. They were at the lowest level of literacy. Their lands were alienated and passed into the hands of non-tribals. Their rights to the forest were definitely encroached upon after promulgation of the Forest Act in 1894. These factors, coupled with other stresses made them exasperated and led them to protest against the administration and as a consequence we find examples of many uprisings of the tribals from time to time in tribal concentration zones.

It has been stated earlier that a large number of schemes were undertaken to effect economic, educational and social development of the Scheduled Tribes. Plan provisions for the welfare of the tribals were made either directly by the Central Government sanctioning money, or by the State Government who also spent money for their welfare. These schemes were of three broad categories as follows :

(i) Education
(ii) Economic uplift
(iii) Health/Housing and other similar schemes
(iv) Removal of social disabilities.

IV

Constitutional facilities were also provided in different Article of which Article 46 is most important, which runs as follows :

> The State shall promote with special care the educational and economic interests of the Weaker Sections of the People, and in particular Scheduled Castes and Tribes, and shall protect them from social injustice and all forms of exploitation.

Article 244 empowers the President to declare any area,

where there is a substantial population of tribal people, as Scheduled Area under the Fifth Schedule or in Assam as a Tribal Area under the Sixth Schedule. Under this Schedule, the executive power of a State extends to the Scheduled Areas, but the Governor is vested with the Authority to modify State and Central Laws and to make Regulations for maintenance of peace and good government. It was laid down that in all States having Scheduled Areas, a Tribal Advisory Council has to be set up. The Governor has to submit periodical Reports to the President. It was also provided that the executive power of the Union shall extend to giving of directions to the States regarding administration of the said areas.

Article 275 of the Constitution provides for financial assistance to the States for the implementation of the provisions of the Constitution.

Articles 330, 332 and 334 provide for reservation of seats for the Scheduled Tribes in the Lok Sabha and the State Assemblies for a certain period. Article 335 provides for reservation in the services for them.

There is a provision that a separate Minister should hold the protfolio of Scheduled Tribes in the States of Bihar, Madhya Pradesh and Orissa.

Formation of a Tribes Advisory Council is provided for in the Fifth Schedule of the Constitution. "There shall be established" it says "in each State having Scheduled Areas there and if the President so directs, also in any State having Scheduled Tribes but not Scheduled Areas therein, a Tribes Advisory Council consisting of not more than 20 members of whom as nearly as may be three-fourths shall be the representatives of the Scheduled Tribes in the Legislative Assembly of the State. The Tribes advisory Council was intended to be a channel of discussion about the stages in which the laws and rules generally obtaining should be applied to the tribal areas. There is also provision for formation of District Tribal Advisory Committees to formulate and implement the projects for the welfare of the tribals.

V

The setting up of the Commissions from time to time as

mentioned before was to examine the nature of welfare works done for the down-trodden by the Government. The Commissioner of the Scheduled Castes and Scheduled Tribes, India, under Article 338 of the Constitution has to present an annual report to the President of India through the Minister for Home Affairs. He has to watch the implementation of the Protective measures by—(1) scrutinizing the legislation existing or proposed to be adopted, concerning Scheduled Tribes, (ii) enquire into the complaints and representations, (iii) undertake case studies, and (iv) maintain extensive contacts through freely mixing with the members of the Scheduled Tribes and their representatives as well as various voluntary and humanitarian organizations working in this field. The Planning Commission has a Social Welfare Division to examine the various welfare activities under operation and for their assessment and evaluation for future planning. So the Commissions thus appointed are expected to examine the tribal problems and welfare situations in a perspective of reality and to suggest to the Government suitable remedial measures. Naturally an approach is needed for the overall betterment and solution of the problems of the Scheduled Tribes of our country for effective implementation of the projects. The author of this paper had the opportunity to discuss four important reports on Scheduled Tribes made by—(1) Dr. Verrier Elwin, (2) U.N. Dhebar, (3) P. Shilu Ao, and (4) Professor L.P. Vidyarthi and his personal assessment and suggestions are contained in it which he thinks will help solve many of the basic problems of the Scheduled Castes and Tribes effectively.

VI

Initially for the purpose of tribal development, Special Multipurpose Tribal Blocks were decided to be set up jointly by the Ministry of Home Affairs and Ministry of Community Development and Co-operation in the most underdeveloped parts of our country where the tribal communities are predominantly in a majority. These are 43 in number. After the introduction of this project there was criticism and naturally the Ministry of Home Affairs appointed a Committee to examine the working and programmes of these Blocks. The Committee began to function with Dr. Verrier Elwin as

Chairman in 1959. The terms of reference of the Committees were simple and were intended to cover the following aspects :

(a) To study the working of the Special Multi-purpose Tribal Blocks.

(b) To advise the Government of India on how to implement the intensive development programmes of the Blocks more effectively and give the programme a proper tribal bias.

VII

The special features of these Blocks were more or less like those of the NES Blocks with greater emphasis on rapid improvement in the economic and social standards of the tribal people by selecting specially undeveloped but compact areas for multi-sided development. The object was to make these programmes of development more intensive in character than those undertaken in the normal C.D. Blocks. The Ministry of Home Affairs sanctioned Rs. 6,45,00,000 during the Second Five Year Plan for these units i.e. Rs. 15 lakh for each Block and a further sum of Rs. 12 lakhs for each Block was granted by the Ministry of Community Development. These Blocks covered 23,340.58 sq. miles with a total population of 16,85,325 of whom 12,10,976 were tribal. The average coverage for each Block was thus 182 villages with a population of 39,193 spread over an area of 547.45 sq. miles. These were distributed as follows : in Andhra Pradesh 4, in Assam 7, in Bihar 8, in Bombay 7, in Madhya Pradesh 1 0, in Orissa 4, in Rajasthan 1, in Manipur 1 and in Tripura 1.

In the report, the general principles of tribal development were framed and focussed. These were on the basis of a statement made by the late Prime Minister Nehru and enunciated as follows :

(a) People should develop along lines of their own genius and we should avoid imposing anything on them. We should try to encourage in every way their traditional art and culture.

(b) Tribal rights in land and forest should be respected.

(c) We should train and build up a team of their own

people to do the work of administration and development. Some technical personnel from outside will no doubt, be needed, specially in the beginning. But we should avoid introducing too many outsiders into tribal territory.

(d) We should not over-administer these areas or overwhelm them with multiplicity of schemes.

(e) We should judge the result, not by statistics or the amount of money spent, but by the quality of human character that is evolved.

The report elaborately discussed the detail of the staffing pattern and made the suggestion for appointment of a Forest Extension Officer and more tribal representation in such schemes. It suggested not to make frequent transfers of staff. The problems of land and agriculture had been examined fully. Considering the landless status of the tribal people, the Committee opined that more land should be given to them through the "Gramdan Movement" along with *patta* or legal deed. Cultivable lands in these areas should be surveyed and unoccupied lands should be distributed to the tribals. It is desirable, it suggested, that every tribal should have at least one-and-half acres of wet land or five acres of dry land. Money should be spent specifically for animal husbandry and agricultural extension along with land reclamation, irrigation and soil conservation. Areas of shifting cultivation have also been thoroughly examined and the Committee suggested to improve the fertility of the *jhum* cultivation land to produce more food, and for growing alternate crops that can be raised in a short time. The problems of communication, health services, drinking water, education, social education were also examined and it suggested establishment of Ashram types of Schools. The Committee critically evaluated the women's programme and suggested the appointment of sensitive Mukhya Sevika and Gram Sevikas for implementation of social and educative programmes for the tribal women and their greater involvement in these programmes.

Progress in rural arts and crafts is not satisfactory among the tribal-folk and this has been very seriously criticised by the Committee. Rural housing and setting up of colonies are important items, but this aspect of development was found not at all satisfactory. The problem of indebtedness and co-operation among the tribals is also a major cause of their exploitation. The tribals are so much in debt to the money-lenders that an individual, even an entire family are often found in bondage to them and have to offer free labour to them for long periods. To overcome these problems the Committee suggested to establish Co-operative societies for providing them with loans and agricultural inputs in times of need. The Committee in making these suggestions took into due consideration the endeavours and research activities done by the Cultural Research Institute, Dept. of Anthropology of some Universities and Anthropological Survey of India in these respects.

Since the tribals, in general, are very poor and most of their problems are intricate and they live in the condition of backward technology, so arrangements should be made with all seriousness by the State Governments on the above lines, for their uplift and proper rehabilitation. All the Departments entrusted with this work should tackle the problems in their proper perspective. Officers, specially the Block Development Officers shou'd know the major tribal languages for easy understanding of their problems and adopting appropriate administrative measures to solve these.

VIII

In Article 339 of the Constitution it has been laid down that the President shall appoint a Commission at the end of ten years from its commencement to report on the administration of what are known as the Scheduled Areas and Scheduled Tribes and accordingly a Commission under the Chairmanship of U.N. Dhebar was set up on 28th April 1960. Popularly this report is known as Dhebar Commission Report. This report examined all facts and the nature of developments achieved through these schemes related to Scheduled Areas and Scheduled Tribes except Assam, i.e. covering the field of operation of the Fifth Schedule of the Constitution. The report began with a brief description of the socio-cultural life of some tribal communities and constitutional arrangements in Part I. Then it dealt with the tribal problems in general, tribal loyalties, integration and development in which emphasis was given on approach to the tribal problems through emotional integration of the tribals with the mainstream of the society. Besides, it discussed in detail the condition of the tribes prior to independence in which the British policy of isolation has been criticised and condemned. In the part "Constitution and the Scheduled Tribes" the drawbacks of the constitutional formulae have been discussed. The population of the Scheduled Areas of our country, i.e. where the tribals are concentrated is more than 50 per cent of the total population. Table below gives State-wise total population and the percentage of tribes.

TABLE 5.1

The Scheduled Areas

State	Area in sq. miles	Total population of the area	Schduled Tribe population	Percentage
1. Andhra Pradesh	11312	820384	767000	93.0
2. Bihar	15611	5865675	2457993	41.9
3. Madhya Pradesh	25652	2812168	1686464	59.9
4. Maharashtra	9380	1346113	733948	54.5
5. Gujarat	6917	1576084	993653	63.0
6. Orissa	22014	3229049	1522527	47.0
7. Punjab	4700	11423	2661	23.2
8. Rajasthan	4077	731986	445394	60.0

The report contained the details of the powers of the Governor and the Tribes Advisory Council which the Commission had recommended, specifying the nature of constitution of the Council which should have a permanent staff and a Secretary.

This report discussed the criteria of administration of the Scheduled Areas as well as responsibility of the States. In Part II of the report detailed assessments have been made pinpointing the nature of achievements during the First Five Year Plan. Land, land reforms and land transfers have been discussed in detail along with the suggestion for the rehabilitation of the displaced tribals. Forest policy and exclusively tribal inhabited forest villages have been suggested. Adoption of agriculture in Scheduled Areas along with animal husbandry and orientation and proper training of the workers who will supervise these schemes have also been suggested. Elaborate discussion has been made in regard to Community Development and Tribal Development Blocks. Problems of indebtedness and how this can be overcome by co-operation, has also been suggested. In course of discussion of the educational aspects, certain types of schools have been suggested along with the mode of selection of the type of teachers who will man these. Discussion of health conditions and suggestion for establishment of Mobile Health Units are other salient points. Housing and communication problems have also been given due importance. Cottage Industry has been suggested as the alternative economic pursuit of the tribals for their upliftment, and as such, the anticipated impact of such industrialisation has been dealt with in greater details.

In Part III of the report elaborate discussions have been made in respect of administration including the role of Voluntary Organisation and training programmes. Representation in the services has also been discussed.

By way of conclusion, the Commission followed the path of Gandhi who said

> I do not want my house to be walled in on all sides and my windows to be stuffed. I want the cultures of all lands to be blown about my house as freely as possible. But I refuse to be blown off my feet by any.

The Commission very sympathetically discussed the condition of the tribals in the following manner :

> We have viewed the tribal problem from this wider angle of the interest of the tribals, the need for maintaining harmony and of integration. We hope and trust that our recommendations conform to that objective and will be helpful in fulfilling it.

IX

A study team headed by P. Shilu Ao as Chairman was constituted on 26 October 1966 for the north-eastern States of

India to examine the tribal development programmes there, with the object of giving practical effect to the recommendations made in the original Fourth Five Year Plan for the welfare of the Scheduled Tribes. The team was required to—

(1) study the problems and needs of the tribal communities in each State;
(2) appraise the working of tribal development programmes, specially during the Third Five Year Plan;
(3) ascertain how far the schemes formulated so far have enabled the tribal communities to secure an adequate share in the benefits accruing from the general development programmes;
(4) make detailed recommendations regarding the lines on which the schemes should be oriented in the Fourth Plan to accelerate progress; and
(5) suggest measures for strengthening the administrative machinery and harnessing tribal leadership and institutions so as to ensure their fullest participation in the task of economic and social development.

The team gave a very clear description of the tribal communities all over the country. While discussing the problem, it explained the tribal welfare policy, and held the view that the tribals should "develop along the lines of their genius" and that nothing should be imposed on them. The view of the team was based on an objective assessment of the progress made so far in the social and economic development of the tribal communities. They have broadly categorised all the tribal groups into three segments—

(i) tribes living in the fastness of the hills cut off from all contact with the outer world, who are still in the hunting and food gathering stage.

(ii) A virile race of freedom-loving politically conscious tribals in north and north-east India, many of whom through the devoted efforts of the missionaries for over a century have reached a stage when they can rub shoulders even with their most enlightened counterparts amongst the advanced communities.

(iii) The tribals between these two extreme poles in varying stages of development mainly distributed in the vast tribal belt of Central India.

The study team discussed elaborately the conditions of the Donotified Communities who were once considered as ex-criminal tribes. According to them they should be scheduled as per their style of life either with the other castes or the tribes for better integration and overall development of the tribal people.

This study team has dealt with the impact of the First, Second, and Third Five Year Plans and the physical targets achieved in all aspects of tribal life including educational benefits through grant of scholarships, construction of school and hostel buildings, provision of books and clothing, setting up of Ashram Schools and provision of mid-day meals. In respect of economic uplift, elaborate discussions and recommendations have been made in regard to development of land and irrigation facilities, supply of bullocks, implements, seeds and fertilizers, soil conservation, cottage industries, colonizations of shifting cultivators co-operation, technical training and communication. Recommendations were also made in respect of health and housing, medical facilities, drinking water supply schemes, provision of legal aid and grants to Voluntary Organisations working at the State level.

The study report deals further with details of agriculture and allied programmes, land tenure soil conservation, animal husbandry, forest and forest policies. Tribal Development Blocks in specific areas have also been studied in detail. Indebtedness, co-operation, education, vocational education, medical and Public health, housing and communication were also covered by this study. Part II of the report is an assessment and examination of tribal problems all over the country and Part III is related to administration and Institutional set-up.

Besides this, the Sixth Schedule of the Constitution is related to the administration of tribal areas of Assam. The last part of the report contains the summary, recommendations and conclusions. By content, this is an exhaustive report relating to the Scheduled Tribes of India.

X

After independence various measures have already been taken but the problem of tribal development has reached a very critical stage without bringing much benefit at least for some tribal communities who remain untouched. Unequal development at different spheres of tribal life has caused tension and as such a fresh look at the tribal situation in the country has become indispensable. Thus scientific reviewing of the strategy of development was made. It was reemphasized that the tribal communities should be the equal partners in all spheres of national life as early as possible. So, the Fifth Five Year Plan was considered a little different from the earlier ones because it envisaged some key programmes on a time-bound basis. Tribal development should be treated as an integral part of social and economic development and as such a new strategy was fixed to attack the problems. Continuous evaluation of the development effort becomes a part and parcel of the administrative structure, so that we are not once again forced to say in respect of tribal development, "we do not know". The new strategy can be summarised as follows :

(i) The problem of tribal development should be defined at the national level and the national effort required for tackling it should be worked out;

(ii) The precise part assigned to each State and to each department in this task should be fully defined and the central sector should pay an important role though essentially one of supplemental assistance :

(iii) A review of important national level policies specially those covering forest, industry, mineral development and excise administration should be taken up;

(iv) An integrated area development approach in consonance with the development of the people should be adopted. The development programmes should give high priority to programmes minimizing incidence of exploitation and help building up the inner strength of local communities;

(v) Strengthening and streamlining of administration and economic institutions should be taken up urgently and evaluation should become an integral part of the administrative structure.

With this view, the Planning Commission set up "a Task

Force on Development of Tribal Areas" (5 April 1972) with Professor L.P. Vidyarthi as the Chairman. The following terms of reference were outlined :

(i) To review the nature and level of development, identify the present bottlenecks and weaknesses in policies and programmes and suggest corrective measures.

(ii) To suggest a perspective of development from 1973-74 to 1988-89 in the light of the overall development perspective envisaged in the Fourth Plan.

(iii) Special schemes for extremely backward areas and for neglected and isolated tribes and also for tribals affected by major projects should be formulated.

(iv) To formulate proposal for the Fifth Plan in the light of the perspectives indicating priorities, policies, programmes and outlays. As far as possible contents of programmes with geographical coverage should be outlined. To facilitate working of the Task Force, as well as to cover all the aspects of tribal life, the Planning Commission constituted five working groups on the following subjects :

(a) Working Group on Identification of Tribal Development Areas and less developed tribal communities (Professor Vidyarthi as Chairman).

(b) Working group on Legislative and Administrative set-up (Dr. B.K. Roy Burman as Chairman.)

(c) Working group on Tribal Development Programmes based on Forests (Sri S.A. Shah as Chairman)

(d) Working Group on general programmes and area-wise programmes of infra-structure and social services in Tribal Areas (Sri D.V. Natarajan as Chairman)

(e) Personnel policy in Tribal Areas (Sri R.N. Haldipur as Chairman).

In course of review of the tribal situation, the Task Force expresses the view that in spite of investment in various ways by the State and Central Governments for tribal development in the successive Plans in regard to the problems of the tribals reflected in primitive methods of agriculture, land alienation, indebtedness, adverse effects if industrialization, low rates of literacy, poor health and nutrition etc. have not been solved. The committee categorically stated that the efforts so far made for social and economic development of scheduled tribes did not bring about appreciable changes in their condition, one of the important factors for lack of impact so far is that the development of "scheduled tribes and tribal areas" has been looked upon as a problem of "Welfare" as distinguished from "Development". Further, there has been a tendency to rely on schematic patterns in the Tribal Development Block Programme in place of adopting a flexible strategy suiting the needs of each Tribal Development Block Area. The elites among the tribals tend to take away all benefits of developmental programmes thus creating vested interests. Therefore, more backward among the tribals have been denied the benefits of plan programmes. Lastly as a result of historical reasons, the administrative structure in tribal areas has continued to lack simplicity and thereby defying comprehension of the tribals and has failed to evoke any response from them. Such a structure of administration may not therefore be suitable for carrying out integrated development of tribal areas".

Thus during the Fifth Plan period a few distinctive policies were suggested and formulated. Integrated Tribal Development Programme (ITDP) covering big areas designated as "macro" generally correspond to a district, a bit smaller designated as "meso", and small equal to that of Block designated as "micro" were demarcated where tribals are present with high concentration. Apart from macro, meso and micro areas there are small pockets of tribal population which need special attention and their development will necessarily have to be given priority in multi-level planning. For development of tribal areas short-term and long-term planning were suggested. Provision of infra-structure of the extension of credit marketing, market link roads and inputs for the development of agriculture were suggested with priority. So the Fifth Plan provides many opportunities for the over-all development of the tribals in all parts of our country. This was termed as Sub-plan with the following objects :

(1) to narrow the gap between the levels of development of tribal and other areas; and

(2) to improve the quality of life of the tribal communities in general with an idea to prevent the exploitation of the tribals, to develop tribal economy of a new type utilising the available resources, generating employment opportunities and

providing a basic infra-structure, through growth centres-communication network, schools, rural, health centres, marketing and credit organisation, rural electrification etc.

Thus the Task Force exercised the kind of sagacity and pragmatism needed most at the moment in offering its suggestions for tackling the problems of the downtrodden. This was reflected in the projects and schemes during the Fifth Plan period.

XI

By way of conclusion it can be said that the Scheduled Tribes in general of our country have become very conscious now. They have realised the advantages of scheduling which gave them sufficient protection and strength for their own cause, Anthropologists are the architects of the society and they know the details of the anatomy of the society. They must act as experts in Committees which undertake the responsibility of introducing welfare measures. There should be good social workers as well as officers to implement these development schemes as they will be in a position to understand the whole situation in reality. They should steer clear of all bottlenecks and formalities or difficulties arising out of impleentation of the formulated projects.

For the overall development, the plans must be region-based with a slant towards ethnicity. The plans should be such that socio-economic barriers and carriers will be focussed to have a desirable change within a limited period. Periodic assessment is necessary and provisions should be made for any changes when required. All schemes should have phases with provision for follow-up schemes and the small and hostile communities should not be disturbed. Local resources should be tapped to develop a sense of belonging among the people concerned. Due respect should be given to their myths/rituals, by which the people can be easily won over and interlaced with the main-stream of the society. Thus, in course of time, the people of the weaker sections will be elevated and be able to complete with their more advanced brethren even when the assistance now given under the plans is discontinued.

SIX

S. P. Sinha

TRIBAL DEVELOPMENT ADMINISTRATION
A Historical Overview

PLANNED CHANGE in tribal areas in India can be understood properly if we begin with study of this phenomenon during British rule. They are rightly credited with having been the first to extend the arms of government most seriously (may be due to imperialistic design) to the inaccessible hilly fastness which were almost consigned to oblivion, paying occasional tribute and professing a loose loyalty when pressed to do so. In historical times during the days of the Imperial Maurya special attention was to be paid by the Crown Prince and there was a separate Minister in the cabinet known as *Ant Mahamatya*. The Rock Edicts of Asoka the Great are witness to this and so are the large number of epigraphical and literary evidences. But in the most effective sense, modern principles of administration whether for colonial or other ends were first brought to the tribals by the British in the territory known as British India.

The constitutional obligation in free India to make the tribals catch up the non-tribals in the race for social, political and economic prosperity, which is the kernel of planned action in the different Five Year Plan periods, cannot be fully appreciated if the special situation in tribal areas. ecologically socially, politically and administratively, is not fully discussed. But paucity of space limits this study to the administrative situation only, which is, of course, the main fountain of all activities directed to bring about change in ecology, society, polity, and economy in any area. Therefore, this article has been divided into two parts : (i) planned change in British Tribal India with the sole purpose of isolating the tribals from the mainstream of national life, and (ii) planned change in free tribal India during the Five Year Plans with the sole purpose of integrating the tribals into the mainstream of national life. The study is limited in its coverage to the situation in the tribal areas of Bihar to be cited as a typical example of what is happening in tribal areas in India today.

PLANNED CHANGE IN BRITISH TRIBAL INDIA

Bringing about transformation of the tribal people living in the hilly fastnesses and out-of-way places, unattended and unknown, had been the special concern of administration right from the days of Warren Hastings, when first governmental attempts were made to bring bandit "Hill men" or Pahariyas of the Rajmahal Hills under the pale of civilization" through an indefatigable Brooke, Browne, or Cleveland in the latter part of the eighteenth century. The nineteenth century say the utilitarians, like Munro, Elphinstone and Metcalfe, the three principal representatives of a patriarchal, unitary system of administration devising the pattern of field administration which was military in form but personal in orientation.[1] They devised a steel frame of administration to bring about a change in tribal areas by discarding Cornwallis' division of judiciary from executive; they would allow no one to be glued to his chair in court or office. The man who collected the revenue was also responsible for order—he was policemen, magistrate, and judge.

Non-regulation System

This system of government stood for different ideals. To the ryot government must be represented simply, not by a multiplicity of officers and a multiplicity of written forms but by a single officer, who has powers to equire, to judge, and to punish without delay and intricacies of western legal process. This officer was not to be a distant and awful figure, presiding in his *cutchery* like a deity in his temple, but a familiar lord, visiting and speaking with them of their quarrels and their crops and looked up to as *Ma-Bap*—father and mother. In practical terms, this meant a union of powers, at least at the district level.[2] The emergence of new ideas, viz., liberalism, utilitarianism, and humanism which called for a new view of the functions of Government, paved the way for the combination of magisterial and revenue functions, in the person of the Collector. It was considered most desirable because it was in consonance with the contemporary philosophy of liberalism which advocated functionalism on the one hand and centralism on the other.[3]

It is to be noted that no civilian officer was preferred for the tribal areas; the criteria seemed to have been efficiency, as a military officer was effective in suppressing the unrest or tribal rebellions as well as the prevailing notion that the military officers were best suited for administration and relief. This attitude came in such a bold relief that the provinces where such military officers were employed were known as Non-Regulation while civilians were exclusively employed in Regulation provinces.[4]

Dent and Wilkinson, Special Commissioners to suppress the Great Kole Rising of 1832, must have been influenced by these ideals. Wilkinson's thinking was more due to the direct experience he had in running administration in tribal areas of Nagpore for more than a decade where he drew heavily on his experiences and upon the ideas worked by Munro and Elphinstone. But his model was W. Blunt, who had considerable experience of tribal administration of civil justice in Arracan[5] in 1828. W. Blunt, who rose to be the third member of the Governor-General's Council, was the most important of the paternalists under the reforming Bentinck.

Thus, the system of administration specially of tribal areas by these utilitarians was paternalistic in mode and depended in a large measure for its successful operation upon the administrator's personal qualities of character, initiative and vigour. Similar to the arrangement at the provincial level, the districts in which military officers were employed were known as Non-Regulation, while those where civilians were exclusively employed were Regulation districts—these where governed by the laws made under the Charter Acts called Regulations till 1834. Elements of administration in Non-Regulation areas (predominantly inhabited by turbulent tribal people, whose pacification was the greatest necessity) were predominantly military with the civilian's part relegated to a secondary position.

The system had certain merits which served the British cause in Arracans in 1828 when Blunt framed the famous Arracan Rules. In Chotanagpur in 1834, when Wilkinson's Rules were promulgated, and in 1855, when a separate Santhal Parganas District under Yule Regulation was created the British policy in those Non-Regulation areas remained isolationist. As the time went on the idea that special arrangements were necessary for the isolated tribal regions gained general acceptance. The whole of the nineteenth century was punctuated by one tribal rebellion or other. This compelled British administrators to experiment with one measure or the other—legislative or executive till such time that these areas were turned into practically "ethnological parks", protected and safeguarded by different tenurial steps and executive actions. Pax Britannica was meaningless without the religion of Christ being the major persuasion of the subject people, and therefore, a thorough and systematic induction of Christian missionaries started in the tribal areas. They were actuated by an "obligation to convert our erring brethren to the faith of Christ".[6] They thought "to make Government effectual to all the good purpose of it, there must be a religion".[7] We are aware of the various Christian missionaries exploits and their persistent approach to keep the tribal converts away from the national movements.

The mutiny brought into bold relief the merits of paternal despotism, because it was considered that the paternal despotism was not only the happiest but the only regime for India.[8] Therefore, in the year 1874 when the Scheduled District Act was passed, or in 1919 and 1935, when Government of India Acts were passed, the tribal areas in different states were kept excluded from the purview of the legislature and were kept as wholly excluded areas and areas of modified exclusion-'Partially Excluded Area' and 'Excluded Area'. This exclusion served to a great extent the British purpose of keeping the tribal areas isolated, away from the mainstream of national life, so that the 'contagion' of the Freedom Movement did not affect the tribal people.

Therefore, extensive tribal tracts in the provinces of Bihar, Bengal, Orissa, U.P., Madhya Pradesh, Bombay and Madras were declared 'partially excluded areas', whereas frontier and border regions in Assam, Laccadive and Minicoy Islands, and the Lahul and Spiti areas in Himachal Pradesh were declared 'excluded areas'.

In spite of the enforced isolation, the tribals responded to the call of Mahatma Gandhi and other nationalist leaders.[9] In Bihar, the Tana Bhagat movement got mixed with the Non-cooperation movement launched by Gandhiji. Some of the valiant Tanas walked on foot to Lahore, Belgaum, Nagpur, Calcutta, Gaya, Ramgarh, etc., to attend sessions of the Indian National Congress and participated in other agitations like Flag Satyagraha at Nagpore, and courted arrest many times. The national leaders got first hand knowledge of their (tribal) conditions and they became anxious to reintegrate the tribal society with the main current of Indian life from whère they (tribals) had been kept away all along by the British masters for reasons suited to their imperialist designs. Protests were raised against the British policy of isolation through protection. After the formation of popular ministries in 1937, committees were appointed in the provinces of Bihar, Orissa, Bombay and Madras to enquire into the condition of the tribals, but the resignation of the Ministries postponed adoption of any new policy for tribal welfare until Independence.

A.V. Thakkar and some other workers of the Servants of India Society did pioneering work among the tribes and they prepared the ground for a new attitude and approach towards the tribals by the national leaders, who were getting conscious by and by of their responsibility towards them (tribals). A vast literature on tribes and castes by early British administrators, like Dalton and Risley, by Census Officers like Grigson and Hutton, by anthropologists like S.C. Roy, B.S. Guha, etc., gave good insights into tribal problems. Verrier Elwin's contribution towards understanding tribal problems is still a landmark which helped Mahatma Gandhi and later on, Pandit Jawahar Lal Nehru in formulating their ideas regarding the tribal problems.[10] Missionaries like Knowles, Wood, Hislop, Nortrott, Bodding, Hoffmann, etc., placed their view points on tribal life and aspirations, though they interpreted these in their own way.

PLANNED CHANGE IN FREE TRIBAL INDIA

When India attained independence, the leaders were greatly benefited by such literature and one of the first acts of the Constituent Assembly was to appoint the 'Excluded and partially Excluded Areas' (Other than Assam) Sub-committee with A.V. Thakkar as Chairman which showed that the new democratic state was aware of its responsibility towards the welfare of the tribal people living in areas however remote and inaccessible they might be.

The Constituent Assembly accepted this and the tribal problem at once became an integral part of the development of the Indian people as a whole. Sardar Patel would not like to rest till every tribal reached the level of Jaipal Singh.[11] Thus, the Constituent Assembly passed some of the provisions, like Article 46, which embodied the new policy, its 'message of hope'[12] for millions of our citizens hitherto neglected. Out of Article 46 flows all safeguards for members of scheduled castes and scheduled tribes. Thus, the goal set by the Constitution assures a progressive life to the members of these weaker sections of our community. Our goal is to 'emancipate them from all forms of exploitation'.

Five Year Plans

In tune with these objectives, the Five Year Plans were launched with some special priority to eradicate different handicaps and disabilities imposed by the working of the earlier governmental machinery. The under privileged groups, such as scheduled tribes, scheduled castes, denotified tribes, nomadic tribes lacked adequate opportunities for group and individual self-development, specially in increasing their income, employment, facilities for health, housing and education.

At the beginning of the First Five Year Plan, there were (they are still continuing unchanged) about 427 Scheduled communities their number is 38.2 million according to the Census of India 1971, at varying levels of development, some of them living in isolated and remote hilly areas which are almost inaccessible. To promote their welfare, Article 275 provides for grants-in-aid from the Consolidated Fund of India to States for implementation of development programmes in addition to general developmental outlays accruing to the tribal people and areas. In 21 years of planned development, a sum of Rs. 358 crores was spent up to 1971-72 on the welfare of backward classes through special schemes alone. The table below would give the idea of plan provision and expenditure incurred on scheduled tribes during the first three plans. Figuies of other places on an all-India basis are unfortunately not available after the Fourth Plan period.

TABLE 6.1

Plan Provision and Expenditure on Scheduled Tribes[13]

Plan Provision	Total Plan Expenditure		Provision	Scheduled percentage to total Plan Provision	Tribes Expenditure	Percentage to total expenditure
	Prov.	*Exp.*				
First	2378	1960	25.00	1.05	20.05	1.03
Second	4800	4672	47.00	0.98	40.93	0.94
Third	7500	8608	59.39	0.79	53.40	0.62

As a matter of fact, the special provision in the Plan for scheduled tribes and other backward classes is not in lieu of the provision in the General Development Programme, but is intended to supplement it. Except Andhra Pradesh no State Government unfortunately has been found alive to this fact. The report of the Task Force on Development of Tribal areas 1973 shows that the proportionate expenditure on scheduled tribes remained diminishing during the Plan period. This is evident from the table below.

TABLE 6.2

Size of Plan for Scheduled Tribes

Plan period	Total plan	Scheduled tribes	percentage
First plan	1960	19.93	1.0
Second plan	4672	42.92	0.9
Third plan	8577	50.53	0.5
1966-69	6756	32.32	0.5
Fourth plan	153902.2 (Outlay)	75.00	0.04

Table No. 6.3 shows the expenditure incurred on different sectors of welfare of the scheduled tribes during the first, second and third five year plan periods and the average per capita expenditure per annum on the three groups of scheme.

TABLE 6.3

Expenditure Incurred on the Welfare of Scheduled Tribes

Scheme	First Plan		Second Plan		Third Plan		Expenditure in Fourth Plan in 1966-69		
	Total Expen-diture incurred (Rs. in crores)	Expen-diture per-capita Rs.	Total Expen-diture incurred (Rs. in crores)	Expen-diture per capita (Rs.)	Total Expen-diture incurred (Rs. in crores)	Per eapita (Rs.)	Total Expen-diture Rs. in crore.	Per-capital (Rs.)	
1. Education	5.10	0.48	7.84	0.78	13.51	0.98	9.32	N.A.	31.50
2. Economic Uplift	4.59	0.41	20.00	1.78	30.71	1.82	24.07	N.A.	42.25
3. Health, Housing, Communication etc.	10.14	0.90	15.08	1.34	6.31	0.78	1.93	N.A.	10.45
Total	19.83	1.79	42.92	3.90	50.53	3.58	35.32	N.A.	84.20

Except the education sector, under which stipends and scholarships were given to the Scheduled Tribe students, invariably the welfare content in other sectors was general and diversified. Therefore whereas the expenditure under the head 'Education' might have helped in throwing up a new elite among the tribes (very beneficial for them, indeed), expenditure under other sectors has reportedly accentuated the tensional situation between the parochial tribals and the exploiting non-tribes causing severe hindrance in integration of the tribes with the mainstream of our national life.

This also shows that there has been increase in expenditure from Plan to Plan but in the Third Plan, expenditure on it is 21.56 per cent more than that during the Second Plan period. In the First Plan, the main emphasis was on health, housing and communication, but in the Second Plan the emphasis shifted to "economic development" (agriculture, cottage industries, forest cooperative societies and setting up of multipurpose tribal blocks). The Third Plan renamed these blocks as Tribal Development Blocks with the priorities for economic uplift, education and health, housing and communications. The Study Team on Tribal Development Programmes, set up by the Planning Commission in 1969, did not feel enthusiastic about giving a clear verdict as to whether the progress was "appreciable or marginal" but it was very clear to the team that "if progress is to be judged by what remains to be done to bring the tribals on par with the rest of the population, the leeway to be made up is still considerable and that the delay in the implementation of considered recommendations, made by the Scheduled Areas and Scheduled Tribes Commission and other high level bodies in the past to protect the rights of the tribals has worsened the position which these recommendations were intended to correct, while the failure to pay attention to and profit by their advice on matters pertaining to the formulation and implementation of tribal development programmes has resulted in the failure of ambitious schemes and consequent waste of valuable resources".[14]

Experience shows that most of the programmes in the backward classes sector in the absence of adequate financial backing and organizational support, had little impact on the poverty, educational backwardness and social disability of backward classes.[15] Even in the cases of area based programmes, such as Tribal Development Blocks (taken up since the Second Five Year Plan), the impact has not been satisfactory on account of the limited area covered and the absence of substantial investment called for on such programmes as minor irrigation, development of communication and electrification, etc.[16] According to a recent report,17 allocation under welfare of backward classes, which was meant to be supplementary to the outlays in the general sectors of development have, in fact substituted the latter. The policy of productive schemes in the Fourth Plan was not only to increase productivity as a whole, but also to remove the huge disparities in development that exist, between different regions and classes. It is regrettable that so far as backward classes are concerned the disparities have tended to increase between them and the rest of the population. As on 18 April 1973, there were 504 Tribal Development Blocks in the country but the philosophy of tribal development has miserably failed.

Fifth Five Year Plan

The current thinking is that in view of the magnitude of the problem of scheduled tribes which has baffled our planners as well as executors in the period of four Five Year Plans, some time-bound programmes have to be formulated to provide increase in the level of literacy, major changes in occupational pattern and development of infrastructure in terms of marketing, provision of credit, communications and irrigation so that they could come up to an adequate minimum level of living, comparable with that of the general population.

Once again, hopes have been pinned on the Sixth Five Year Plan. Perspective plans have been prepared up to 1988-89 through which least minimum facilities of civilized existence to the members of scheduled tribes and other backward communities are also provided so that disparities that exist between them and the general people can legitimately be narrowed and finally eliminated. With such an end in view, the Fifth Five Year Plan strategy of development of backward classes places greater emphasis on the role of the general sector in providing major developmental programmes. The public consumption programmes specially in regard to the minimum needs will give high priority to scheduled castes and scheduled tribes.

In the Fifth Five Year Plan, it was considered that utmost priority was to be accorded to drawing up an integrated area plan after identifying specific tribal areas. In formulating plan programmes, review of legislative measures regarding prevention of land alienation of both scheduled castes and scheduled tribes, providing infra-structure for economic and social service, and modification of personnel policy in tribal areas should receive prior attention. This however could not be achieved very successfully. The efforts are being continued with some force during the Sixth Five Year Plan.

Some Pre-Conditions

But no plan strategy can work well unless we pragmatically honour some of the compulsions of the tribal situation. The imbalance in development not only requires comprehensive planning, but also a different type of administrative edifice. There are yet certain pre-conditions for the success of the Fifth Five Year Plan to be launched.

For drawing up a comprehensive development plan for tribal areas, identification of specific tribal areas is essential. Taking the criterion of concentration of tribal population, compact areas can be demarcated at macro-, meso- and micro-levels. Macro-areas could generally correspond to a sizable scheduled area; meso-area may be coterminus with a district or taluka; and micro-area may be a Tribal Development Block. Even after identifying and categorizing as macro-, meso- and micro-tribal areas,[18] there would still be a large number of tribal pockets scattered throughout the country which deserve special attention and multi-level planning at the district level or even taluka level.

By and large, we have some clear-cut segment of tribal areas throughout the country; some of them have attained their status of statehood recently. We have the tribal areas in the north-eastern regions, like Meghalaya, Nagaland, Arunachal Pradesh and Mizoram where state plan benefits are largely for the tribal population. They have presently no problem of getting step-motherly treatment from the dominant group of people, but nonetheless it is very difficult to say that in those tribal states the dominant groups of tribals are not maintain-ing some sort of hegemony over less dominated ones.

Of the remaining States (except Haryana, Jammu & Kashmir and Punjab, which are mostly without any sizeable tribal population), the districts with substantial concentration of tribal population can be listed and comparable administrative units of taluka or block level can be identified for graded backwardness on the basis of economic status in the district and their literacy rates as compared to the general level of literacy of the district.

There is therefore, the need for declaring more areas as scheduled areas having more than 40 per cent of tribal population so that ameliorative measures could be taken on the lines suggested in the Fifth Schedule of the Constitution. According to the 1971 census, there are 17 districts having 70 per cent or more tribal population (Laccadive and Minicoy Islands and Mizoram have 90 per cent tribal population), 13 districts with 50-69 per cent, 18 districts with 39-49 per cent, 46 districts with 10-29 per cent, and 89 districts with 1-9 per cent tribal population. The last two categories of the districts could be suitably grouped into a compact development zone and special develop-ment projects could be tried there for their all round develop-ment. The report of the Scheduled Castes and Scheduled Tribes Commission had already suggested some more areas in the states of Gujarat, Kerala, Madhya Pradesh, Manipur and Union Territories of Andaman and Nicobar islands for schedul-ing, since tribals living in the areas have similar conditions as of those in scheduled areas under Scheduled Area Order, 1950.

In this connection, mention could be made of some of the state governments setting up Area Development Authority. Bihar State Legislature, in 1971, constituted the Chotanagpur and Santhal Parganas autonomous development authority for "formulating short term and long term plans for this region as well as advising the State Government on matters connected with the preparation and implementation of development programmes for this region, for the first time in the history of the Authority areas. Some special attempts to identify the special problems of development of this region were made and are being made when groups of bureaucrats and technocrats formulated and revised the Rs. 10.33 crores draft plan of the Authority. There is every chance of this plan being a wasteful exercise if it fails to arouse, popular enthusiasm (which is difficult in view of the unwieldiness of deliberative bodies of the Authority) and the greater sincerity to execute it on the part of the powers that be at Patna and Delhi. The need of the hour is that when a plan has been prepared the executing machinery should be yoked with all seriousness to take out the backward people living in the Authority areas from the morass. The important question of development of any such area could not be decided on the political plane only (analogies from Telengana with regard to earmaking separate funds); rather it is by the policy of ruthless implementation through a resolute will that we can expect the Authority to deliver the goods. It is said that procedural wrangles, mutual bickerings, wilful apathy, a solthful bureaucracy and people's representatives has made this Authority a paper tiger which has not been in a position to check the rising extremist and separatists' fissiporous tendencies. which can run diametrically against the interest of the people of the area and the State. Therefore, the Government, it seems, requires greater alertness in setting its own house in order. Recently, the Authority was supplanted by three Authorities, one each for South and North Chotanagpur Divisions and one for Santhal Pargana. A Branch Secretariat has been opened in the office of T.R.D.C. and has started functioning. The RDC is the Principal Secretary and Chief Functionary of Development on the Plateau. Authority has perhaps died a natural death. An office of T.W.C. has also been opened and is functioning independent of R.D.C. but the TWC has not been given the power of the Tribal Welfare Commissioner, Madhya Pradesh, Andhra Pradesh and other places.

About 85 per cent of the tribal population are engaged in agricultural pursuits, and therefore, their relationship with land, legislative and administrative measures and their execution is very significant. A thorough understanding of tribal customary land and forest right vis-a-vis changes which are taking place in the socio-economic tenure system in the tribal areas due to social contact between the tribals and non-tribals is imperative. Tribals and non-tribals have the tradition of living together peacefully over thousands of years; but the follies of neo-settlers during the aftermath of the Permanent Settlement of 1793 and subsequent waves of outsiders in the wake of urbanization and industrialization after Independence have created a tensional situation between them creating a cleavage among the people as *Diku* and *Hor,* and "We group" and "they group". The problem of land alienation and indebtedness have assumed grave proportions.[19]

Therefore, there is need for having a uniform approach in different parts of the country for identifying the tribal rights about land and forests through a thorough survey and settlement operations and preparation of records of rights. Measures to protect the tribals against the exploitation of money lenders, land alienations and resetting of land and other facilities would definitely better their lot.

Since transactions between the tribal and licensed and non-licensed money-lenders are oral, it is very difficult to meet the situation. Some State governments have passed laws leading to debt redemption and control of money-lending activities by setting up of Conciliation Boards and putting a moratorium on tribal loans, but the implementation side is very bleak. The long-term remedy can be found in providing wider coverage of institutional credit in tribal areas and undertaking social economic and educational programmes for the tribals with the assistance of official and non-official agencies. Tribal Development Corporations are merely sinking ships. T.R.D.C. have been opened in some of the states, but they have not been able to acquit themselves in better ways. Land Mortgage Banks have not been able to help the tribal mass. The Cooperative as a movement, has totally failed. Forest Labour Cooperative Societies everywhere, except in Maharashtra, are the handmaidens of forest contractors. State Tribal Cooperative Development Corporations are merely sinking ships. Government taccavi and other loans are practically useless for resourceless tribals. Existing legal and medical aids to the tribals have not been able to mitigate sufferings of even one per cent of them.

What is the reason for this dismal and bleak achievement of the administrative machinery charged with responsibility to provide all these facilities and advantages to the tribals? The answer is given in the recent Report of the Planning Commission which found for "the existing administrative and personnel policies for the tribal areas are far from satisfactory". It felt that unless there is a single agency administration and it is within the comprehension of the tribals, whom the administration intends to serve no amount of development planning would deliver the goods.[20] For example the tribal areas of Bihar in the District of Chotanagpur and Santhal Parganas have been experiencing the worst experimentation. Ever since independence and the inauguration of the Community Development Programme, the single-line system of administration vested in the Deputy Commissioner under Non-Regulation system started getting diversified so much that the plethora of administrative personnel bewildered the simple tribals. An army of officials in tribal areas executing one programme or another without being very much responsible have, far from serving the tribals, alienated them to the full. The plans which these officials execute, are sometimes misunderstood and are taken as a clever device to entangle the tribals and dispossess them of their land which they value so much. Moreover, the unsympathetic dealings of these officials with the tribals keep them practically on inimical terms with each other.

Fists and blows, wordy duels, and acrimony prevail in the administration at the Block and other levels. Tribals, alienated from this administrative machinery have not been able to reconcile themselves with their present position and wistfully look to the days when their *Abua Raj* (their rule) would come.

In Bihar the tribals are fast losing content of their traditional autonomous system of tribal administration in Damin-i-Koh in Santhal Parganas and Kolehan in Singbhum, granted to them hundreds of years ago. They are now feeling the strain of disintegration due to unsympathetic recommendation of the State Law Commission. The matter is pending with the Tribal Advisory Council of Bihar. The author has conducted a survey on this issue. The consensus is that the system should continue of course with certain amendments in Administration of Civil Justice.

While the Circuit Court of Patna High Court has been brought to the city of Ranchi, presumably to bring the highest but costliest justice to the very doors of the tribals, the rough and ready justice meted out to the tribals in the Small Cause Courts in Santhal Parganas under Santhal Rules and

Kolehan Courts under Wilkinson's Rules with little cost are facing closure in the name of bringing uniformity to a people who are still on a different footing of development.

The Panchayati Raj Act has been creating some complications. Zila Parishads have been opened in all the tribal districts of Bihar where *Adhyakshas* have emerged as the co-sharer of powers with the Deputy Commissioner. The *Adhyaksha* is being assisted by one Senior IAS officer and several officials of Additional District Magistrate's rank in matters of development. The Deputy Commissioner is now left with Revenue and Law and order responsibilities only. Even here the Commissioner has to contend himself with some big issues and acting as the supreme court in the Kolhan cases. The need of the hour is to create a new cadre of leadership, which could realize the call of the time to integrate and replace those parochial elements which are vociferously demanding innumerable privileges at the cost of others just to perpetuate backwardness.[21] Backwardness has become a vested interest.

The Prospect

In the light of the forgoing discussion we can safefly see that the prospect of tribal administration is grim. So long as we do not remove the above mentioned failings most pragmatically, the dreams of our Constitution makers to emancipate the tribals from all source of exploitation and to integrate them with the mainstream of national life, will remain unrealized. We do not get tired of proclaiming advantages and privileges to the tribals but, being based on the criteria of ethnic groupings, these are expropriated by the clever sections among the tribals. Any move to recognize economic crteria as the sole guidance of planning has been opposed tooth and nail by the vested interests but the *Garibi Hatao* from the tribals cannot be done without taking a drastic step of excluding those who are economically better off among them. A ranking of the backwardness among the tribal groups, based on a thorough socio-economic study can help us, but we should not allow ourselves to become victims of sadistic pleasure of crying for the amelioration of tribals at the cost of the teeming millions while at the same time actually doing nothing for them.

NOTES

1. Haridwar Rai, "Politico-Administrative Bases of India: Field Administration", the *Indian Journal of Public Administration*, Vol. XVI, No. 4, p. 474.
2. Eric Stocks, *The English Utilitarians and India*, Oxford : Clarendon Press, 1959.
3. B.B. Misra, *The Central Administration of the East India Company 1773-1834*, Bombay : Oxford University Press, 1959.
4. L.S.S. O'Malley, *The Indian Civil Service*, 1601-1930, London : Frank Cass, 1965 (2nd edn.), p. 53.
5. Communication from W. Blunt, Special Commissioner for Arracans to H. Shakespeare, Acting Chief Secretary to the Government, Fort William, dated 19th June, 1828.
6. Rev. Alexander Duff, *India and Indian Missions*, London, 1840 (second edition), p. 308.
7. Ibid., p., 294.
8. Thomas R. Metcalfe, *The Aftermath of Revolt, India 1832-1870*, Princeton :Princeton University Press, 1965, pp. 250-252.
9. S.P. Sinha, "Mahatma Gandhi's Impact on Chhotanagpur Tribes (1920-30)," *Gandhiji and Social Sciences and Other Papers*, New Delhi, 1970.
10. Verrier Elwin, (1) *Philosophy of NEFA*, (2) New Deal.
11. Constituent Assembly Debates (Discussion on 30th April 1947), Vol. 3, p. 467.
12. Ibid.
13. Report of the Study Team on Tribal Development Programmes, Planning Commission, 1969.
14. Shilo Ao Committee Report, New Delhi, 1969 (Mimeographed), p. 25.
15. Approach to the Fifth Plan (1974-79), Planning Commission, 1973, p. 57.
16. Report of the Steering Group on Development of Backward Classes and Social Welfare for the Fifth Five Year Plan (Planning Commission), 1973, p 10.
17. Ibid., p. 11.
18. *Report of the Task Force on Development of Tribal Areas*, New Delhi. Planning Commission, 1973.
19. S.P. Sinha, *The Problem of Land Alienation in and Around Ranchi City*, Patna, 1968.
20. *Report of the Steering Group on Development of Backward Classes and Social Welfare for the Fifth Five Year Plan*, New Delhi, June 1973.
21. Prime Minister, Indira Gandhi, in her address to Welfare Ministers, in *Newsletter*, July 1971, Department of Social Welfare, New Delhi.

SEVEN

S. N. Ratha

TRIBAL DEVELOPMENT PROGRAMME
An Appraisal

NEXT TO Africa India has the largest concentration of a tribal population. The Census of India for 1971 counted 427 tribes and 38,015,162 tribal persons. This constitutes 6.9 per cent of the total population of the country. Among these there are tribes like the Bhil, the Gond, and the Santhal with populations around four million each, large enough to people a nation. In fact they are larger than many contemporary nations.

The distribution of this population in the country is greatly uneven. There are states where they constitute the majority, as in Nagaland (88.61%), Meghalaya (80.48%), Mizoram (94.26%), Arunachal (79.01%); whereas in states like Tamilnadu, Uttar Pradesh, and Karnataka their contribution to the demography is less than one per cent.

The literacy among the tribes is very low: only 11.29 per cent of them can read and write. Close on the heels of non-literacy are superstitions and ignorance.

Occupationally 89.10 per cent of the tribal population is locked up in agriculture, either as cultivators or as agricultural labourers. Though precise figures on tribal land holdings are not available, it can safely be assumed that most tribal land owners are marginal and small farmers.

Consequent upon the contact with the non-tribal world, wide socio-economic differences are observed in tribal populations. Tribal groups around industrial and urban complexes have different problems from their brothers who live in comparative isolation. Religious conversion has added another factor of differentiation into the tribal way of life.

II

The poverty of the tribals is appalling. Poverty, however, should not be taken to mean only inadequate food in quantity and quality but also ignorance, illiteracy, immobility, unhygienic living conditions causing suffering from easily curable diseases, early death and the like. This condition of a large section of the population should not be allowed to continue for long. It is no wonder that the popular government in the country seized upon this problem almost immediately after it assumed office. This spirit led the constitution makers to envisage a fast enough pace of development for the tribal areas so that they could be brought to the level of development in the surrounding regions in the concerned states within 10 years after the commencement of the Constitution.

III

Article 46 of the Constitution of India states that "the state shall promote with special care the *educational and economic* interests of the weaker sections of the people and in particular of the scheduled castes and scheduled tribes and shall protect them from social unjustice".

Article 244 empowers the president to declare any area where there is a substantial population of tribal people, as a Scheduled Area under the 5th Schedule or in Assam as a Tribal Area under the 6th Schedule.

The 5th Schedule aimed at safeguarding the interests of the tribes in land, to give them protection against exploitation, to protect their way of life, and to develop the Scheduled Areas and Scheduled Tribes.

Consequently areas in the states of Andhra Pradesh, Bihar, Madhya Pradesh, Maharashtra, Gujarat, Orissa, Punjab and Rajasthan were declared as Scheduled Areas and the Union government took the decision to establish Tribal Development Blocks.

IV

Special programmes for these areas, therefore, were taken up in the early fifties in the form of Special Multipurpose

Tribal Blocks and, subsequently as Tribal Development Blocks. These programmes continued till the end of the Fourth Plan which could cover only 40 per cent of the total tribal population of the country.

In the beginning of the Fifth Plan, a new approach was adopted for tribal development where all areas with more than 50 per cent tribal concentration were clearly identified and special plans were prepared. This "new strategy" covered about 65 per cent of the total tribal population of the country. The remaining 35 per cent remained outside the orbit of the developmental plan and no special attention was given to their problems.

The Sixth Plan sets objectives for tribal developments as follows :

(i) The entire tribal population, whether living in the areas of tribal concentration or outside will be covered by suitable developmental programmes during the Sixth Plan period;

(ii) The gulf between the level of development in the tribal areas and the surrounding areas will be generally bridged by the end of the Sixth Plan and, in the case of more backward tribal areas, in the course of another five years, i.e. by the end of the Seventh Plan; and

(iii) The tribal communities outside the tribal areas will be helped to attain the general level of development in the area by the end of the Sixth Plan, or latest by the end of the Seventh Plan in the case of more deprived communities.

Thus it is envisaged that the problems of the tribal communities be solved in 12 years from now, i.e., by the beginning of the year 1989 (G.O.I. 1977 : 1-2). The plan has not started yet. Three years have already passed from the stipulated twelve.

As the socio-economic situation of tribal communities varies considerably from one area to another, it is neither possible nor desirable to have a uniform prescription for all of them. Therefore, even the broad approach to tribal development should be formulated on the basis of the distribution pattern of the tribals in an area and the level of their socio-economic conditions.

The post Fifth Plan strategy, therefore, tries to attack the problem from three angles classifying the tribals into three categories :

(a) Tribals in the areas of tribal concentration
(b) Dispersed tribals in other areas; and
(c) Primitive tribal communities.

The developmental measures for these three categories of the population are designed to be area oriented, community oriented and individual family oriented respectively.

V

The concern for tribal development, therefore, appears to be oriented towards bridging the gap between the tribals and the non-tribals so that the latter can become partners in the new productive processes and developmental programmes. This obviously means that the income level of the tribals must increase. Their economic development must be the first concern; without economic development the rest cannot follow. The first step in increasing the incomes in the tribal context is to save the average tribal from deprivation from a *multitude* of exploitative processes which tend to get strengthened as developmental programmes are initiated in these areas. The Fifth Plan accorded a high priority for the elimination of exploitation which needs to be followed in right earnest as we proceed with development. Elimination of exploitation does not require large financial investment. Only the administrative machinery has to tighten its belt a little more firmly. Certain government policies, such as the forest policy, excise policy, land alienation, marketing especially of forest produce, which in the past generated exploitative forces, need to be closely examined and their validity in the tribal context should be empirically tested.

Though development is popularly regarded as an economic process equal emphasis should be placed on the qualitative aspects of the human development. Sociologically speaking, development should be looked upon as an organized activity with the aim of satisfying certain basic needs and to psychologically orient the tribals to adopt new skills, attitudes, and life styles, so that they build up the inner strength, and appropriate social and cultural infra-structure to stand the pressures of the new situation and accrue benefits from the new programmes and maintain higher levels (Belshaw, 1972). From this point of view, development is a multidimensional process to progressively improve the social, cultural, economic, and human conditions of the people—all vital sectors necessary for a balanced growth of the society. Due emphasis should be paid to establish a meaningful link between the local and national levels of development and of the world at large (Schneider, 1975).

The developmental strategy should also discover the ways and means to utilize the latent resources of unused or under-used labour, skills and knowledge; and to increase motivation in the individual to produce better. Development should also mean a tangible effort to bring effective freedom to this important segment of society in order to unify the people for the greater task of nation building.

Effective development is, therefore, a comprehensive, balanced or integrated development; and it is obviously a dynamic process signifying goal oriented, guided and gradual change from something considered to be less desirable to something thought to be desirable or more desirable (Sparkman, 1961).

A goal oriented development should be ultra realistic. It should fix up achievable targets to be formulated on the basis of adequate and complete data. Plans formulated on inadequate or fragmentary data and ambitious goals lead to the creation of impossible expectations, and therefore, inevitable disappointments. The failure gets built in.

VI

Therefore the formulation of the development projects requires a clear methodology of approach not only in delimiting or defining the beneficiaries of the programmes, but also a clear knowledge of their socio-cultural base and their physical environment. An additional requirement is to clearly establish the priority of the sectoral programmes for each micro-area concerned; may it be area approach, community approach or individual approach.

There is no single cause for economic under-development or cultural stagnation. Forces—economic, social, political, religious, historical and cultural—that act at any given point of time or place may be mutually reinforcing or contradictory.

No single social science can provide the data or conceptual apparatus necessary to identify, analyse and understand the problems of the tribes who are at different levels of technological, economic and cultural development.

The anthropological approach to the formulation of the development programmes and policies suggests to involve specialists from all fields of study relevant for development including social workers and administrators. Anthropologists have special skills to offer (Mandelbaum, 1978). They can provide adequate data to identify the cultural forces. But that does not seem to be adequate enough to formulate an infallible policy for development. The planner should be provided with all the necessary data regardless of which sector of social reality they come from. The analyst must identify all relevant forces at woık so that integrative forces of the culture of the group considered for development can possibly be used as effective tools; head-on-collision with resistant spots of tribal life can be tactfully avoided and the people can be brought to associate effectively with the development programmes rather than keeping them passive and indifferent onlookers which might generate active resistance.

VII

A sociologist views tribal development as :

(i) a movement emphasing upon building up organizational structures;
(ii) a programme emphasing on activities;
(iii) as a method emphasing on certain achievable ends;
(iv) as a process emphasing upon what happens to people not only economically and socially but also psychologically; and
(v) institutionalization of newly discovered skills and procedures leading to social change without completely breaking away from the past (adopted from Sanders, 1958 : 6).

The government agencies have considerably exerted

themselves and over the years have evolved an organizational structure ; formulated action and end-oriented programmes in such important sectors of life as education, health services, agriculture, marketing, forestry, nutrition, communication etc.

Without going into the details of each of these sectoral programmes let us examine the fourth requirement, namely, what has happened to the people economically, socially and psychologically during the last thirty years of developmental activities. The achievements of these special programmes were greatly uneven. Some progress was, no doubt, made in some areas, but in many cases, the differences in the levels of development of the tribal areas and the remaining regions in the states even accentuated.

A Government of India document issued by the Ministry of Home Affairs laments :

> In the name of tribal development we have spent a lot of money during the last several plans but when accounting was made at the end of the last period of the safeguards to the tribal in the Constitution, it was found that actual benefits trickling down to the tribals have not been consistent with the promise we have made. Expenditure has not resulted in the benefits that should have accrued to this population. Unfortunately, the developmental programmes for tribal areas did not yield the desired results . . . (p. 98).

It further adds that more than 75 per cent of total benefits have not reached the tribals and cautions that "we can not have development at this rate".

Evaluating the impact of animal husbandry it records, "In this sector, . . . lot of money has been spent in the name of tribals and the benefits never reached them" (p. 100), and this also is true in other sectors.

Consequently tribal development resulted in widening the gap between the tribals and the non-tribals in the area and in all probability made the tribal exploitation more effective and organized. *This is what has happened* to the tribals economically.

The same document refers to a report that "some responsible tribal bodies have refused to accept a larger programme in the tribal areas for fear of exploitation". This is one of the most telling observations by the tribals and does no credit to anybody who talks of tribal development and specifically to the executing agencies. The organizational structure has failed to ensure that the programmes meant for the tribals really benefit them. The developmental programmes, if this observation is true, has also widened the psychosocial gap between the tribals and the non-tribals including the government. This is a dangerous situation and needs to be set right. Undoubtedly this is one of the most difficult tasks of tribal development. Such thoughtless promises that all their problems can be solved at the end of 1989 also psychologically alienate them; and even programmes launched in good faith are frowned at. In an atmosphere of distrust and apathy development cannot take place.

The problem of tribal development, then boils down to not one of carving out an exclusive destiny for tribal society. Here is a section of humanity simple, tough and hardy, convinced of the wholesomeness of its own way of life. Their existence has depended during the centuries of their forest and mountain existence, upon the principles of challenge and response. Rigours of climate have not driven them away from their homelands nor obliged them to abandon their way of life. But then they do not suffer from the obstinacy of adherence to the beliefs. They are open and frank and willing to change when faith and reason convince them that a change is necessary" (Elwin 1963 :1).

SUGGESTED READINGS

Belshaw, C.S., "Development : The Contribution of Anthropology", *International Social Science Journal*, 1972. 24:83-94.

Elwin, V., "A New Deal for Tribal India", Government of India, Ministry of Tribal Affairs, 1963.

Government of India, "Approach to Tribal Development in the Sixth Plan : A Preliminary Perspective", Occasional Papers on Tribal Development No. 17. Ministry of Home Affairs 1977.

Mandelbum, David G., "The Potentials of Anthropology". In *Anthropology for the Future*, D.G. Simkin, Sol Tax, J.W. Morrison (ed) pp. 24-41, Department of Anthropology, Research Report 4, University of Illinois, Urbana 1978.

Sanders, Irwin T., "Theories of Community Development", *Rural Sociology* 23 (March) : 1958 : 1-12.

Schneider, Harold K., "Devclopment and Anthropology", In *AnnualReview of Anthropology*, B.J. Siegel et al. (ed): 1975, 271-292, Palo Alto : Annual Reviews Inc.

Sparkman, John J., "Economic, Social, and Political Implications of Community Development", *Community Development Review* 6, 1-9, 1961.

EIGHT

K. B. Srivastava

ADMINISTRATION THROUGH STAGES AMONG THE TRIBALS OF CHOTANAGPUR*

THE PLATEAU region known as Chotanagpur had four districts, viz. Hazaribagh, Singhbhum, Manbhum and Lohardaga till the last decade of the 19th century. In January 1891, the district of Lohardaga was divided into two, viz. the districts of Ranchi and Palamau.[1] In 1973, "a new district, Giridih, was carved out of Hazaribagh district". When the Autonomous Development Authority was created in 1971, the Santhal Parganas of Bhagalpur Division also formed a part of the Plateau Region "for all round development of the area".[2] In March 1974 Chotanagpur-Santhal Parganas (Autonomous Development Authority) created a sub-plan area consisting of the districts of Ranchi and Singhbhum, portions of Santhal Parganas and Palamau, and individual Blocks in Giridih, Dhanbad and Rohtas districts.[3]

The Rev. Fr. J.B. Hoffman, in his *Encyclopaedia Mundarika* writes that the tribals are "the descendants of the original clearers of the soil and are in possession of a land system, based on undeniable ethical principles and most rationally regulated down to the minutest details".[4] Dr. Davidson, in his report of 1839, says that they were "an intelligent people, as much, if not more so than the labouring class of any part of India which I have visited".[5] It is established that "they were the first clearers of the soil, they became the first owners of the land and

*Read at the Silver Jubilee Celebration of the Indian Institute of Public Administration, Ranchi Local Branch, in which the trainees of the Tribal Development Administration Course participated.

meant to keep its ownership for themselves and their descendants. For centuries they remained undisturbed by the outside world, walled off by the geography of the region. This immunity from hostile disturbances over a large period, enabled them to build up their social, administrative, and political systems".[6]

Ownership of land had a very important place in this system. "When the Mundas first came into the country, they were neither a pastoral nor an agricultural people. They had to live by hunting and on the fruits and herbs they could find in the jungle. A family or a group of related families made a clearing in the forest. They called this clearing a *hatu* and later it came to be known as a *khuntkatti-hatu*—the village of the family of the original settlers. The family thus owned the land, for the one who cleared the land and settled on it was regarded as the owner."[7] Rev. Fr. J.B. Hoffman writes, "The title to personal ownership, i.e. the proprietory right rises in the first instance naturally out of creative or formative work. Hence the man who first turns a piece of jungle or a plot of waste land into arable land even as he who shapes a piece of wood into an axe-handle or a plough, becomes the owner of that blade or plough".[8] The boundaries of the village were marked by the paterfamilias and within these bounds all the lands, arable as well as waste, all the hills, jungles and streams—everything above ground and underground—became the common property of the village family. Some sections of the jungle were specifically reserved for the village bongas and spirits, and called *Sarnas* (sacred groves). The real owners of the land were the whole family—both past and present, deceased ancestors and living members. There was a kind of continuity and communion between the living and the dead. This was also the reason why a woman could not inherit property because if she did, the land would pass out of her father's family to that of her husband's and that was not allowed in the Munda system. So once she married, a girl could no longer take part in the sacrificial offerings to the spirits of her own family ancestors. Being excluded from this sacrifice, she lost all right to a share in her father's property. On the other hand, as a married woman, she was also debarred from offering sacrifices to the ancestors of her husband's family. Hence she was not entitled to inherit property belonging to his family either. Thus ownership was closely linked with male descent from the ancestors who cleared the soil.

The family of the Munda was patriarchial and a joint family. The father was not only the head of the family, but also the priest. The sons stayed with the father even after marriage. This helped to establish ties of unity and of group solidarity between the brothers and between their families. When the father died, the married sons often separated and built houses for themselves in the same village. In this way the original home broke off into a number of separate families still within the same village. As the number of families grew and the village became too small to contain them all, some of the sons went out to clear forests nearby and to start other villages. All these villages acknowledged one common ancestor and were linked to one another in their clan organisation. Thus the basis of the social organisation of the Mundas was the clan. Munda Society was made up of separate clans or sects, called Killis, many deriving their names from some animal, plant or material object. In the beginning they appear to have buried their dead in the common *sasan* or burial ground of the present village. This brotherhood of allied and associated villages constituted a *parha* or *patti* which became the unit of their socio-political organisation. Their sons were expected to place a *sasandiri* or burial stone over their remains. Under the same stone, the remains of succeeding generations were placed until the family became so large that new sasandiris had to be set up. This stone was regarded as permanent proof of real membership in a given clan and the highest evidential value among those people and the title deed of the Munda race.

Similarly the Oraon made extensive clearance in the north-western parts of the plateau. They copied from the Munda their village and patti organisation. The mode of subsistence of the Oraon was agriculture. They selected a particular jungle area, and cleared it. The pioneer families were called *bhuinhars* term corresponding to the Mundari term khunt-kattidar). The lands cleared by them were called the Bhuinhari lands of their respective families. Hence an Oraon of Chotanagpur always claimed some village as his bhuinhari village. They reserved a portion of the forests for the spirits and called it the Sarna or the Jatu. As in the case of the Munda, the customary rules governing inheritance and succession among the Oraon resulted from their ideas of ownership. They also resulted from their belief in the state of the human soul after death. The property and the title to it had to be kept in the family. Hence only sons could inherit. Among the Munda the village community as a whole owned all the lands within the village area; among the Oraon the joint ownership of the *bhuinhars* was recognised only in respect of the public lands. To the Oraon the living and the dead members of the clan form one large family. The deceased ancestors reside in the underworld where the spirit of all the deceased Oraon of the same clan live. Like the Munda the property must remain in the hands of their male descendants The women are denied the right to inherit. The remaining tribes followed either the Munda or the Oraon.

In the 17th century the *jagirdari* system was introduced by the Maharaja of Chotanagpur. Landlordism thus entered Chotanagpur. Prior to this the Munda and the Oraon knew themselves as *khuntkattidars* and the bhuinhars of their villages. With the introduction of jagirdari they were reduced to the position of rent-paying tenants when the tenants in the traditional set-up were the less privileged of the Munda and the Oraon. The jagirdars introduced the idea of rent in cash. They also introduced rents in kind (*rukumats*) and levies or cesses (*abwabs*) of various sorts. The tribals resisted these exactions. "The tribes, in their anxiety, to protect their sacred birth-right, the ancient village organisation and land system, made a gradual tour of the entire country from one end of it to the other".[9] "Once it started, the appropriation of the land of the Mundas and the Oraons continued, and nothing seemed to be able to stop its progress".[10]

In 1765 Chotanagpur became a part of the territory ceded to the British and with it ended the Mughal Rule in the area. The situation aggravated further when the Maharaja of Chotanagpur began granting villages on temporary lease (*thika*). These leaseholders (*thikadars*) soon followed the example of the jagirdars and ousted the aboriginals from their villages. In resentment the aboriginals started calling the jagirdars and the thikadars as *Dikkus* and refused to admit that they had any rights to the land. "Our fathers cleared the forest. Singbonga sends the rain and gives us the harvest. What have these dikkus done that they should own the land ?"[11]

Under the Mughals the revenue of tribute-paying districts were called *Dewanis*. After the Mughal Emperor was defeated by the British, the Emperor was allowed to keep his throne but had to cede to the British East India Company the Dewanis of Bengal, Bihar and Orissa. Chotanagpur, as part of the Dewani of Bihar, thus came under British Rule. Under the Mughals the revenue collectors were called *zamindars*. The East India Company began to regard the revenue collectors (zamindars) as landlords. Till 1834 the British did not interfere in the internal administration of the area. The first entry of the British into this region took place in 1772 when the Maharaja requested them to help him in revenue matter. In 1780, the British established what was known as the Ramgarh Hill Tract. Chotanagpur was one of the areas under this administration. The Headquarters were alternately at Shershati and Chatra. In 1800 the Collectorship of Ramgarh was abolished. Meanwhile in 1793 the Permanent Settlement was introduced in Bengal which extended to Chotanagpur. Against the payment of a fixed sum, it gave the zamindars the lands for which they had till then collected revenue. In 1806 a zamindari police system was established. The Maharajas and the landlords were asked by the British to establish police stations and appoint police officers. Dalton says that the changes of government up to 1831 were not beneficial to the tribals. "They were neglected by their new masters, oppressed by the aliens, and deprived of the means they had formerly possessed of obtaining redress through their own chief".[12] Only those of the regional heads of the village who were strong enough to inspire "were able to keep their villages" while the others were entirely dispossessed and replaced. The tribals became restless and they rose against the landlords in 1789, 1797, 1807, 1812 and 1820. These risings were, however, suppressed. Once again in 1832 there was a rebellion which convulsed the whole region. The Thikadars had managed to obtain temporary leases of the villages from the Maharaja of Chotanagpur against payment for their goods. These thikadars took the lands of the tribals and took rents and other services, including the forced labour or *beth begari.* The Munda and the Oraon rose as a body and declared, "Our lives are of no value, and being of one caste, let us stand fast to each other and commence to plunder, murder, and loot".[13] The Company appointed British officials to investigate the causes of the unrest and to report. The officials reported that the tribals were likely to resist the authority of the Government for slight causes of discontent or complaint. Mr. Blunt, a member of the Governor General's Council, in his Minute of April 4, 1832, noted about the people that "ignorant, poor, and uncivilised as they are, they have ever been regarded as a peaceable and inoffensive race of people who possess few wants, and who are patient and unresisting in an extraordinary degree".[14] Major Sutherland has remarked on Blunt's report that the Munda and the Oraon were a people "who have a character for truth and honesty beyond that of many of the people of India".[15] If they rose, it was because of the discontent caused by the actions of the landlords aided by the police. In 1834 it was decided to put an end to the indirect administration by the East India Company in Chotanagpur and to introduce a new system of administration, and Chotanagpur became a part of the South Western Frontier Agency under the management of the Agent to the Governor General.

The Agent to the Governor General was assisted by other British officials who were called the Principal Assistants to the Agent to the Governor General. These Principal Assistants came to be called Principal Assistant Commissioners from 1855, and later Deputy Commissioners (1861). In 1861, the Deputy Commissioner of Chotanagpur was called Judicial Commissioner and the Principal Assistants became Deputy Commissioners. In 1854, a Commissioner was appointed for the whole of Chotanagpur under the Lieutenant Governor of Bengal. At that time Chotanagpur consisted of four sub-divisions—Lohardaga (including Ranchi), Hazaribagh, Manbhum and Singhbhum—each under a Deputy Commissioner. Since 1861, the chief court of Chotanagpur was that of the Judicial Commissioner who was in charge of both civil as well as criminal suits. The Deputy Commissioners had special powers since 1861 to try all cases not punishable by death. There were two Commissioners—the Commissioner of the Division who was the chief executive, and the Judicial Commissioner who was in charge of the judiciary.[16] The headquarters of the administration was at Wilkinsonpur (popularly known as Kishanpur), Ranchi. A system of civil justice was introduced, police stations were established and maintained at Government expense. The zamindars too were encouraged to establish police stations and to appoint police officers. The ordinary Regulations that had hitherto been in force in the district were withdrawn from it. Chotanagpur and some of the surrounding territories were separated from the Ramgarh Hill Tract and formed into a Non-Regulation Province. The word "regulation" was the name given to the laws and judicial rules passed by the Government between 1793 and 1834. Regulation XIII of 1833 exempted certain areas, among them Chotanagpur, from the regulations and placed them under special and new rules for the administration of civil and criminal justice and for the superintendence of Police, land revenue, etc. For the administration of justice, the district of Lohardaga was constituted as a centre for dispensing justice. Mr. Wilkinson, the Agent, granted the Munda and the Manki of certain areas official documents confirming their title to the land and fixing the rent for ever.

There was no Record of Rights to show what belonged to the Tribals and what belonged to the new classes of landlords. About it Dalton wrote "during the administration of South-Western Agency the greatest disturbance of present proprietory tenure occurred".[17] To save the Tribals and to bring peace to the area, Major Hammington, the first District Commissioner of Chotanagpur, requested the drawing up of a Record of Rights which would make clear what lands belonged to the Tribals. In 1853-54 Mr. Ricketts, a member of the Board of Revenue, made an inspection tour of Chotanagpur and he also asked for an investigation into the land tenures and for the drawing up of a Record of Rights for the protection of the people. He also suggested that the zamindari police be abolished. In 1858 the Mundas rioted against the landlords again. As a consequence, the Government seriously discussed the question of registering the land tenures of Chotanagpur. Accordingly, on April 15, 1858, the Government appointed Lal Lokenath Sahi, a local landlord and Sub-Assistant Commissioner, to prepare a register of all Bhuinhari lands. The officer died in harness and without completing his work. In 1869, the Chotanagpur Tenures Act (11 of 1869) was passed for settlement of the title to Bhuinhari lands. It is also known as the Bhuinhari Survey and Settlement or simply the Bhuinhari Settlement. By this Act the Lieutenant Governor was empowered to appoint one or more persons as Special Commissioners to carry out the provisions of the Act. Actually only one Special Commissioner was appointed. He was Rakhal Das Haldar, a Calcutta Barrister, and he submitted a report at the end of the proceedings. Unfortunately the Act itself did not define the term "Bhuinhari land" and the fact remains that the Act was a failure. The Mundas and the Oraons, instead of gaining anything, lost more in their lands. Naturally unrest in the area increased. The net result was that the communal ownership of land was transferred into individual ownership. Father J.B. Hoffman has summed up the situation as "the general inability of two entirely different civilizations to understand each other.[18] The British with their background of private property, could not understand the land system of Chotanagpur.

The unrest among the tribals, particularly the one known as Birsa rising, gained momentum after the failure of the Chotanagpur Tenures Act, 1869, and of the operations following on, it namely, the Bhuinhari Survey and Settlement operations. The oppression by the landlords to eject the tenants from their lands, destroying their crops and houses, increasing rent collections several times over, refusing to give receipts for the rents paid, increased the misery of the tribals manifold. They filed lots of petitions to the Government at all levels. The leaders among them, called the Sardars, collected money from them to defray the expenses of engaging the lawyers at Calcutta to draw up the petitions. They persuaded the tribals to refuse rent to the landlords on a wrong impression created by them that the Queen of England had given a decree establishing the region of Chotanagpur as a free and independent region. Naturally the Government regarded the activity of the Sardars as political agitation. Slacks, the Settlement Officer of Ranchi, observed in May 1903, that it was the growing discontent among the Mundas against the landlords that brought about the movement. The report of the land Revenue Administration of the Lower Provinces for the year

1897-98, said, "In Lohardaga, the zamindars are said to take all they can in the way of rent and labour out of the raiyats, especially the aboriginal raiyats, whom they coerce by threatening to oust them from their lands. The raiyats, on the other hand, try to evade payment of their just dues". And in the Report of the following year, we are told,—"There is no change to report in the relations of landlords and tenants (of the Lohardaga District), which continues most unsatisfactory, the landlords trying to get all they can out of the raiyats, legally or otherwise; the raiyats where they resist at all, refusing to pay their lawful dues . . . Dispute as to rights in jungle are also becoming very common, and unless something in the way of a settlement of such rights can be made, either the old rights of the cultivators or else the jungles themselves will wholly disappear over a great part of the district".

The authorities, naturally, became very anxious to devise some radical cure for the discontent among the Munda. Sir John Woodburn, the Lieutenant Governor, visited the district, studied the situation, and came to the conclusion that "the essence of the whole business was to get a correct record of existing facts in tenants' holdings". It was decided, in 1901, to effect a survey and settlement of the Munda country. By the Bengal Government order of the 18th February 1902, survey and settlement operations commenced in the 1,346 square miles constituting the Munda country. This comprised the whole the thanas Tamar, Khunti, and Bano, one-third of each of the thanas of Basia and Karra, and one-fourth of thana Kolebira, besides 645 acres in the south of the Ranchi thana. And in the light of the results of the investigations made by Mr. E. Lister, the eminently able officer to whom the settlement of the Munda country was entrusted, the Chotanagpur Landlord and Tenant Procedure Act of 1879, and the Commutation Act of 1897, were amended by Bengal Act V of 1903. The Rev. Father Hoffman did yeomen's service to the cause of the Munda by explaining most lucidly to the authorities, the true nature and extent of their rights in Khuntkatti villages and lands. The amending Act dealt chiefly with the rights of the Mundari Khuntkattidars on the original clearers of the soil, as the treatment hitherto according to them, was, in the words of the Select Committee, "one of the chief causes of the agitation wich has long disturbed the people locally known as the Mundaris."

When these amending Acts were being discussed and passed, it was understood that a consolidated Act would be passed at an early date. It was reserved for Sir Andrew Fraser's Government to give the long-promised Act to the district. Sir Andrew evinced almost a personal interest in the welfare of the Ranchi District, and, by his wise measures, succeeded in quieting the unrest of a century. It was decided to re-arrange and consolidate the whole of the principal enactments relating to landlord and tenant in Chotanagpur in an entirely new amending Bill. The Bill was introduced in Council and passed into law in 1908.

The Chotanagpur Tenancy Act, 1908, came into force from 11 November 1908. It reproduced with certain modifications the provisions of the Commutation Act (Act IV of 1897) and of Act V of 1903. The Chotanagpur Tenancy Act, however, was not an unqualified success, particularly in its provisions about transfers in raiyati holdings. The Chotanagpur Tenancy Act, has, on the whole, been a failure as far as transfer in raiyati lands is concerned. Its chief success is that it has undoubtedly given the raiyats a greater security of tenure as against their landlords than they had previously. "On the whole it can be fairly said that although the Chotanagpur Tenancy Act has not been an unqualified success the balance is on the credit side".[19] "Landlord's privileged lands were defined and provision was made for a final and conclusive record of their rights".[20]

There have been several amendments in the Chotanagpur Tenancy Act. The revisional Survey and Settlement operations were undertaken with a view to make a survey and an up-to-date record-of-rights. On the conclusion of the Survey and Settlement operations, in spite of the levy of Dak Moshara by some landlords and persistence of abwabs and begari in some forms, the relations between the landlord and the tenant generally improved. But about the year 1921-22 the Tana Bhagat and the Unnati Samaj movement under the influence of non-co-operation movement launched by Mahatma Gandhi, adopted an attitude which was antagonistic to landlords and distrustful of Government, the Tana Bhagats particularly crusaded against payment of rent to landlords.[21] The Kisan

Sabha Movement was started in Ranchi District in 1931 under the leadership of Theble Oraon and Lorentius Barla. It aimed at improving the economic and agricultural condition of the tenancy and creating better relationship between them and their landlords.[22] The Bihar Restoration of Bakast Land and Reduction of Arrears of Rent Act were also passed in 1938. Under these Acts the tenants began to assert their claims, usually extravagant, against their landlords and this often created the problems of law and order.[23] The rent reduction operations led to a spate of civil suits, but they did not bring about much benefit to the tenants as in most cases reduction in favour of tenants was restored in appeal by the Commissioner.[24] As regards the effect of Sections 3 and 6 of the Bihar Restoration of Bakast Lands and Reduction of Arrears of Rent Act, 1938, the general relationship between landlords and tenants tended to deteriorate considerably.[25] Both Ranchi and Porahat estates in Singhbhum had a common starting point to their fiscal history, in that both the original systems were almost identical in so far as they related to aboriginal village. In both rent was originally assessed on the person of the cultivator in the form of *chanda* (subscription) and not on the land he held in the form of rent proper. In both, with the influx of a governing class from outside the idea gradually grew that the sum of money paid by the cultivator was attached to the land he held and not to his person i.e. the idea of a territorial rent ousted the previous idea of a personal *chanda.* In Porahat, circumstances led to a regular series of rent settlements and recognised rates of rent. But in Ranchi the rent history proceeded without guidance or form.[26]

During the tenure of the first National Government in Bihar (1937-39), aproposal to abolish the zamindari system was mooted and this spurted the local zamindars, like their counterparts elsewhere in the State to organise to resist this move. On the cessation of the Second World War the popular government, which came in the wake of Independence, enacted the Land Reforms Act, 1950, which ended the permanent settlement made in 1793 by Lord Cornwallis and established a direct link between the State and the tenants.[27] It provided for the transference to the State of the interests of proprietors and tenure holders in land and of the mortgagees and lessees of such interests including interests in trees, forests, fisheries, jalkars, ferries, hats, bazars, mines and minerals, free from all encumberances (Section 4a) on payment of appropriate compensation and for the constitution of a Land Commission for the State of Bihar with powers to advise the State Government on the agrarian policy to be pursued by the State Government consequent upon such transference and for other matters connected therewith. It came into force over the State on 25 September 1950.[28] As the number of small intermediary interests in the State was very large, much difficulty was experienced in acquiring them through individual notification. So provision was made in the Bihar Land Reforms (Amendment) Act, 1953 (Bihar Act XX of 1954) for taking over all estates and tenures within a particular area by issue of a single notification. Thus by notification, area-wise, all the remaining estates in Ranchi district vested in the State.[29] All the intermediary interests except the Mundari Khuntkatti tenancy within the meaning of Chotanagpur Tenancy Act, 1908 (Bengal Act 6 of 1908) and the Bhuinhari tenure were vested in the State.

The agency of collection became as follows : At *halka* (a group of villages) level a Karamchari was appointed to be responsible for collection of rents, cess, and sairats, maintenance of registers and accounts, submission of reports and returns, and holding enquiries relating to mutations, assessment of compensation, and interim payment of compensation to the ex-landlords and allied work. A Circle Inspector is posted in each Circle or Anchal to supervise the work of Karamcharis in his jurisdiction. A gazetted officer, designated Anchal Adhikari, is in charge of a Circle. The Sub-Divisional officer is responsible for revenue collection in his sub-division. He is assisted by a Deputy Collector in charge of Land Reforms and Development. The Additional Collector is responsible for revenue collection as well as other matters connected with land reforms at the District level and is under the general control and supervision of the Collector. The Collector is responsible for revenue work in the district to the Commissioner of the division and ultimately to the Revenue Department of Government. Thus a halka is the unit of revenue administration in a district, and a Circle is a group of halkas. The Circle Officer now discharges all the functions and duties of a Khas Mahal Officer under the provisions of the Bihar Government Estates Manual, 1941.

At about the same period the Government decided to take over control of the forests and transferred all the powers to the Forest Department of Bihar so much so that even the Forest Settlement Officers were brought under the effective control of the Divisional Forest Officers. This being the position, the judge became a subordinate administrator placed at the beck and call of one of the parties to the disputes and, naturally, it is too much to expect justice by the other party in the court of Forest Settlement Officers who exercise all the powers of a Civil Court in the trial of suits.[30] Forests, being the integral part of the day to day existence of the tribals, interference in their way of life in respect of forests makes them absolutely miserable and they cannot exercise even the rights given to them in Khatian part II. The tribals have similar difficulties with regard to the way in which the Bihar Excise Act, 1915, is enforced. As a rule, the Adibasis, excepting the Tana Bhagats, take beer as a necessary part of their food. It is not considered a sinful act. And no Adibasi would hesitate in confessing frankly that he takes beer as a food and as a restorative. Still, everyday the Adibasis are caught for infringing the provisions of the Excise Act and they are prosecuted in Law Courts. The Adivasis have yet to be convinced if they have really committed any offence.[31] One thing they cannot understand why so much stress is laid on "prohibition". Pure *handia* made at home is fit for offering to their gods and ancestors, is health giving and invigorating and it must not be encroached upon in the name of prohibition. To keep themselves healthy both in body and mind, they must remain free from such treatments.

Administration has played an important part in the system of the graingolas among the tribals. "It has a history of its own which dates back to more than 50 years. The idea of starting graingolas for the benefit of Damin raiyats in Santhal Parganas occurred to C.H. Bompas, Deputy Commissioner of the district who in August, 1902 got seven graingolas in Dumka Damin and three graingolas in Godda Damin constructed at a cost of Rs. 1,16,000. There is every reason to believe that C.H. Bompas borrowed the idea of graingolas from the Marwaris who were acquainted with this system of money lending through grain transactions. Later on in the forties, Government of Bihar started graingolas in other parts of the State with the object of creating central stores of grains which might be readily available in time of scarcity or famine and which in ordinary times would be utilised to provide aboriginals with seed grains for cultivation and short-term loans for subsistence during the period before the harvest . . . It is a fact that grain loans occupy an important place in the economy, and the credit transactions in kind are very significant in terms of the number of borrowers as well as the relative value of borrowings. Advancing grain loans from the graingolas is the simpler and straighter form of credit which is popular and clearly understood by the tribals. Still it cannot be said that reactions of the tribals to the working of the graingolas in Bihar have been satisfactory, because in a number of cases, the scheme had been abused by the Thana Welfare Officers in charge of the graingolas who carried on malpractices like issuing loans in fictitious names, recovering loans but not crediting them to the account of loanees, obtaining thumb impressions of the applicants on agreements and receipts without making actual disbursement of paddy, etc".[32]

After independence, we have given ourselves a Constitution that ensures equally to all of us and offers equal opportunity to every son of the soil. Through the Constitution (Scheduled Tribes Order 1950), certain classes of people, among the population of India have been declared to be Scheduled Tribes. The Government of India have provided special safeguards for these tribes. A separate Welfare Department has been set up for the Tribals. Special educational concessions are given by the Government to the students of the Scheduled Tribes, such as free tuition, stipends, scholarships, provision of books, special scholarship for three classes of students including overseas scholarships. A Tribal Research Institute has been started at Ranchi. The Department of Anthropology is also carrying out extensive research on the social and cultural life of the tribes. The need for weaning away the tribals from the primitive forms of agriculture and settling them permanently on land are engaging the attention of the Central and the State Governments. The scheme for controlling the practice of shifting cultivation has been started.

With the concept of the Welfare State, the Government have launched a series of Five Year Plans and the Community Development programmes. Visible changes in their life and conduct have taken place. They have ambitions and they are marching ahead and they are trying to assimilate themselves with all the rest of the Indians. In recent years some important pieeces of legislation of far-reaching effects have beenpassed. The most important of them are (1) the Bihar Bhoodan Yagna Act, 1954, (2) The Bihar Consolidation of Holdings Act, 1956, and (3) The Land Reforms (Fixation of Ceiling Area and Acquisition of Surplus Land) Act, 1961 (Bihar Act XII of 1962). For development projects under the Five Year Plans and rapid industrialisation of the area, vast areas of land have already been acquired and more and more are likely to be acquired even now. Therefore, the question of rehabilitation of the displaced persons has arisen, The Chotanagpur-Santhal Parganas Autonomous Development Authority, Ranchi, have put emphasis on irrigational facilities, industrial prospects, development of power, integrated development of rural roads, land development, for the purpose '15 Meso Areas, which will together form Macro Areas".[33]

Administration is a big experiment in man's laboratory. The experiment has been a trial and error method. The medium of experiment in Chotanagpur is actually the tribals. Therefore, it must be understood well the material one has to use in his experiment. The tribals "possess many virtues for which mankind has been striving for ages. They are essentially honest, truthful, hardworking, self-reliant and highly co-operative. On such a good soil, democratic decentralisation will surely flourish in an abundant measure. The real need is that we should go the maximum distance with the tribals and then re-orient them in such a manner as to make them worthy citizens of India. If one means business, if he has the will to discharge his obligations, the tribals are anxious to give maximum co-operation to the administration".[34]

REFERENCES

1. Fidelis de Sa, *Crisis in Chotanagpur.*
2. Draft Fifth Five Year Plan, Part I—Chotanagpur-Santhal Parganas Autonomous Development Authority, Ranchi.
3. Draft Sub-Plan for Tribal Region of Bihar 1976-79—Chotanagpur-Santhal Parganas Autonomous Development Authority, Ranchi, March, 1974.
4. Rev. Fr. J.B. Hoffman, *Encyclopaedia Mundarica.*
5. Dr. Davidson, Report of 1839 (cited in Selections from the Records of the Bengal Government, Vol. XX, Chotanagpur, Calcutta, 1855, page 14).
6. Fidelis de Sa, *Crisis in Chotanagpur.*
7. Ibid.
8. Rev. Fr. J.B. Hoffman, *Encyclopaedia Mundarica.*
9. S.C. Roy, *The Mundas and Their Country.*
10. Fidelis de Sa, *Crisis in Chotanagpur.*
11. J.B. Hoffman, *Encyclopaedia Mundarica*, Volume 11, page 515.
12. Dalton, *Descriptive Ethnology of Bengal*, p. 170.
13. Bengal Government Resolution, November 25, 1880.
14. B.C. Vol. 54227 No. 46.
15. Ibid.
16. Imperial Gazetteers, Provincial Series, Bengal, Vol. II, pp. 356-357.
17. Chotanagpur Agrarian Reports, Calcutta, 1890, Part 11, page 21.
18. Rev. Fr. J.B. Hoffman, *Encyclopaedia Mundarica.*
19. Final Report on Revisional Survey and Settlement Operations, 1927-35, 1940. p. 56.
20. M.G. Hallett, Ranchi District Gazetteer, 1917, pp. 196-99.
21. Revisional Survey and Settlement Operations, 1927-35, p. 3.
22. Ibid, p. 4.
23. Land Revenue Administration Report for Ranchi, 1938-39 and 1939-40.
24. Ibid., 1941-42.
25. Ibid.
26. Revisional Survey and Settlement Operations Report, 1940, pp. 70-71.
27. Ranchi District Gazetteer, 1970.
28. Notification No. 5067-LR, dated the 24th September, 1950.
29. Notification No. 1022/LR, dated the 1st January, 1956.
30. The Indian Forest Act, 1927, Section 8.
31. K.B. Srivastava, Article in The Indian Nation, Patna.
32. K.K. Leuva, *Graingolas in Bihar : A Critical Review about their Working.*
33. Draft Sub-Plan for Tribal Region of Bihar, 1974-79.
34. K.B. Srivastava, "Present Position of the Tribals", *Economic Times.*

PART II

STRATEGIES OF TRIBAL DEVELOPMENT

NINE

Bhupinder Singh

TRIBAL DEVELOPMENT
Strategy and Approach

The Tribal Setting

ON THE BASIS of geographical distribution, ethnic characteristics and linguistics affiliations in India the tribal groups can be broadly divided into three distinct zones viz., north-eastern, central and southern. The first one is the habitat of the Naga, Mizo, Khasi, Garo, Rabha, Dafla, Apatani, belonging to Mongoloid racial stock and speaking dialects of Sino-Tibetan and Tibeto-Burman family of languages but for a little admixture of Mon-Khmer speech. They are spread over the States of Arunachal Pradesh, Meghalaya, Mizoram, Manipur, Assam, Himachal Pradesh, etc. The central zone spans the States of West Bengal, Bihar, Orissa, Madhya Pradesh, Rajasthan, Maharashtra, and Gujarat in which major tribal groups like the Oraon, Santhal, Munda, Bhil, Gond, Kolam, Khond, Baiga, Bhil, Savara live. In general they speak dialects of either Austric or Dravidian family of languages, their physical features being mostly proto-Australoid. The tribal areas of Andhra Pradesh, Karnataka, Tamilnadu and Kerala form part of the southern zone where the Chenchu, Koya, Bagata, Gadaba, Kadar, Irula, Toda, Kota, Yerukula, Yenadi inhabit. They belong to the proto-Australoid racial stock and speak dialects of the Dravidian family.

According to the 1971 Census, the scheduled tribe population in the country was 380.15 lakhs (about 38 million) constituting 6.94 per cent of the total population. Consequent upon the amendment of the list of scheduled tribes in 1976, their population in 1971 was estimated at 410.96 lakhs (about 41 million) constituting 7.5 per cent of the total population. There are scheduled tribes in 25 States and Union Territories. Of these, six States and Union Territories are tribal-majority States. These are Meghalaya 80.48 per cent, Nagaland 88.61 per cent, Arunachal Pradesh 79.01 per cent, Dadra and Nagar Haveli 86.89 per cent, Lakshadweep 92.85 per cent and Mizoram 94.26 per cent. The total number of scheduled tribes in these States is small, being 20.49 lakhs (about 0.20 million). However, the State of Madhya Pradesh has the largest concentration of scheduled tribes numbering 98.15 lakhs or about 9.8 million, followed by Orissa 50.75 lakhs or about 51 million, Bihar 49.33 lakhs or about 4.9 million, Gujarat 37.57 lakhs or about 3.8 million, Maharashtra 33.41 lakhs or about 3.3 million and Rajasthan 31.35 lakhs or about 3.1 million. This east-central-west belt has about 300 lakhs or 30 million of scheduled tribes according for 73 per cent of their population in the country.

Nine major tribal groups account for about 20 million scheduled tribes. The major tribes and their distribution in States are roughly as follows :

The Bhil, about 5.2 million, in Madhya Pradesh, Maharashtra, Rajasthan and Gujarat;
The Gond, about 4.8 million, in Madhya Pradesh, Maharashtra, Andhra Pradesh, Gujarat and Orissa;
The Santhal, about 3.6 million, in Bihar, Orissa and West Bengal;
The Oraon, about 1.7 million, in Bihar, Orissa, West Bengal and Madhya Pradesh;
The Mina, about 1.5 million, in Rajasthan and Madhya Pradesh;
The Munda, about 1.2 million, in Bihar, Madhya Pradesh, Orissa and West Bengal;
The Khond, about 0.9 million, in Bihar, Orissa, Madhya Pradesh, West Bengal and Maharashtra;
The Ho, about 0.5 million, in Bihar, Orissa and West Bengal;
The Naga, about 0.5 million, in Nagaland and other north-eastern States.

The 41 million scheduled tribes have been identified as belonging to about 250 different big and small groups, speaking over a hundred different languages.

Whatever may have been the state of the tribal economy in the distant past, there is no doubt that in recent decades, the tribals have been practising a subsistence economy. As a consequence, indebtedness, both for consumption and production items, has been common. A survey in Gujarat in 1961 by the Reserve Bank of India (Report of Study Group on Relief of Indebtedness, 1975) revealed that 72 per cent of the tribals had outstanding loans. The extent of indebtedness of tribals was commented upon by the Study Team on Tribal Development Programmes headed by Shilu Ao (1969) who cited a detailed study of Tribal Research Institute, Madhya Pradesh, which showed that 52.5 per cent of the families were indebted, the average debt per family being Rs. 367; in 63 per cent of the cases the rate of interest was more than 25 per cent. Earlier, the special Working Group on Co-operation for Backward Classes appointed by the Ministry of Home Affairs headed by M.P. Bhargava observed in the report (1962) that indebtedness had far outgrown the repaying capacity of the debtors in tribal areas and was acting as a serious drag on their economic development. In the 1974-75 Report of the Commissioner for Scheduled Castes and Scheduled Tribes (pages 115-116), mention has been made of a survey conducted by the United News of India that about 65-70 per cent of small farmers, scheduled castes and scheduled tribes in rural areas are steeped in debt and are at the mercy of village money-lenders; the average debt of a family varying from Rs. 250 to over Rs. 500. It further showed that while agricultural needs constitute more than half the debts incurred by the concerned families, domestic consumption, marriages, death, birth, religious and social ceremonies account for the rest. The tribals' subsistence economy dependent on slender resources and scantier savings is well understood by a non-tribal money-lender who does not hesitate from extorting usurious rates of interest. Sometimes, indebtedness is handed down through generations. In the process, a tribal family may lose the only capital resource it has i.e. the land. Alienation of tribal land takes place in other illegal ways also. They are exploited in the price of the consumer goods they purchase or the farm and forest produce they sell. The liquor vendors frequently defraud them. Hence, exploitation of tribals by outsiders is a marked feature of the situation.

Tribal Development and Rural Development

Tribal development is sometimes thought to be synonymous with rural development. The difference between the two has to be clearly appreciated. The scheduled tribe population in the country is, by and large, concentrated in certain tracts called "Scheduled Areas".[1] In the first place, many of the tribal areas are remote, inaccessible, forested, hilly or slopy. Their natural resource endowment is vastly different from that of the alluvial plains which have for all these centuries been the bastion of the country's agriculture production. The schemes for their development have to be related to the regional resource availability. Secondly, their requirements of infra-structure are large and distinctive. Thirdly, on account of their age-long seclusion, the tribal communities have been cut off from the mainstream, and, hence, cross-fertilisation of ideas has been restricted hampering technological advancement. Further, again as a consequence of their isolation, the scheduled tribe communities have developed a certain culture and psyche of their own in tune with their own environment. These factors make it incumbent to set planning for the tribal people and area, apart from rural development.

Constitutional Provisions

In the Indian Constitution, special provisions have been enshrined for the protection and development of the scheduled tribe population, constituting about 7 per cent of the total population of the country. In Article 46, the State has been enjoined to promote with special care the educational and economic interests of the weaker sections, in particular of the scheduled tribes, and to protect them from social injustice and exploitation. To ensure that the intention of special care does get translated into concrete action, the Centre has been charged with the responsibility of providing funds to State Governments for meeting the costs of schemes of development for promoting the welfare of scheduled tribes in the States and for raising the level of administration of areas predominantly inhabited by scheduled tribes, called "Scheduled Areas" in the Constitution (Article 276). Further, reservations have been made for representation in the Parliament and the State Legislatures as well as in public services roughly proportional to their population percentage.

Recommendations of Committees and Commissions

Under Article 339 (1) of the Constitution, a Commission was appointed headed by U.N. Dhebar in 1961 to investigate and report on the problems of scheduled tribes. The Commission observed (1961) that there was diffusion of effort in the welfare work. It was necessary to concentrate on a few essential items like drinking water, food all the year round, employment at least for 300 days in a year on reasonable wages, education, health and village roads. They stressed that an integrated and planned approach based on these few essential items would give the plan a more realistic touch in the eyes of the tribals.

A Study Team headed by T. Shilu Ao remarked in its Report (1969) that during the First Plan (1951-56), the main scheme undertaken related to education and economic development, improvement of roads and communication and provision of economic and public health facilities. In the Second Plan (1956-61) the emphasis was on economic development like agriculture, cottage industries, forest co-operatives. In the Third Plan (1961-66) the priorities were in the order of economic uplift, education, health, housing and communication. The Team was in broad agreement with the priorities adopted in the Third Plan, recognising that deviation might be necessary in the light of needs disclosed by a socio-economic survey. The Team made the observation that while some advance had been made, the expectation that substantial outlays in the Tribal Development (TD) Block[2] by themselves would make a dent was belied. In fact, the revelation was that funds earmarked for tribals had been diverted for non-tribal benefit, in the TD Blocks, since no device had been evolved to secure them specifically for tribals' interest. Thus, while some sections of Indian society marched forward as a result of planned efforts though the rural mass lagged behind, the tribal people were, by and large, stagnating while the harvest of investment was being garnered by others. The violent Naxalite movement of the late sixties and early seventies would appear to have discovered in the circumstances fertile ground in the tribal areas in the country and swept through it.

It appears in retrospect that unless it was ensured that the fruits of physical and financial effort actually reached the tribals, there would be no means of preventing the gains being siphoned off by the more powerful sections of the society. The second drawback of the programmes introduced for tribal benefit seems to have been that the developmental prescriptions for non-tribals were sought to be applied verbatim to the tribal context. The situations were different. The socio-economic, psychological, technological and cultural milieu were at variance. Even now, many tribal communities retain strong social and communal ties particularly at the village level. Some tribal communities are insular and xenophobic; some communities practise shifting cultivation using not even a plough, but merely a hand-hoe.

Some Planning Imperatives

In a country like India, where disparities in socio-economic levels between the sophisticated, westernized urban sections of society living in metropolitan towns like Delhi, Bombay, Calcutta and Madras and the traditional, undifferentiated, forest-dwelling sections is vast, the general premise that micro-planning should be a reflection at local level of macro-planning will not be tenable. Further, the presumptions made in any planned effort that (a) growth stimuli have more or less an even spread effect, (b) in a planned economy the benefits automatically percolate to the lower strata of society, are likely to go away in the tribal situation. The fact of the matter is that the socio-economic topography of the tribal region is characterised by unevenness. Further, their socio-cultural matrix is different. Another significant parameter of the tribal situation is that life is lived by a tribal community as a whole, in which social, economic and institutional dimensions are delicately interwoven. Their universe responds to external stimuli more or less as a single entity; individuals belonging to the non-tribal system find it difficult to appreciate it.

In concrete terms, the nature of the tribal universe dictates that the repercussions of each of the programmes sought to be introduced therein should be assessed in terms of the universe as a whole, and not in Sectoral Fragments.[3] If, as is the case, simultaneously a number of sectoral programmes are set in motion, an attempt at anticipating their results in overall terms, considering the system as one integral whole, should be made. The various sectoral programmes should be tied up in a package and the impact of the package on the universe of the community adjudged before-hand. This sets the tribal areas apart from the rest of the national planning ground which indeed can absorb individual sectoral programmes (like major industry or commercial forest plantation) without manifestation of any strain.

The planning process for scheduled tribe communities in particular and of Scheduled Areas in general should be regarded as an input projection for well-integrated communities, practising as well as preserving the ecological balance. This aspect has been dealt with by Vidyarthi while studying the Maler where he spoke of Nature-Man-Spirit complex (Vidyarthi, L.P., 1963). The inputs have, therefore, to be selected with care and discrimination. The inter-penetrating equilibrium of pursuits is partly expressed in agricultural and forestry occupational patterns wherein social, ritual, religious and political dimensions each plays its due part. A planning effort which ignores or flouts the comprehensive view is likely to deal a blow to the tribal sensitivity and seal the chances of rapport between the planners (or implementors) and the target groups.[4]

There is another area which requires the discriminating apprehension of the tribal context. At the national and State levels, sometimes it is overlooked that with differing cultural backgrounds, the tribal areas have nurtured their own political and social ethos. Long after the rest of Indian society came under British sway, aided by their isolation the tribal communities continued to sustain their own institutions and systems. After Independence in 1947, notwithstanding some muffled dissent, there has been an attempt to superimpose the national institutional framework on them. The case in point is that of Panchayati Raj (decentralised decision-making) institutions which have been statutorily introduced in tribal areas. It would appear that the results of such superimposition have not been adequately studied. Perceptive observers feel that even now it is not too late to retrieve for the more "backward" communities the traditional tribal Panchayats and similar organisations for the purpose of growth and development of these communities. The institutions could be adapted to the new emerging situations.

Chance, howsoever well-intentioned, has at times clanged harshly with the harmony of life in the tribal world. As a part of communications programmes, some roads laid in the interior tribal areas became the carriers of exploiters like the money-lenders, the liquor vendors, the forest contractors and their kin; earlier, they could enter the tribal areas, through hill-paths. The implanting of the administrative apparatus, as a change agent, into the tribal world has, in part, signified addition of more exploiters. Introduction of high-yielding varieties of seeds of crops like paddy brought in a little economic comfort but because of concomitant lack of irrigation facilities, coordination and proper follow-up spelt disaster for some tribal families.

The personality and the characteristics of the different two hundred and odd scheduled tribe communities in the country present a wide range of diversity bearing on their reaction to development process and assimilative power. Taking the example of the State of Orissa, there are 62 scheduled tribe communities numbering roughly 5 million out of the total population of about 21 million. At the one end, are the Gond, advanced and almost indistinguishable from the non-tribals; some members of the tribe have been land-owners and even rulers. At the other are members of the primitive groups like the Juang of Keonjhar, the Kharia of Mayurbhanj and the Saora of Ganjam-Koraput. It needs hardly any argument to appreciate that a blue-print for the Gond will not be relevant for the Juang or the Kharia or the Saora. Further, when we consider declining groups like the Onge of Andaman and Nicobar Islands, this point becomes clear; this tribe has about a hundred souls now living and unless the most well-considered and concerted steps are taken, it will vanish. This is true of a few other tribes also not only in the Andaman and Nicobar Islands, but in some other States too. Such tribes present a case of mere survival and the prescription for a tribe like the Onge must surely be different from plans for other rural and even other tribal communities. Taken to its logical end, it means that there should be 250 distinct blue-prints for planning the development of the roughly 250 scheduled tribe communities of the country. This cannot be laughed off as utopian. The compulsion of realities might sooner or later veer planning that way.

Fifth Plan (1974-79) Period

The Fifth Five Year Plan 1974-79 will be regarded as a watershed in the history of tribal development. Much thinking and preparation went into the concept of tribal development before the commencement of that Plan period. In 1972, a Task Force on "Development of Tribal Areas" was set up with Professor L.P. Vidyarthi as the Chairman to (a) review the nature and level of development that had taken place so far, (b) suggest a perspective of development for a fifteen-year period, and (c) formulate proposals for the Fifth Plan indicating priorities, policies, programmes and outlays in the light of the perspective. Based on the report of the five working groups, the Task Force observed (1972) that the problem of development of tribal areas was primarily linked to the backwardness of these areas, the poverty of the people and the integration of tribals with the rest of the population. They remarked that the tribes of different areas faced different problems: those of the northern zones arising mostly out of remoteness of the habitat and difficult climatic conditions; those of the north-eastern zone on account of a disrupted economy following the formation of East Pakistan (now Bangladesh); those of the eastern, central and western zones related to pressure of population on land, land tenure, indebtedness and rights in forest along with a low level of productivity; those of the southern zone based on shifting cultivation. They suggested that areas with a high concentration of tribal population should be identified and grouped, a combination of ecological, occupational and social parameters properly assessed for policy formulation and implementation and a steady flow of benefits assured to the scheduled tribes. In their view the obvious emphasis would have to be on the primary sector of the tribal economy, i.e. agriculture and forestry; at the same time, there should be a frontal attack in the fields of alienation of land, indebtedness, credit and marketing, excise policy.

A little later the same year, an Expert Committee on tribal development headed by S.C. Dube, constituted by the Central Department of Social Welfare, submitted its report (1972) defining the new strategy for tribal development in the Fifth Plan as follows :

(a) The problem of tribal development should be defined at the national level and national effort required for tackling it should be worked out.
(b) The precise part assigned to each State and to each department in this task should be fully defined and the central sector should play an important supplemental role.
(c) A review of important policies especially those covering forest, industry, minerals development and excise administration should be taken up.
(d) An integrated area development approach in consonance with the development of the people should be adopted. The development programmes should give high priority to programmes minimising the incidence of exploitation and helping local communities to build up their inner strength.
(e) Special schemes for extremely backward areas, neglected and isolated tribes and tribals affected by major projects should be formulated.
(f) Strengthening and streamlining of administrative and economic institutions should be taken up urgently and evaluation should become an integral part of the administrative structure.

Tribal Development Agencies—four in Orissa, two in Madhya Pradesh, one in Andhra Pradesh and one in Bihar, totalling eight—came into being preceding or coincident with the beginning of the Fifth Plan. Their aim was to make massive investment exclusively for tribals from Central funds, while making use of the State outlays for development of both tribals and non-tribals. Their important feature was that they were concerned solely with the development of tribals, leaving the other segments of the population alone. Notwithstanding these handicaps, they made notable contributions, particularly in creating an infra-structure. However, the Fifth Plan period will be remembered more for the birth and evolution of the concept of a sub-plan for the tribal regions of a State within the overall frame of the State plan. *The objective of the tribal sub-plan has been spelt as development of the area with focus on the scheduled tribe population within the sub-plan area.* Briefly, the concept consists of identification of Development Blocks within a State having more than 50 per cent scheduled tribe population and launching of a massive effort for tribal development within that "sub-Plan Area". The effort has been conceived as total in the financial and physical senses. This means that the totality of financial resources available is required to be channelised as investment in the tribal areas and a total matching physical effort is to be mounted to translate the investment into concrete benefits for the tribal families. The unit of planning, an Integrated Tribal Development Project (ITDP) in a State, comprised an aggregate of Development Blocks. The ITDP being smaller than a district and bigger than a Development Block appears more feasible for planning. The lowest unit of execution of the programme is the Development Block; it has a development team with the Block Development Officer as the leader. Programmes have to be planned for an ITDP in the shape of a project report and for a State in the shape of a sub-Plan for the tribal region of the State. Guidelines laid down that planning should be based on the needs of the area and the people and, hence, the process has to be commenced at the grass-root level i.e. the Development Block, and funnelled upwards to ITDP, State and national levels.

The idea of totality needs some elaboration. Taking the financial aspect first, in a State the chief financial source of development is the State Plan funds of the Centrally sponsored schemes and Central schemes being an addition thereto. In the tribal sub-plan areas, these funds are supplemented by special Central assistance provided by the Centre in pursuance of the constitutional provision making tribal development the special responsibility of the Union Government. For family-oriented schemes, while the subsidy component is drawn from Government funds, the loan component is provided by financial institutions, thus, making the latter a very important source. This pool of funds has to be used for undertaking a synergistic package of schemes in a Development Block, keeping in view the natural resource endowment and the needs of the people. It is the intention that the Five Year Project Report and the Annual Plans of an ITDP should reflect the socio-economic aspirations in the ITDP, the total quantum of resources available and the means to be adopted for achieving the objective. Area planning approach has been adopted as the tribal sub-plan areas have poor infra-structure and contain non-tribal population in addition to the tribal population. About 65 per cent of the total scheduled tribe population in the country was covered in the Fifth Plan period.

Financial Arrangements

One shortcoming which stood in the way of receipt of benefits of development by tribal areas was that these areas secured inadequate allocations in the past. The argument used to be that the poor infra-structure in the tribal areas did not permit absorption of funds therein and since no funds were being invested to reinforce the infra-structure, non-utilisation of funds was common, resulting in a vicious circle. This has been sought to be rectified by stipulating that a proportionate part of the State Plan funds should be quantified for the tribal sub-plan. Thus, since the Fifth Plan period, the State Governments have been undertaking in each sector like agriculture, animal husbandry, minor irrigation, cooperation, forestry, small and village industries, education, health etc., the exercise of earmarking funds for the sub-Plan areas in their budget. The funds quantified for the tribal sub-Plan area are reflected under a minor head or a sub-head of a major head in the budget demand of the concerned sectoral department. In some States, e.g. Madhya Pradesh, Rajasthan, Maharashtra, Gujarat, the process has been carried further by opening a new demand for the Tribal Development Department whereunder the allocations of the various sectors are placed. This enables a broad financial investment picture to be obtained every year in advance. Further, the arrangement confers the advantage of making re-appropriation difficult. Non-divertibility in the normal circumstances should make it difficult to starve the tribal sub-Plan areas easily of funds.

During the Fifth Plan period, the question of tribal development was placed in proper focus and attempt was initiated to bend governmental machinery, both at the State and the Centre, in unison in its favour. The tasks were identified and the broad contours of the plans emerged. For the first time, 16 States and 2 Union Territories prepared the tribal sub-Plan highlighting the objectives and the priorities as well as earmarking funds. The twin objectives were spelt out as prevention of tribal exploitation and positive economic development. The most important fields which needed attention were identified as countering of exploitation, raising productivity level in agriculture and allied sectors, provision of cheap production and consumption credit, marketing of minor forest produce, rehabilitation of shifting cultivators etc. The total investment made during 1974-79 was the order of over a thousand crore or ten billion rupees.

The Sixth Plan (1980-85) Prospect

The gains of the Fifth Plan period can broadly be described as, firstly, acceptance of the idea of accelerated tribal development by the tribal concentration States, Andhra Pradesh, Assam, Bihar, Gujarat, Himachal Pradesh, Madhya Pradesh, Maharashtra, Orissa, Rajasthan, West Bengal; secondly, evolution of the concept of the tribal sub-Plan; thirdly, the raising of the administrative scaffolding for implementation and, fourthly, the support of the operation of the idea and the concept. Some financial investments and some physical efforts have gone into it.

We face the Sixth Plan period 1980-85 a little more confidently. In the first place, the conceptual framework has acquired more clarity. In respect of anti-exploitative measures, many States have passed enactments against alienation of tribal lands, tribal indebtedness, bonded labour, liquor vending in tribal areas. These laws have to be reviewed, reinforced and brought up-to-date wherever necessary and where they have not been introduced they have to be enforced. For ensuring marketing of surplus farm and minor forest produce of tribals, and a reasonable return on it, co-operatives at the primary and secondary level have been set up. Though about 2400 primary large-sized multi-purpose societies (LAMPS)[5] have been set up, many of them are in a nascent state and need to be nurtured and strengthened. Proper linkages between LAMPS, the Tribal Development Corporations (TDCs), the District Central Cooperative Banks (DCCBs), the State Co-operative Banks (SCBs) and other such secondary or apex institutions have to be properly and firmly forged. LAMPS at the primary level are multi-functional for production and consumption credit, purchase of tribal farm and forest produce and sale of consumer necessities. At the secondary or apex level, the credit functions are handled by the DCCBs and SCBs, non-credit functions by other bodies like the TDCs. Credit at differential rate of interest (4%) through commercial banks as well as co-operatives has to become a full reality.

Some steps have already been taken for raising the technological level in agriculture, horticulture and animal husbandry fields. This effort will be intensified. Minor irrigation should continue to engage special attention. Research and experimentation, particularly in those crops which have traditionally been grown by tribals, should claim priority. Forestry policy will be reoriented to involve the tribal as a partner and a beneficiary. For the rehabilitation of shifting cultivators, an integrated plan of action in which agriculture, animal husbandry, horticulture, irrigation, education and health components are all tied up neatly, alone can meet the problem. The experiment of *in situ* horticultural plantation on shifting cultivation slopes as well as in other areas has caught the imagination. One should not be surprised if, in future, the tribal areas steal the limelight from States like Himachal Pradesh in fruitgrowing. Some impact has been made in the fields of education and health, but it cannot be regarded as significant. There is wide-spread recognition now that mere economic measures and even legislative steps may not succeed unless the capability of the tribal himself is built up through education. It is for this reason that the Sixth Plan would accord a much higher priority to education than it received during the earlier Plan. Adult education and youth training should underpin the socio-economic programmes and improvement of health should play a significant role in furthering them. This is the broad policy framework for the Sixth Plan.

On the financial side, during the Sixth Plan period, flow from State Plans is expected to treble, i.e. go up to about Rs. 2,700 crores (or 27 billion). The investment from the Central Ministries is projected to be of the order of Rs. 750 crores (7.5 billion), while that of institutional finance of the order of Rs. 550 crores (5.5 billion). The quantum of special Central assistance is projected to be of the order of Rs. 1000 crores (10 billion). Thus, the total size of the tribal sub plan during the Sixth Plan period is estimated to be of the order of Rs. 5000 crores (50 billion).

Administrative Structure

The instrument or execution is as important as the policy framework. Since attention was engaged during the Fifth Plan period in so many diverse fields particularly of a basic character, its full elaboration has not so far been possible.

Broadly speaking, if we leave aside the north-eastern States like Nagaland, Arunachal Pradesh, Meghalaya, Mizoram which are predominantly tribal, we have two types of States from the demographic point of view. Firstly, those of Central India, i.e. Andhra Pradesh, Assam, Bihar, Gujarat, Himachal Pradesh, Madhya Pradesh, Maharashtra, Rajasthan, Tripura, which have a concentration of tribal population forming a sizable percentage ranging from 8 to 29. Second, those States where the tribal population is more dispersed in character and percentage-wise also it is lower e.g. Karnataka, Kerala, Tamilnadu, Uttar Pradesh and West Bengal. In the former category, during the Fifth Plan period, Development Blocks containing more than 50 per cent tribal population were identified and a group of two or more Blocks was aggregated to form Integrated Tribal Development Projects or ITDPs. As already indicated, an ITDP is a unit of planning;

and a Development Block is a unit of execution. Generally, a Project Administrator has been placed in charge of an ITDP and a Block Development Officer (BDO) remains in charge of a Development Block. By and large, the ITDPs have not been converted into Agencies functioning under the Societies Registration Act as was the case with TDCs except in the States of Andhra Pradesh and Orissa. Administrative linkages in the ITDPs would roughly be as follows :

	Village Level Worker	
Extension Officers	B.D.O.	Extension Officers
District Level Officers (DAO, DAHO, DFO)	Project Administrator	District Level Officers (Ex-Engineers, CMO)
	Collector or Deputy Commissioner	
Divisional Technical Officers	Divisional Commissioner	Divisional Technical Officers
Development Departments	Tribal commissioners	Regulatory Departments

In this manner, a unified line of command has been sought to be set up, though it cannot be said that it has been fully established.

At the project level, a committee comprising both official and non-official elements, has been constituted for planning and overseeing functions. The non-officials mostly are Members of Parliament (MPs), Members of State Legislative Assemblies (MLAs), Panchayat Samiti Chairmen and prominent tribals. In some States, this committee functions as an implementing agency also, but in some other States e.g. Madhya Pradesh, a separate Project Implementation Committee has been set up. At the State level, there are again two types of committees, one a Cabinet sub-committee and the other an official committee. In some other States, one committee combines both these functions. These committees lay down broad policy decisions and review implementation from time to time.

It is fully realised that implementation of the policies and programmes depends on the quality of personnel engaged in their execution. The men and women entrusted the responsibility have to be chosen not only for their competence but also for their sensitivity and dedication. They should be imparted suitable training germane to planning, implementation and evaluation of tribal development programmes. For the achievement of any degree of success, the knowledge, experience and participation of tribal experts in the fields of administration, anthropology, sociology and other related disciplines should be sought.

Till the tribal leadership comes of age, voluntary organisations will have to play an important part working alongside Government machinery. The dedicated workers of the voluntary organisations can exercise a healthy influence on the bureaucratic set-up. The endeavour is to encourage the growth of selfless voluntary organisations which will adhere to the ideal of human service. Fortunately there are still a few of them extant. It is to be hoped that they will also induce young men and women to follow the ideals. The Government machinery and the voluntary agencies should be complementary to each other and should work hand in hand.

The great adventure of tribal development was commenced earnestly in the Fifth Plan. Now the sea is a little less uncharted than it was then. For the task to be accomplished successfully, for the process of change and development to be smooth and meaningful, it has to be approached with empathy. There is no doubt that the steam-roller of development would perhaps disturb the fine balance of the tribal life and world. Our effort would be that a new golden balance is struck and the transformation is congenial harmonious and happy.

NOTES AND REFERENCES

1. *Scheduled Areas*

   The Fifth Schedule of the Constitution envisages special administration for the under-developd areas having a preponderance of scheduled tribes. The idea that distinct and special arrangements are necessary for the isolated tribal regions gained acceptance over a period of time. The extent, total population, scheduled tribe population etc. of the scheduled Areas are indicated in the two Presidential Orders of 1950. At the time of issue of these Orders, the total area covered was about 1 lakh (one hundred thousand) square miles covering 86 lakhs (8.6 million) scheduled tribe population (1951 Census); presently the area covered is about 3.6 lakhs (0.36 million) square kilometres and scheduled tribe population as per 1971 Census is about 189 lakhs (18.9 million). Special provisions have been made in the Constitution for the protection and advancement of scheduled tribes, the most important of them being in Article 244 which provides for the administration of "Scheduled Areas" in accordance with the Fifth Schedule. The Scheduled Areas are administered as part of the State in which they are situated, but the Governor of a State has been given powers to (a) modify Central and State laws in their application to them and (b) frame Regulations for their peace and good Government and, in particular, for the protection of rights of tribals in land, the allotment of waste land and their protection from money-lenders. According to the Dhebar Commission the Scheduled Areas have been constituted with two clear and straightforward objectives. One is to assist the tribals in enjoying their existing rights unhindered or unobstructed by others through summary process. The second is to develop the Scheduled Areas and promote the economic, educational and social progress of the scheduled tribes. According to Article 339 of the Constitution, the President may, at any time, and shall, at the expiration of ten years from the commencement of the Constitution (1950), appoint a Commission to report on the administration of Scheduled Areas on the welfare of Scheduled tribes in the State. A "Scheduled Areas and Scheduled Tribes Commission" was appointed in 1960 under the Chairmanship of U. N. Dhebar. They submitted their report in 1961 after investigation into the problem of scheduled tribes. They observed that there was diffusion of effort in the welfare work. It was necessary to concentrate on a few essential items like drinking water, food all the year round, employment at least for 300 days in a year on reasonable basis: education, health and village roads. They stressed that an integrated and planned approach based on these few essential items would give the plan a more realistic touch in the eyes of the tribals.

2. *Tribal Development Blocks*

Blocks were originally chosen with a population of a lakh (a hundred thousand) to become the units of formulation and execution of development programmes. Popular representatives were associated with the Blocks' governmental machinery so that the programmes could be reflective of the needs and aspirations of the people. In the Third Five Year Plan period (1961-1966) Tribal Development Blocks came into being, based on the general pattern of Community Development

Blocks, but more intensive in character. The object was to bring about rapid improvement in socio-economic standard of tribals. Till the end of 1966-67, 484 Blocks had been set up in various States. Though no rigid schematic pattern was laid down, the guidelines prescribed that 60 per cent of funds should be earmarked for economic development programmes, 25 per cent for communications and 15 per cent for social services. High priority assigned to communications programme was in consideration of the difficult terrain and inaccessibility of tribal areas. An assessment of the programme made by the Vidyarthi Task Force indicated that it had fallen short of expectation though it brought in a change in outlook of tribals, particularly in the fields of education and agriculture. They thought that the main reason of the shortcoming of the programme was the relatively small size of the tribal Blocks which cannot accommodate schemes like soil conservation, major and medium irrigation, secondary and technical education. Further, it was thought that a large number of standardised schemes in vogue among advanced communities had been applied to tribal areas without scrutiny of their appropriateness and that 60-70 per cent of the funds were being spent on "brick and mortar schemes". With some changes, the T. D. Blocks continued into the Fourth Plan and beyond. Presently, the T.D. Blocks as well as the Community Development Blocks are a part of Integrated Tribal Development Projects in States which have some tribal concentration.

3. *Sectoral Programmes*

In the context of a Development Block, in the initial stages a total outlay along with earmarked outlays for each sector was fixed. Thus, in each of the Blocks in the country during the First and Second Five Year Plans a fixed sum of money was available for agriculture, animal husbandry, irrigation, roads, education, health etc. sectors. The amounts for each sector had been decided at the national level in the light of the priorities sensed. Subsequently, it was realised that such uniform inter-sectoral allocations of the total might not be strictly relevant. This is particularly true of the tribal areas. At the same time, if the matter is looked at merely from the point of view of sectoral allocations, there is a possible tendency to isolate each sector from the other and judge its relevance and importance unrelated or leastly related to other concerned sectors. The need in tribal areas is to assess the priority requirements of each sector in the ITDP perspective and enmesh each sector firmly with the others so that a coordinated holistic over-view plan emerges. Hence, the two pitfalls of nationally pre-determined routinised budgetary sectoral allocations and excessively sectorally weighted allocations have to be avoided, in favour of locally-attuned resources linked aptitude-based balanced inter-sectoral allocations.

4. *Target Groups*

In this country, planning process proceeded initially on the broad assumption that economic growth would bring prosperity to the people. In other words, expansion of infra-structure and programmes of increased production would automatically lead to rise in living standard. At a later stage it was realised that increase in gross national product may not, ipso facto, contribute to rise in the standards of the poor people. Hence, in planning the principle of growth with distributive justice has been adopted thereafter. This implies that along with the thrust towards infra-structural development and production programmes, a strategy for addressing programmes of socio-economic development to the poorer and weaker sections of the society should be implemented. It has been generally accepted that about 40 per cent of the total population of India lives below the "poverty-line", i.e. without adequate resources for normal upkeep. In addition, certain weak groups e.g. scheduled tribes and scheduled castes have been recognised by the society and even in the Constitution to whom special attention requires to be paid. The poorer segments of the population and the weaker sections of the society constitute target-groups for special attention for planning and development.

5. *Large-Sized Multi-purpose Societies* (*LAMPS*)

These co-operative societies have been set up since 1974 in tribal areas in the country with a view to supplying under one roof the various requirements of tribal people. Their credit-cum marketing needs are particularly looked after by LAMPS. The policy of LAMPS is sought to be tribal-oriented by having a majority of tribals on the Board of Directors and making one of the tribals as a Member of the Board of Directors. Adequate share-capital is being provided. Cadre management of plan is an important aspect and this is being attended to.

SUGGESTED READINGS

Govt. of India, Ministry of Law, Justice & Company Affairs : The Constitution of India.

Govt of India : Report of the Scheduled Areas and Scheduled Tribes Commission headed by U.N. Dhebar, 1960-61.

Govt of India, Ministry of Home Affairs : Report of the Special Working Group on Co-operation for Backward Classes, 1962.

Govt of India, Planning Commission: Report of the Study Team on Tribal Development Programmes, Committee on Plan Projects, 1969.

Govt. of India, Ministry of Home Affairs: Tribal Development in the Fifth Plan, some basic policy papers, Vol. I, 1975, Report of Task Force on Development of Tribal Areas headed by Prof. L.P. Vidyarthi, pages 65-100.

Govt. of India, Ministry of Home Affairs : Tribal Development in the Fifth Plan, some Basic Policy Papers, Vol. 1, 1975, Report of Expert Committee under the Chairmanship of S.C. Dube, pages 33-63.

Govt. of India, Ministry of Home Affairs : Tribal Development in the Fifth Plan, some Basic Policy Papers Vol. I, 1975, Report of the Study Group on Relief of Indebtedness, Land Alienation and Restoration in Tribal Development Agency Areas, pp. 142-152.

Govt. of India, Controller of Publications : Report of the Commissioner for Scheduled Castes and Scheduled Tribes, 1974-75, pages 115-116.

Singh, Bhupinder : Tribal Development at Cross-roads; A Critique and a Plea, *Man in India,* Volume 57, Number Three, July-September, 1977.

Vidyarthi L.P. : *Malers* : *Study in Nature-Man-Spirit Complex of a Hill Tribe,* Bookland, Calcutta, 1963.

TEN

B. K. Roy Burman

STRATEGY OF TRIBAL DEVELOPMENT
An Anthropological Approach

1. CONSIDERATION of the strategies of tribal development should cover the following aspects :

(i) Scope of tribal welfare and development activities,
(ii) Integration of tribal welfare and development activities in the national development plan,
(iii) Role of government and statutory bodies,
(iv) Role of voluntary agencies,
(v) Role of tribal institutions.

2. Welfare and development activities are expected to be concerned with :

(i) Satisfaction of minimum needs,
(ii) Control and management of productive resources,
(iii) Employment optimisation,
(iv) Broad based participation of the population in development process,
(v) Socio-cultural and political aspects of national integration. Each of these aspects will be briefly touched upon here.

SATISFACTION OF MINIMUM NEEDS

1. Broadly the minimum needs in the tribal areas include food for work in the lean season, potable water, health and sanitation, housing, fodder, fuel, communication and primary and non-formal education.

The most important strategic question in the matter of satisfaction of minimum needs is whether it should be done as a welfare measure or by rescheduling the productive activities. Generally the approach has been to satisfy the minimum needs as a welfare measure. This tends to destroy the self-reliance of the tribals and make them dependent on bureaucratic management. Also this leads to a distortion in the utilisation of the productive resources at the disposal of the tribal communities. A complete reversal of the approach is called for. In other words as far as possible the minimum needs of the tribals are to be satisfied through harnessing the forces of production and orienting the social relations of production in conformity with the tribal ethos of self-management and national objective of building up a socialistic pattern of society.

CONTROL AND MANAGEMENT OF PRODUCTIVE RESOURCES

From the preceding enunciation, control and management of productive resources assumes a great importance in the tribal welfare and development administration. This includes :

(i) Determination of the nature of rights including communal rights over productive resources, through systematic enquiries.

(ii) Preparation of record of rights after giving due recognition to the traditionally prevailing categories of rights.

(iii) Systematic enquiries on the factors and processes of transformation of the traditional categories of rights and consequences thereof on the standard of living of the tribal population, patterns of interaction with the tribal communities and with the rest of the nation.

(iv) Phasing of administrative, legal and political action to reinforce the trends of transformation of the categories of rights which harmonise with the national objectives and with the broader humanistic goal of development.

(v) Elimination of the hang-over of the colonial forest policy of imposing state or state sponsored capitalist mode of production on primitive social and technological base.

(vi) Prevention of alienation of tribal productive resources—primarily land—through appropriate administrative, legal and political processes and supplemented by the rescheduling of the productive activities and mode of functioning of financial institutions.

(vii) Augmentation of productive activities which are primarily meant to serve the essential needs of the local communities and creation of a system of circulation of commodities in a manner, that, only after meeting the needs of the progressively expanding communities (in social boundary and in number) the surplus goes to the market.

(viii) Adoption of a technology and production schedule of maximum recycling of non-renewable resources.

An obvious criticism that can be made against this inventory of aspects involved in the management and control of the productive resources is that, there is an underlying assumption that they would smoothly dovetail with one another. Criticism of a different order can be that this more reflects a philosophy than a programme.

It is not proposed to brush aside these criticisms. But in a rapid over-view like the present one, it is also not possible to go into a detailed probe. In a general way, it can be stated that the philosophy or rather the ideational thrust of the present formulation is based on an understanding of the implication of the persistence of the tribal communities in the contemporary world. Hardly any of the tribal communities of today are primitive communities, they retain the moral bindings of the primitive community and at the same time try to harmonise the same with the organisational structures of modern technology. They are post-primitives,—the builders of a new social order, which is not primarily dependent on the coercive power of nation-state. Their persistence provides a hope that perhaps alternative frameworks for organised living can yet be found, without the modern man being all the time haunted by the spectre of alienation from his surroundings.

As regards inter-relations among the different aspects, it is quite possible that they will not always easily fit with one another. In those cases the optimun fit is to be found giving priority to the satisfaction of the minimum needs of the population. The order of priorities among the other items will depend on the specific historical and ecological contexts.

EMPLOYMENT

Coming over to employment, it would first be necessary to categorise the tribal labour as follows—

(i) Self-employed and family labour in agricultural sector.
(ii) Self-employed and family labour in non-agricultural sector.
(iii) Employees in agricultural sector.
(iv) Employees in non-agricultural household sector.
(v) Employees in plantation.
(vi) Employees in public sector industrial, commercial and other enterprises.
(vii) Employees in private sector industrial, commercial and other establishments.
(viii) Government service.

The problems of the different categories of tribal workers are broadly as follows—

Self-employed and Family Labour in the Agricultural Sector

Frequently they are displaced from their traditional activities as a sequel to changes in land use pattern, cropping pattern, mode of production and production technology.

The first task in such cases is to examine the rationale of the changes. If they are inevitable, it would be necessary to help the tribals to raise the level of productivity in their traditional work and/or provide other socially desirable and culturally compatible productive and non-productive activities.

Self-employed and Family Worker in Non-agricultural Sector

Frequently such workers are displaced as a sequel to changes in the pattern of relationship with the other sectors of economy or in the availability of requisite inputs, production technology and channels of disposal of products. In their case also first it is to be examined whether the displacement is unavoidable; in that case socially desirable alternative productive and non-productive activities are to be thought of.

Employees in Agricultural Sector

This category would include agricultural labour. Strictly

speaking the share-croppers are not employees; but where the share croppers work under feudal obligations, they can be considered under this category.

In case of the agricultural labour the task is primarily that of ensuring continuous employment and improvement in the terms and conditions of their work. In determining the types of employment, the political economy of the region, social mobility, trends and the aspirations of the communities concerned are to be kept in view.

In case of the share croppers, the major task is that of getting their right of cultivation recorded in the record of rights. The second task is that of improving the terms and conditions of obtaining the requisite imputs and ensuring that they get the commensurate share of the output.

Employees in Non-agricultural Household Sector

Frequently the non-agricultural household sector of production forms the weakest sector in tribal economy. Correspondingly the tribal workers in this sector constitute the weakest section of the workers. It is difficult to improve their lot without improving the condition of the specific productive activity itself in the total economy. If on systematic enquiry resuscitation of the productive activity is not found possible, it would be necessary to rehabilitate the workers in other sectors of economy.

Employees in Plantations

Frequently the tribal plantation labourers are migrant labourers, living away from their traditional habitat. Continuation of their cultural communication with traditional habitat, extension of cultural communication with the indigenous population of the area of migration are major problems. At the same time, their solidarity with other plantation workers and organised and unorganised workers for safeguarding their common interests is to be ensured.

Employees in Public Sector Industrial, Commercial and Other Enterprises

Very frequently the tribals are found in such enterprises in sizeable numbers only as unskilled labour. The major task is to ensure their proportionate representation at various levels and promote occupational mobility. Improvement of the terms and conditions of their work, including where they are employed by contractors is another important task. Apart from these, frequently great social distance prevails between tribal and non-tribal labourers in the same industry. This seriously impedes the establishment and functioning of industrial democracy. This matter requires careful attention.

Employees of Private Sector Industrial, Commercial and Other Establishments

The tasks are more or less same as in case of the employees of public sector establishments. But here more efforts are to be made to build up inter-ethnic harmony and to ensure that the tribal workers discharge their responsibility as members of organised working clan.

Reservation in Government Services

Apart from insuring proportionate representation, the tasks are those of socialisation in job situation and promotion of occupational mobility.

PARTICIPATION OF THE POPULATION IN THE DEVELOPMENT PROCESS

The participation can take several forms :

(i) Participation of selected individuals in planning/implementation or both in planning and implementation stages.

(ii) Participation of tribal representatives in various stages according to the discretion of the officials.

(iii) Participation of tribal representatives as required by the statute.

Again the participation may be confined to giving advice or may be extended to policy making and operational control functions.

Each approach has its own socio-political implications. But over a length of time the ideal would be to ensure the participation of the tribal representatives as required by the statute in policy making and operational control functions.

SOCIO-CULTURAL AND POLITICAL ASPECTS OF NATIONAL INTEGRATION

In determining the strategies of tribal development one must also have a well thought out conceptual framework about national integration.

The framework may relate to the socio-cultural aspects centring the questions of tribal language (as a cultural activity and as a medium of instruction); literature and creative activities, education, symbolic actions and ways of life. In these matters there are variant models, namely (a) identification with dominant culture or assimilation in national mainstream, (b) melting pot or cross-cultural fertilisation, (c) cross-cultural co-existence, (d) common strivings towards universalistic goals. By and large at the conceptual level many do not support the first model, but all the same at the operational level frequently it prevails.

Of late the problems of tribal integration are also being examined from a different angle. This covers political communication, with due understanding of the specificities of tribal history and co-existence of diverse modes of production in tribal areas. This also takes into consideration the responsibilities of a country like India as a secular democracy and as a co-participant with other third world countries in the common struggle for a just social order.

Integration of Tribal Welfare and Development Activities in the National Development Plan

After defining the scope of welfare and development activities in the tribal areas the question of integration of the same in the national plan is to be considered. This would cover the following aspects :

(a) Orientation of the national programme to the political economy prevailing in the tribal areas.

(b) Adjustment of legal, administrative and political frameworks to the specific historical and socio-cultural contexts of the tribal areas.

(c) Preparation of integrated area plan and incorporation of needed outlays in respective sectoral plans.

(d) Amalgamation of sectoral plans for tribal areas based on fund available from respective sectors (with such weightage as the conditions demand) in the proportions that the tribals bear to the total population.

Going into details, it is to be noted that functional integration of development activities in respect of the tribals in the national plan is also oriented to the political economy prevailing the tribal areas. There are historical rights of the tribal and other indigenous people in the hill and other outlying areas of the country. In drawing up the national plans in respect of forestry, power, industry, horticulture, animal husbandry etc. these historical rights are to be kept in view. If the national plans are based merely in infra-structural and raw material requirements of commercial and industrial establishments and other elite sections of the society at the national level, the tribal communities are very likely to be alienated.

Apart from reorientation of the productive activities, it is also necessary to formulate a well conceived population policy. In respect of tribal and border areas keeping in view, the constraints of ecology, history and political economy. This is necessary to alley the misgivings of the tribals that they are being cornered in their home by continuous influx of migrants; at the same time a balance is to be made with national security and social and economic needs.

As regards the adjustment of legal, administration and political frameworks, to the emerging needs, one of the major tasks is that of extension of the provisions of Indian succession Act, Hindu Marriage, Succession and Adoption Acts by notification wherever necessary and codification or authentication of customary laws in other cases, keeping in view their instrumental value and compatibility with public policy. It is also necessary to re-examine whether the existing administrative and political units in the tribal areas require to be modified so as to enable the tribals to articulate their aspirations and expectations more purposefully in the national life.

As regards integrated development provision should be made for the satisfaction of the minimum needs to the full, during the Sixth Plan. At the same time perspective plan is to be drawn up for building up productive infra-structure and generating productive activities to such an extent and in such a manner that the existing human resources are fully utilised, their historical association with the productive resources are reinforced, the exploitative relations in the systems of production and exchange are eliminated, functional specialisation contributing towards the improvement of the quality of life are strengthened and such linkages with the rest of the country are established, as would optimise the utilisation of the national productive resources and reduce regional disparities.

Subsumed within the perspective plan short-term integrated development programme is also to be drawn up so that the different schemes are linked up with one another in time and space in a logical sequence and the total outlay remains within a reasonable limit.

Role of Government and Statutory Bodies

While at the national level the roles of the Commission for Scheduled Castes and Scheduled Tribes, Commissioner for scheduled Castes and Scheduled Tribes, Planning Commission, Union Home Ministry, Rural Development Department require to be reviewed, at the local level the roles of the organs of Panchayati Raj, commercial banks and other financial institutions are of considerable importance. Frequently the Panchayats are controlled by the rich peasants and rural money-lenders and traders who are also the exploiters of the tribals. In such contexts recognition of the traditional organisations, representing the corporate identities of the tribals may serve to countermand the negative features of the panchayati bodies. The commercial banks frequently adopt norms of economic viability of schemes which are not related to management experiences, consumption and saving habits and decision-making processes of the tribals. Large-scale adaptations to tribal situation based on careful research are needed.

Roles of Voluntary Agencies

The following types of agencies may be considered :—

(a) Philanthropic and welfare agencies
(b) Political parties
(c) Peasant organisations in tribal areas

(d) Trade Unions among the tribals

(e) Other voluntary agencies.

In each case the extent of rigidity or flexibility of the approach of the agencies concerned on ideological consideration is of paramount importance.

Roles of Tribal Institutions

Roles of traditional institutions like tribal panchayats or of formally created bodies like tribal association in mobilisation of the tribals for various activities are also to be kept in view in generating development programmes among the tribals.

An Overview of Integrated Approach

Taking an overall view the development activities among the tribals can be categorised as follows :

(i) Paternalistic and welfare oriented.

(ii) Self-reliant and basic-need oriented.

(iii) Universalistic and oriented to social transformation.

In the first case the development programmes follow type-plans drawn up externally and implemented mainly by official agencies of non-official agencies whose social bases are outside the total communities concerned. Frequently in such approach welfare activities take place along with extension of profit maximising market economy in tribal areas. In the second case, a greater emphasis is given on the satisfaction of basic needs through productive activities and also on participant management of programmes by the tribal themselves. After meeting the basic needs the residual resources are linked up with the market and the tribal elites are helped to articulate their interests in the common platform within national elites. In the third approach the tribals function as self-managing corporate identities at the same time they share the common platforms along with the other deprived sections of the society for ushering in radical social transformation.

ELEVEN

K. K. Srivastava

PLANNING FOR TRIBAL DEVELOPMENT

PLANNING for development of tribals and tribal areas has to keep in view the ethnic diversity of tribal people who form 7 per cent of the total population, their habitations, as unlike the scheduled castes they are mostly concentrated in certain areas, and the diverse socio-economic levels of tribal societies. The planning strategy, therefore, has to be carefully framed so as to take into account these peculiarities. In this context tribal areas, their problems and earlier attempts at tribal development will need recapitulation.

General Problems Relating to Scheduled Tribes

The total tribal population in the country was 38.2 million according to the 1971 Census. This figure has been estimated by the Registrar General of India to have risen to 41 million as per the Scheduled Caste and Scheduled Tribes Order (Amendment) Act, 1976. The tribal population is widely spread over the whole country. The largest concentration is found in the North-East and Central regions. The individual tribes and sub-tribes vary in their numbers from a bare handful to several millions. They present a varied spectrum of development and a diversity in their ethnic and cultural background.

The mainstay of tribal economy was, and still is, agriculture which exists usually in a rudimentary form and provides a subsistence level of economy. Quite a large number of tribals practise shifting cultivation. The majority of them supplement their economy by gathering minor forest produce which is used to buy their daily requirements like clothing kerosene, salt, agricultural implements etc., at the weekly or fortnightly *hats* in the villages. The forests are, therefore, very closely linked with the tribal economy. The forest policy as followed by the colonial Government led to the disruption of the tribal economy leaving them at the mercy of the lower forest functionaries and contractors.

The main areas of tribal concentration and their general problems may be summed up as follows:—

(i) Northern zone stretching from Ladakh in North-west to Terai region of Uttar Pradesh have tribes who have remained neglected mostly due to remoteness of their habitat and difficult climatic conditions.

(ii) The north-eastern zone comprising the hinterland between Assam and Tibet, have tribes whose economy was disrupted, because of severance of communication between rest of the country on account of carving out what is now Bangladesh. This led to almost halt to their trade with plains areas and commercial centres in West Bengal. The tribals of these zones are mostly shifting cultivators (or *Jhumias*) due to a dearth of level land and steep hill slopes. *Jhuming* and communication are, therefore, major problems in this zone.

(iii) In the eastern, central and western zones comprising the States of West Bengal, Bihar, Orissa, Madhya Pradesh, Gujarat, Maharashtra and Rajasthan, problems of tribal development are related to pressure of population on land, problem of land tenure, indebtedness and rights of tribals in forests and practice of shifting cultivation coupled with low production level. Tribals of this area also suffer from chronic scarcity of food, water and employment. Added to these is the problem of modernisation due to growth of industrial complexes in the heart of tribal areas which has disrupted the traditional style of life. This has also led to group tensions due to large scale population movement which industrialisation entails, compounded by resettlement of refugees from what is now called Bangladesh among the tribal people especially in Dandakaranya.

(iv) Problems of tribals living in the southern zone (Andhra Pradesh, Tamil Nadu, Karnataka and Kerala) are mostly based on their primitive economy of *Podu* culture (shifting cultivation) or food gathering habits and prevalence of *Muttadari* system of land tenure.

(v) Some of the tribals living in the Andaman Group of islands are facing the problem of a dwindling population. They are very primitive and largely depend on fishing and hunting. The tribals of Nicobar Islands, although not primitive, have subsistence economy based mostly on coconut plantations, banana gardens, piggery and fishing. The problems of tribals living in Lakshadweep Islands also arise out of their subsistence economy largely based on cultivation of coconut and fishing.

In spite of these varying problems that the different groups of tribals have to face, there are certain specific problems which are common to almost all the tribals, such as alienation of land, large scale indebtedness, romoteness, and shifting cultivation. Shifting cultivation or Jhuming/Podu, as it is variously known in different areas, whereby forests are cut down, burnt and seeds sown and later harvested by tribals, is widespread. A patch is cultivated for a few years then abandoned for a new patch of forest. Gradually the cycle of Jhuming gets shorter and whatever soil is there, is endangered by soil erosion which results in loss of forest wealth. A large number of tribals practise this type of rudimentary agriculture in North-East and Central India. Shifting cultivation is a complex problem, a solution to which requires joint efforts of forestry and agriculture departments and integration of the tribal economy with social services. Another general problem is connected with the traditional practice amongst most tribal communities of brewing indigenous liquor which is consumed on certain social occasions. The Excise Administration in the tribal areas resulted in introducing the liquor vending system in these areas through contractors. This policy of selling distilled liquor through the contractors caused tribals to fall in the vicious clutches of money-lenders. Also the liquor shops have proved to be easy channels for introduction of anti-social elements in these areas.

The Approach to the Problem

Prior to Independence the policy of isolation and drift left the tribals to themselves and almost no efforts were made to develop their lot except to administer those areas as "excluded" and "partially excluded" areas. It resulted in reducing the tribals to a state of penury in most parts of the country. Their lands were alienated or heavily encumbered and their rights in the forests were encroached upon. Outside elements introduced for the purposes of Government and forest work continued to exploit them. It was only after the attainment of Independence that the Government became fully concerned about the welfare of the scheduled tribes. The Constituent Assembly set up a Sub-Committee under the Chairmanship of A.V. Thakkar for "excluded" and "partially excluded" areas (other than Assam). The most important recommendation of this Sub-Committee which was accepted by the Constituent Assembly was that the new democratic State had a responsibility towards the tribal people and the development of tribal areas, howsoever remote or inaccessible they might be. The task that confronted the nation was to devise methods which would protect the economic interests of the tribals, safeguard their way of life and ensure their rapid development in accordance with their own genius, to enable them to take their legitimate place in the general life of the country.

Article 46 of the Constitution enjoins upon the state to promote with special care the educational and economic interests of the weaker sections of the people, and, in particular, of the Scheduled Castes and the Scheduled Tribes, and to protect them from social injustice and all forms of exploitation. Article 244 of the Constitution prescribes special provisions for the administration of Scheduled Areas, Scheduled Tribes and Tribal Areas. The special provisions indicated in the Fifth Schedule govern the administration and control of the Scheduled Areas and Scheduled Tribes in the States other than what was then called the State of Assam. The special provisions of the Sixth Schedule govern the administration of the Tribal Areas in what was then called the State of Assam. For the purposes of these special provisions, the President, in orders issued in 1950 (and subsequently amended in 1976) declared certain areas of tribal concentration as Scheduled Areas in the States now known as Andhra Pradesh, Bihar, Gujarat, Himachal Pradesh, Madhya Pradesh, Maharashtra, Orissa and Rajasthan. So far as tribal areas are concerned, they have been defined in the Sixth Schedule of the Constitution. The President, by orders issued in 1950 (subsequently amended in 1956 and 1976) has declared certain tribes as Scheduled Tribes in accordance with Article 342 of the Constitution. Article 275 provides for Central grants-in-aid to States for undertaking development work for the purposes of promoting the welfare of the Scheduled Tribes or raising the level of administration of the Scheduled Areas to that of the administration of the rest of the State. There are also provisions for the reservation of seats in the Houses of Legislature both at the national level and the State level (Articles 330 and 332). Article 335 of the Constitution enjoins upon the Government for safeguarding the claims of the members of the Scheduled Tribes, as also Scheduled Castes, in the services and posts in connection with the affairs of the Union or of a State. Article 339 lays down that the Central Government can give directions to a State as to the drawing up and execution of schemes specified to be essential for the welfare of Scheduled Tribes in the State.

The national effort for the development of the Scheduled Tribes and the Tribal Areas has two prominent components, namely, protection and development. Such a two-pronged approach was necessary because elimination of exploitation coupled with rapid socio-economic development can alone bring lasting benefits to these groups. The scheduling of tribes and tribal areas which derives authority from the Constitution, has the following advantages :

(1) Political—reservation of seats in legislatures and local bodies.

(2) Protective—special legislations for protecting economic interests and eliminating exploitation.
(3) Development—implementation of special programmes for educational and socio-economic development.

The Concept of Development of Areas of Tribal Concentration

Since the First Five Year Plan, efforts were made to provide for the welfare of Scheduled Tribes and Tribal Areas through special sector of development, namely, welfare of Backward Classes. The programmes under this sector were meant to supplement the general development efforts for Backward Classes including tribal population. Programmes providing direct benefits to Scheduled Tribes and Scheduled Castes were taken up under the State and Central sectors for economic, educational and social development of these communities. However, attempts at integrated development of the tribal population was started in the second Five Year Plan by establishing Special Multi-purpose Tribal Blocks. Forty-three SMPT Blocks were set up in the Scheduled Areas and the programme of each Block was given an additive thrust by a special allocation of Rs. 15 lakhs for five years from the Government of India (Home Ministry) in addition to Rs. 12 lakhs available to normal Community Development Blocks. At the end of the Second Plan, the work of these SMPT Blocks and other programmes relating to tribal development were reviewed by the Elwin Committee and the Dhebar Commission. On the basis of these reviews, the programme of SMPT Blocks was modified during the Third Plan and 415 Tribal Development Blocks were set up. Each T. D. Block covered a population of 25,000 with two-third tribal population and got an additional allocation of Rs. 10 lakhs in Stage I and Rs. 5 lakhs in Stage II from the Central Government (Home Ministry). The schematic pattern of earlier SMPT Blocks was given up though the main emphasis of the programme continued to be on economic development.

Review of the Tribal Development Programme was taken up by a Study Team set up by the Planning Commission under the chairmanship of Shilu Ao which submitted its report in 1969. The findings of this team had made it clear that it was necessary to adopt a flexible policy for tribal development. The main observation of this Team regarding the Tribal Development Blocks was that although the achievement under the programme had generally fallen short of expectations, the programme had helped "to bring about a psychological change in the outlook of the tribals". Some of the main drawbacks pointed out by the Shilu Ao Team were :

(i) The Tribal Development Blocks failed to get any significant support from the general development programmes including the C.D. Programme.
(ii) The schemes formulated for these Blocks were not adopted to the felt needs of the specific areas.
(iii) The benefits had mostly accrued to the more advanced among the tribals.
(iv) The T.D. Block was too small a geographical entity for coordinated planning. Programmes like education at secondary and higher levels, soil conservation and other programmes relating to infra-structural development cut across blocks, district or even State boundaries and could not be financed out of the meagre allocation for the Tribal Development Blocks.

The Team suggested that the programme for the tribal development should be based on an "area approach" and should be financed out of the general plan supplemented in suitable cases by special allocation for tribals.

By the Fourth Five Year Plan 43 per cent of tribal population was covered in 504 T.D. Blocks. For further intensification of programmes, supplementary allocations were made by the Central Government, as in the past, and the life of each Block was extended for another five years constituting Stage III. While the programmes were in operation, there was a renewed effort to have a fresh look at the problems of rural development and provide a decisive thrust for achieving a breakthrough. In this period, a number of programmes were taken up for small farmers, marginal farmers as also crash employment and rural employment schemes. With this emphasis on the rural poor, some of the more backward tribal areas also received attention. The focus was now turned to individual families, a new programme of Tribal Development Agencies was taken up by the Ministry of Agriculture which was a variant of small farmers programme. Six projects (Tribal Development Agencies) were started in the country—two each in Madhya Pradesh and Orissa and one each in Andhra Pradesh and Bihar. Two more projects were taken up in Orissa in the Fifth Plan. The core programmes of economic development were taken up. An important feature of these projects was that a special agency was constituted and the total developmental outlays were placed at its disposal.

Fifth Five Year Plan

On the eve of the Fifth Plan, the Planning Commission set up a Task Force in 1971 which reviewed the tribal situation comprehensively and recommended a perspective for the development of tribal areas in the country. These were kept in view while formulating the policy, approach and strategy for the Fifth Five Year Plan. The problem of Tribal Development basically pertained to the development of three categories of tribals :

(a) Areas of tribal concentration;
(b) Dispersed tribals; and
(c) Primitive tribal communities.

While evolving the strategy for the Fifth Plan, it was felt that attention had to be focused on the specific problem of each identifiable group and area. The situations in regions of tribal concentration and in areas of dispersed tribal population would be quite distinct and would require different approaches. In the regions of tribal concentration, area development approach had to be adopted, keeping focus on the problems of the tribal people. In the case of dispersed tribal population, family approach would have to be adopted. It was also felt that category (c) which included certain very backward and isolated smaller groups faced problems of their very survival and they would have to be treated as a special category, both within the areas of tribal concentration and outside, and special group-oriented programmes would have to be formulated for them.

The basic approach towards tribal development adopted in the Fifth Plan was to identify larger areas of tribal concentration which included the Scheduled Areas, contiguous T.D. Blocks and other blocks/areas having 50 per cent tribal concentration. All such blocks/areas in a State were to be brought under a sparate sub-plan under the overall State Plan. However, States and Union Territories which have predominant tribal population like Nagaland, Meghalaya, Arunachal Pradesh, Mizoram and Lakshadweep were not required to draw up separate sub-plans, because the entire State Plan in these cases was basically for the welfare of the tribals.

For the preparation of the Tribal sub-plans, Planning Commission issued a set of guidelines to the States. The guidelines spelt out the long-term objective of the tribal sub-plan as (1) narrowing the gap between the levels of development of tribals and other areas, and (2) improving their quality of life. Among the immediate objectives were (1) elimination of exploitation in all forms, (2) speeding up the processes for social and economic development, (3) building up inner strength of the people, and (4) improving their organisational capabilities. The guidelines laid down the criteria for identification of the sub-plan areas, the approach and strategy for their development and also the pattern of funding and formulation of programmes in these areas. The guidelines also stated that the sub-plan areas in each State should comprise a number of viable projects. For each such Integrated Tribal Development Project (ITDP), an integrated area development plan focussing attention on the specific problems of the area and the tribal people, was to be formulated. The sub-plan areas in each State thus comprised a number of viable projects.

Identification and Demarcation of Sub-Plan Areas

In addition to the scheduled areas, each State identified the Tehsils/Talukas/Blocks having a tribal concentration of 50% or more. From these suitable planning areas were carved out at macro-,meso- and micro-levels, keeping in view the natural resources, physical features, level of development of the tribes inhabiting the region and other socio-economic considerations to suit the planning functions at these levels. It was laid down that these areas should, to the extent possible, conform to the existing administrative boundaries. For instance, macro areas were constituted in a manner in which they conveniently fell into separate revenue Divisions/Districts. Similarly, micro areas normally coincided with CD/TD Blocks. As a general rule, a TD/CD Block was taken as the lowest unit except in States which have large dispersed tribal population. Between the macro areas and the micro areas, was the meso area, popularly called the "project area" (ITDP), which was formed by grouping of contiguous development blocks and is generally co-terminus with a Taluka/Tehsil/Sub-Division and in some cases District also. In the case of Madhya Pradesh, Orissa and Bihar, more than one district tribal region spread over a number of districts formed Sub-Plan areas. These States have thus, more than one macro region for tribal development. By the end of the Fifth Plan 179 projects (ITDPs) had been identified in the entire tribal Sub-Plan area in the country.

The planning functions at the macro/meso level, depending on local conditions, included overall planning and detailed project formulation for rural electrification, major and medium irrigation projects, arterial roads, apex cooperative organisations, processing industries etc. At the micro level, which is the Block level, planning for social services, minimum needs programme, minor irrigation, agricultural extension and household industries were to be undertaken.

Strategy in the Fifth Plan

A general strategy was evolved by each State for the development of its tribal areas keeping in view the special problems of the tribal regions, in consultation with the Planning Commission and the Ministry of Home Affairs of the Government of India. The entire legal and institutional frame, the inter and intra-sectoral priorities were reviewed keeping welfare and development of scheduled tribes as the primary focus in the Plan Programme of the area. Some of the main points of the strategy in the Fifth Five Year Plan were :

Prevention of Exploitation

It was realised that no developmental activity could be of benefit to the tribal population unless their exploitation was prevented and integrated credit-cum-marketing services developed in the Sub-Plan areas. These services covered marketing of agricultural and minor forest produce, supply of inputs and essential consumer commodities. Credit for productive, consumption and social needs was made available to the tribals in the Sub-Plan areas. The credit and marketing structure in these areas was reorganised into Large Agricultural Multi-purpose Societies (LAMPS) in accordance with the recommendations of the Bawa Committee set up by the Ministry of Agriculture, Government of India, to study the problem. Efforts were made for past debt redemption of the tribals through legislative and executive measures. Programme for prevention of land alienation, restoration of land already alienated and rehabilitation of bonded labour were taken up. Attention was also given to solution of problems created among the tribal society on account of modern industries being developed in these areas. The Excise and Forest policies which directly affected tribals, were also reviewed in order to protect the interests of these people.

Development of Tribal Agriculture

High priority was given to tribal agriculture. The most important aspects of tribal agriculture development are ownership rights, completion of land records, land development and introduction of improved methods of agriculture through extension services. Special attention was given to shifting cultivators, forest villages and forest labourers through schemes of plantation, afforestation, Forest Labour Cooperative Societies, etc.

Generation of Employment Opportunities

Opportunities for better utilisation of available manpower were created through programmes which could be easily inducted into tribal economy like horticulture, animal husbandry, poultry, piggery, etc., and cottage industries based on local raw materials.

Provision of Basic Infra-Structure

In order to accelerate socio-economic development, special attention was given to creation of basic infra-structure legal, institutional and physical. Growth centres, communication net-work, schools, health centres, marketing and credit organisations, rural electrification, manpower resources and training facilities were required to be planned in an integrated fashion keeping in view the special conditions of the tribal areas.

Special Groups and Their Problems

Even within the tribal areas, the primitive tribal groups in extremely backward pockets, shifting cultivators and tribals affected by major industrial projects were given special attention by drawing up different schemes which would help these groups.

Each Sectoral authority was required to review sectoral programmes being implemented in the Sub-Plan areas in order to adapt them to the special needs of these areas. The programmes in these areas were categorised as core programmes and other programmes. The core programmes included credit and marketing, preparation of land records, restoration of alienated land, crop husbandry, training of farmers, minor and medium irrigation, forest based programmes, special problems, primary road net-work linking important market and growth centres, rationalisation of administrative structure and techno-economic survey and evaluation studies.

Funding Strategy for the Sub-Plan

The resources available for the tribal Sub-Plan comprised :

(a) State Plan outlays,
(b) Sectoral outlays in the Central Ministries for the tribal Sub-Plan areas,
(c) Special central assistance for the tribal Sub-Plan areas, and
(d) Institutional Finance.

The basic frame for the development of these areas was provided by the State Plan. The flow of funds from the State Plan for the Tribal Sub-Plan was worked out on the basis of total population of the Sub-Plan area, its geographical area, its comparative level of development and of social services. The actual share of the Tribal Sub-Plan out of the State Plan was quantified out of the divisible pool of State Plan resources with a weightage for the backwardness of the Sub-Plan area. The investment out of the non-divisible pool such as power, major irrigation and industrial projects, were generally in accordance with the actual benefits accruing to these regions. A Special Central Assistance meant to augment the efforts of the State was added to the State Plans on the basis of an accepted formula. The Central Ministries were also required to identify Central and Centrally-sponsored schemes which would benefit the tribal areas.

Another important feature regarding the outlays for tribal development was that the funds should be made non-divertible. So far as the Special Central Assistance is concerned, it is already a charge on the Consolidated Fund of India and has a special status. The first step towards non-divertibility of the State Plan outlay has been to introduce separate budget sub-heads under each major head of development. This was on important step for systematising and consolidating the developmental efforts in the tribal Sub-Plan areas and bringing some accountability. In some States like Madhya Pradesh, the entire sub-plan outlay for tribal development has been brought under one single demand. The Secretary, Tribal Welfare Department or the Tribal Development Commissioner has been nominated as the Chief Controlling Officer for this single demand. This has helped in greater flexibility in inter-sectoral re-allocations and ensuring non-divertibility. A workable mechanism in those States where the sectoral sub-plan outlays continue to be budgeted under the separate demands is gradually being evolved to ensure non-divertibility, flexibility and accountability.

Administrative Structure

The tribal areas were, till Independence, administered only minimally, where only forest guards and occasionally police were in charge of some sort of administration. Obviously the needs of the tribal people were neglected. Their exploitation by the middlemen, excise and forestry personnel impoverished the tribal society. After Independence and with the development programmes being implemented, a multiplicity of administrative agencies came into existence. When TD Blocks were set up, the right type of development personnel were not forthcoming for lack of incentive to work in remote areas, as well as lack of understanding of the problems of the tribal people amongst whom they were required to work. Therefore, a suitable administrative set-up was devised by each State for the Sub Plan area depending upon the particular requirements of the area and the existing infrastructure. Multiplicity of agencies was required to be avoided in the tribal areas as it led to diffusion of responsibility, inadequate control and lack of coordination. Efforts were made to build into the system adequate flexibility along with specificity of responsibility and individual authority.

Fifth Plan Efforts

By the end of Fifth Plan, 18 States and Union Territories had drawn up Tribal Sub-Plans covering 65 per cent of the tribal population in the country. The entire Tribal Sub-Plan area in the country had been divided into 179 projects (ITDPs). Although the Sub-Plan strategy was a new one and Sub-Plan started taking concrete shape only in 1975-76, even then by the end of Fifth Plan period project reports had been prepared for 129 out of the 179 projects. In terms of financial investment, the State Governments had quantified Rs. 601 crores as outlays from general sectors of development and the special central assistance for the Sub-Plan amounted to Rs. 120 crores. Investments from Central Ministries Plans could not, however, be clearly identified. As will appear from the following figures, the percentage of flow of funds from the State Plans has been steadily going up from year to year and from Fifth Plan to Sixth Plan.

The preparation of Annual Sub-Plans became a concurrent exercise with the State Annual Plans. Thereafter, the Annual Sub-Plan so prepared were disaggregated projectwise. The ideal situation would have been that the sub-plans were prepared from the project level upward. This could not, however, be done in most of the States. In the early stages of a new strategy, some divergence between the normative frame and the actual programme profile is inevitable for some time. However, it has been possible for the States to

TABLE 10.1

(*Rs. in crores*)

	Total State Plan	Total State Sub-Plan	Percentage of Sub-Plan to total Plan	Special Central Assistance
1974-75	1844	43*		5.00
1975-76	2660	109	4.10	20.00
1976-77	3215	192	5.96	40.00
1977-78	3874	257	6.64	55.00
1978-79	4975	344	6.92	70.00
1979-80	4987	394	7.90	70.00

*Rough estimates made recently on the basis of programmes implemented.

narrow this gap with the successive Annual Plans and greater association of the project authorities in the planning process.

The Sub-Plan strategy lays emphasis on administrative structure and proper personnel policy. The concept that tribal development is the responsibility of all development departments has now been reasonably settled. At the ITDP level, the collective responsibility of different departments has also been accepted. Almost all States have appointed or agreed to appoint senior officers as project officers. The Project Authority, comprising various Heads of Departments, the Collector and the Project Officer has been charged with the responsibility for implementation of the total development programme. However, the integration of all sectoral programmes at the project level has still to be fully achieved.

The first Sub-Plan spelt out the broad strategy and priorities in different States. A broad consensus was arrived at regarding the various issues affecting the tribal population. Elimination of exploitation was given the highest priority. It was agreed that the problem of land alienation needs to be tackled as a time bound programme. Priority was also to be given to marketing and credit to do away with the middlemen and the money-lender. 2216 Large Agricultural Multipurpose Societies (LAMPS) were organised.

A review done by the Working Group on Tribal Development constituted for the preparation of the Sixth Plan revealed that although the approach and priorities in the programme had been clearly worked out, the programmes had not yet picked up. Elimination of exploitation has limited success. Although there had been a spectacular success in relation to the level of investments in these Tribal Sub-Plan areas, programmes of infra-structural development such as roads, electricity, buildings etc, dominated over smaller programmes of direct benefit to the tribal families. The Working Group observed that administrative preparedness had come up "as an important constraint in the effective implementation of tribal development programmes and protective policies".

The Fifth Plan had also envisaged special programmes to be taken up by State Governments for the primitive tribal groups at pre-agricultural levels of technology, or who had remained extremely backward due to social and economic reasons. Though not much headway could be done in this direction, a total number of 52 communities or groups had been identified for whom the project reports were required to be prepared.

Draft Sixth Plan

The experience of planning in areas of tribal concentration indicated that the broad approach to tribal development will have to depend on the pattern of distribution of tribals in an area and the level of their economy. In areas of tribal concentration, an area approach with focus on tribal communities will have to be continued as in the Fifth Plan; the dispersed population would be covered by family-oriented programmes; and community-oriented special programmes will have to be evolved and implemented for primitive groups. Since a CD/TD block was adopted as the smallest unit for inclusion in the tribal sub-plan, a substantial portion of dispersed tribal population could not get the benefits of the area approach. The Draft Sixth Plan, therefore, provides for extension of sub-plan approach to additional areas of 10,000 population with tribal concentration of 50 per cent and above. It is estimated that an additional 10 per cent of country's tribal population will be covered by the extension of the Sub-Plan strategy.

The long-term objectives in the Draft Sixth Plan continue to be the same as in the Fifth Plan, viz. (i) narrowing the gap between the level of development of tribal areas and others, and (ii) improving the quality of life of the tribal people. The strategy of development lays emphasis on consolidation of the gains of protective measures, programmes of full employment, education and health services. The programmes under different sectors of development are required to be intensified with suitable modifications to remove the present inadequacies in implementation.

The States have to give due importance to the integration of programmes in the field and effective delegation of powers to the Project Authorities in ITDPs. Since implementation of programme depends largely on the quality of personnel, some institutional arrangement has to be made by States for posting of suitable officers in these areas who can work with devotion and understanding. Orientation training of personnel has to be given special attention.

The approach in the Draft Sixth Plan 1978-83 for development of backward areas in general, is to rely to a greater extent, on the development of agriculture, village and small-scale industries, subsidiary occupations and related services and also Minimum Needs Programmes and area development programmes. As the tribal regions fall in different agro-climatic regions, a clear strategy for agriculture development of each region has to be worked out. Adaptive research, large-scale field trials of proved techniques and identification of major thrust areas have been considered essential. Improvement of economic status of the tribals should be the first concern and suitable programmes of horticulture, cattle development, poultry and piggery etc., should be taken up. Shifting cultivators have to get due attention which they have failed to get so far. The forest policy in its various aspects affecting the tribals needs to be implemented. In respect of these economic programmes, the role of the marketing and credit organisations such as LAMPS has been re-emphasised. This would help to eliminate the middlemen and the money-lender and thereby give economic benefits direct to tribal population. The economy of tribal artisans is getting adversely affected on account of competitive market. Promotion of tribal crafts and family-based programmes for helping these groups including marketing facilities have to be formulated. Integrated development of tribal communities under the zones of influence of the industrial projects requires to be taken up. Some areas like hinterland of industrial and mining complexes, forest rich regions and areas with high landless population will need special attention and for them separate plans will have to be prepared. These regions should be identified and special provisions made for them in the Sub-Plans.

TWELVE

Hari Mohan Mathur

STRENGTHENING ADMINISTRATIVE CAPABILITY FOR DEVELOPMENT OF TRIBAL REGIONS

UNTIL RECENTLY the issues related to strengthening the administrative capability for development work in tribal areas did not somehow receive the attention they certainly deserve. Even to this day erroneous notions persist in some quarters that the expenditure on administrative development is unproductive and wasteful. The view that seems to have prevailed all these years is that by and large the existing administrative system is adequate and that with minor modifications, especially a further addition in the numbers of staff, it would be in a position to meet the challenges of development on the tribal frontiers.

The emphasis in planning for development of tribal peoples has therefore been on formulation of plans for their socio-economic progress and on mobilising resources necessary to implement the various schemes. Since the beginning of the Fifth Five Year Plan, 16 States and 2 Union Territories have been operating the meticulously framed tribal sub-plans and considerable financial resources have also been committed there in pursuance of the planning exercise.

However in the absence of simultaneous planned approach to administrative development all this planning effort, coupled with an investment programme of a rather high order, does not seem to have produced on the target groups an impact that the policy-makers originally envisaged. Dissatisfaction with the way development worked in the past has frequently been voiced on many occasions now. Some development undoubtedly has occurred even in the remotest tribal villages. But a close look at the outcome of the development effort will immediately bring to the fore the fact that it is the non-tribals living in the area who have tended to benefit most. Development programmes ostensibly meant for the tribals have failed to serve them fully.

Administrative Development Support

On the consequences of not gearing up the administrative machinery for the expanding developmental task entrusted to it, an expert group recently observed :

> Sub-Plan for tribal regions have been operative since the beginning of the Fifth Five Year Plan . . . . For the first time since Independence, massive physical and financial inputs have been made available in these areas. While these investments have been rising, a corresponding adequate matching administrative framework has not been brought into existence in many States, with the result that outlays meant for the sub-plan areas have not been utilised fully. Thus, the objective of benefits accruing to the tribals has been incompletely realized. It appears that the main difficulty has been in the field of programme in implementation.
>
> In some states, the concept of a full-fledged administrative machinery has been visualised but the concept has not become a full reality. In some other states, even the concept has been lacking.[1]

It is becoming increasingly obvious that socio-economic planning and administrative development planning will henceforth have to move forward hand in hand together. A high-powered working group which recently studied problems and programmes of tribal development made this specific recommendation. "The Government of India, in consultation with the State Governments, may take up a review of level of administration of the tribal areas and suitable schemes may be prepared for upgrading it within a reasonable time frame.[2] Indeed matters pertaining to aspects of administrative development can no longer be relegated to the sidelines without detriment to the development process itself. The kind of development strategies being presently pursued with the avowed objective of raising the living standards of the tribal segment in our society would entail administrative capability of a qualitatively different and higher order.

The Development Task

The problems of development in tribal areas are of a different kind than those encountered ordinarily. Often this is not adequately realised. It also must be borne in mind that the administrative techniques and skills which normally produce good results elsewhere frequently prove inadequate to the task here. These are the lessons learnt from a long administrative experience in tribal areas.

The task of development in tribal region is not easy, as it is not limited to raising their income levels, bringing them on par with the levels obtaining in other more advanced regions. This itself would be a stupendous job. Hence it is important to ensure that economic development does not take place at the cost of characteristically tribal values which these people have cherished from time immemorial.

Tribal peoples have long been living in far-flung hilly and forest habitations—somewhat cut off from the mainstream of Indian society. And it is not this physical isolation alone which planners of development have to consider. These people have their own distinctive culture, and they are legitimately proud of it. Their cultures add an important element to the totality of the Indian culture as it is known today.

It would be desirable neither to deny these people benefits of modern civilization simply because development tends to threaten the traditional tribal culture nor to go forward full steam with development in a way that the people lose those elements of culture which give them an identity all their own. Their age-old isolation certainly has to go if they have to move on the development path along with others, but the objective is not to achieve the kind of development which leaves them culturally impoverished. The twin goals of accelerating economic development as well as of seeing that these peoples do not lose their heritage in the process look impossible, but are not unattainable.

Personnel for Tribal Areas

If this is the development task to be accomplished, it is clear that it cannot be entrusted to the general run of administrators. Indeed, the tribal areas offer challenging opportunities to the administrators who would want to do some creative work, different from the routine kind. It surely is not a job for those who are content to follow the beaten path. To a large extent the success of the development effort here would depend on the kind of personnel deployed. Therefore it is of the utmost importance that administrators for tribal development task are selected with the greatest care. Only those with a sense of commitment are likely to be effective. Late Prime Minister Nehru's observations are especially worthy of note in this connection :

> We ought to be careful about appointing officers everywhere, but we must be doubly so when we appoint them in tribal areas. An officer in the tribal areas should not merely be a man who has passed an examination or gained experience of routine work. He must be a man with enthusiasm, whose mind, and even more so, whose heart understands the problem it is his duty to deal with. He must not go there just to sit in an office for a few hours a day and for the rest curse his fate at being sent to an out of the way place. That type of man is completely useless. It is far better to send a totally uneducated man who has passed no examination, so long as he goes to these people with friendship and affection and lives as one of them. Such a man will produce better results than the brilliant intellectual who has no human understanding of the problem. The man who goes there as an officer must be prepared to share his life with the tribal folk. He must be prepared to enter their huts, talk to them, eat and smoke with them, live their lives and not consider himself superior or apart. Then only can he gain confidence and respect, and thus be in a position to advise them.[3]

With years of administrative experience among the tribal peoples of the north-east, N.K. Rustomji lists traits which go to make up a successful administrator. These are similar to those Nehru had spelt out. A profile of the successful administrator in the words of Rustomji is as follows :

> Together with a sympathetic approach of the people, the workers amongst the tribals must be man of adventure and elastic intellect. The mind must be constantly on the alert to discover ways and means of overcoming the hundred and one problems of administration in such unusual areas and amongst such unusual people. The successful administrator will be ever experimenting. For it is through experiment that, in the last resort, the most practical solution can be found to the knottiest problems. And if only a small percentage of the experiments meet with success, it will be something gained. But the worker who plods along the beaten track, hesitant to undertake any venture lest it might not meet with immediate success, will be of little use for work in areas where the commonly accepted rules and practices are impractical of implementation and are a hindrance to the development and growth of the people.[4]

Unfortunately administrators with such description are not to be found in sufficient numbers. In fact it is proving to be a problem to get people to a fill in many critical positions in tribal areas. Doctors, engineers, teachers, nurses, compounders and others, badly needed for work in tribal areas, just hate to go there and often succeed in their effort to get postings in towns and cities. Roughly 600 out of 5000 posts in tribal areas of Rajasthan recently were reported to be lying vacant.[5] Very similar conditions should be prevailing in other states.

How have things come to such a pass ? Why do not officials respond to this challenge ? Is there no challenge in the job ? Are personnel policies to blame ? The answers to such questions are not likely to be simple or easy. But an effort must be made to understand the issues involved.

Certainly, the job is full of excitement and challenges. There should be enough people who will be simply fascinated by the kind of work that awaits them in tribal areas. But often it is the personnel policies and practices which fail to attract, retain and motivate the best people. Partly the urban bias in recruitment, training, placement, career pattern, etc., accounts for the lack of attraction for these assignments. It looks that the existing personnel policies will need to be modified to reflect a greater concern for the tribal development programmes.

If the postings in the tribal regions go to only those who cannot manage to get on to the more attractive assignments in the cities, and if those posted to work for the tribal people are not accorded adequate recognition, it will indeed become increasingly difficult to find for this challenging job the kind of people who are really needed.

Officers in the tribal areas sometimes get transferred rather quickly. They lack enough exposure to training programmes either. Once in tribal areas, many find it difficult to get postings in cities and towns even on justifiable considerations. It is such policies or lack of them which create the situation in which authorities find it hard to deploy the best trained, motivated personnel on development jobs located in the tribal regions.

Needed Changes in the Policy

The fact must be faced that there are good reasons for people to avoid postings in tribal areas and to seek placements in the urban areas instead. The tribal areas lack even the basic facilities for living. There are places where there are no schools, no dispensaries, no markets, no potable water facilities, no housing. Officers dislike such places not because they are not prepared to serve in difficult areas but because some members in the family—old parents, children and other dependents—do need the basic amenities to which they are accustomed. And when they find that some people can get away from such assignments, they do develop a certain dislike for such jobs.

On the other hand, advantages of posting in the cities and towns are very obvious. All the facilities exist there. Compensatory allowance is attached to postings in cities. They are close to their immediate superiors and peers. Career-wise this work carries greater weight.

There are always some highly dedicated people who do

well no matter what the personnel policies might be. But it would be futile to expect that everybody would do so remarkably even in the absence of a right kind of institutional support. It is very necessary to have a clearly stated policy regarding personnel for less developed areas.[6]

The recruitment pattern must change, to start with. For work in tribal areas the people selected should be those with rural or tribal background. A large number of jobs can easily be entrusted to such people. Then, it could be made clear to the newly recruited officials that they are being recruited specifically for service in the tribal areas. Or, at least, all people should be required to serve in the tribal areas in the beginning of their career. The experience they will gain will stand them in good stead later when they assume responsibilities at the policy making level.

Training which can be an effective tool in developing the human resources for development can play a useful role here. It does not seem to have been utilized imaginatively. A fresh look at the existing training set-up is necessary. There is considerable scope for improvements in this sector. Training should be confined not at only lower levels, but must cater to the identified needs of personnel at all the levels. It would be better to identify training needs of various categories of personnel, and then design training programmes so that they genuinely fulfil the knowledge, skills and attitudes gaps.

The two things which training must hope to do is : (a) to familiarize the officers with the aspects of tribal culture that impinge on their development work, and (b) to instill amongst them right attitudinal and behavioural patterns for service, as outside people are still not perceived as agents of change, but as agents of the groups who have traditionally exploited them.

An important thing to do is to restore to the field postings their old status and prestige. Somehow the secretariat jobs have become more prestigious than the jobs on the ground. People who work in the tribal areas should be given recognition, and their careers should not suffer simply because they are not placed in the secretariat.

Even monetary incentives should be given to those who volunteer to work in difficult regions. The compensation must not be notional, but real enough to offset the disadvantages of a posting in the tribal areas.

About transfers there should be a clear policy. Once posted, the officer must ordinarily be allowed to complete his full tenure of 2 or 3 years. Unless that is done, he will not pick up the details of the areas and the people, and consequently will not be able to do justice to his work. He should not be transferred simply because his action taken in right earnest has upset the position of elite groups. Even when promotion becomes due, the man must be given promotion on the job he is doing. Disruption for whatever reason is not good.

Suggestions have been made in the past for the creation of a separate cadre of workers for tribal development work. There are both advantages as well as disadvantages in this proposal. The main advantage is that a corpus of trained personnel becomes available to tackle the complex problems related to development of the tribal populations. The disadvantage is that the personnel desiring to work outside the tribal areas later may not find it easy to move to those jobs. In fact, no rigid stand can be taken on this subject, and all the pros and cons need to be given consideration before a decision is made.

Organizational and Procedural Changes

Currently great stress is being laid on developmental tasks. The regulatory functions of the government have receded into the background as a result. But this should not be allowed to happen. The role of regulatory departments is very important and if their functionaries do not change their methods of work along with the development workers the tribal people will continue to look at the government personnel with a degree of suspicion.

In the past the tendency has been to introduce organizational structures and procedures of work that have developed in more advanced regions. This not only adds to the cost of development, but proves unhelpful to the people. One quality of the administration in tribal areas should be its simplicity so that the simple folk understand it and do not hesitate to avail of the services it offers them.

When a number of departments, each providing its own particular input and each working more or less independently of the other, come into existence, the tribal people are forced to run from pillar to post to get what they need. The Planning Commission in this connection had observed :

> Multiplicity of agencies has resulted in diffusion of responsibility, inadequate control, lack of coordination and, from the people's angle, difficulty in identifying the officials concerned with specific programmes. The pattern of administrative organization will have to be worked out in detail for achieving functional coordination and efficiency. Delegation of authority, specificity of responsibility and adequate flexibility should be bulit into the system so as to enable the implementing authority to effect changes in the on going programmes on the basis of concurrent evaluation.[7]

It is important to ensure that various agencies created to serve the development needs of the tribal people work in a coordinated manner. At the higher levels coordination is more effective than at the lower levels. But the need for effective coordination is greatest at the grassroots level.

Both administrative and financial powers should be delegated to the lower levels to the extent possible. This will obviate the need for lower level functionaries to look up to the higher levels for sanction of every single paisa. This will then speed up the development process. The higher level officials must not only delegate their powers, but see to it that these powers are in fact exercised, and exercised in a proper manner. Senior level officials need to develop more trust in their field level staff, and to learn to make better use of their capabilities.

Between various levels of administration the communication is formal and infrequent. Usually it is of the top-down kind. The two-way channels of communication should be strengthened.

Involving the People

The Panchayati Raj institutions were introduced to evoke

popular enthusiasm for local development. They did generate considerable local interest in development. But they cannot be said to have succeeded in fully involving the people in the efforts to promote their development.

It must be realized that development in tribal areas will occur rapidly only when officials and local people work together in close cooperation with one another, to achieve the development goals. If the people do not cooperate with the government agencies, the pace of development is bound to slow down. Development, which should lay stress on development of human resources, can achieve this objective only by involving the tribal people in the development effort.

There are no simple solutions to this problem of drawing the tribal people in the planning and implementation of development. But it is fairly clear that the personnel which is willing to treat the target groups of people as partners in progress will achieve better results than the disgruntled officials who will not only mar the image of the government, but might retard the whole process of development.

REFERENCES

1. *Report of Group on Administrative Arrangements and Personnel Policies in Tribal Areas.* New Delhi : Ministry of Home Affairs, Government of India, 1979, p. 1.
2. *Report of the Working Group on Tribal Development during Medium Term Plan, 1978-83.* New Delhi Ministry of Home Affairs, Government of India, 1978, p. 40.
3. Jawaharlal Nehru, "The Tribal Folk", *The Adivasis,* Delhi : The Publications Division, Government of India, 1955, p. 6.
4. N.K. Rustomji, "Tribal Administration in the North-East Frontier Agency", *The Adivasis.* Delhi : The Publications Division, Government of India, 1955, pp. 145-146.
5. *Report of Group on Administrative Arrangements and Personnel Policies in Tribal Areas,* New Delhi: Ministry of Home Affairs, Government of India, 1979, p. 11.
6. Some measures to attract officials for work in difficult regions are discussed in Michael Lipton, 1977, *Why Poor People Stay Poor : Urban Bias in World Development,* London : Temple Smith, pp. 340-341.
7. *Sixth Five Year Plan,* New Delhi : Planning Commission, Government of India.

PART III

TRAINING PROGRAMMES

THIRTEEN

K. K. Srivastava

ORGANISATION OF TRAINING PROGRAMMES IN TRIBAL DEVELOPMENT ADMINISTRATION

Need Based

TRAINING is a pre-requisite for the performance of any job efficiently, whether administrative or technical. Administrators in the States and at the Centre have to undergo a period of academic as well as field training to equip themselves to discharge their duties properly. The technical personnel dealing with banking, forest, revenue and customs, labour welfare, engineering etc., are all given training for their particular job requirements. The need for this training for various categories has been well recognised. However, the need for specialised training for tribal development administration was not thought about till the end of the Second Plan. But even then, it did not receive adequate attention. Without a thorough knowledge of the life and needs of the tribals and the areas inhabited by them, no plans and programmes are likely to succeed, in spite of heavy financial investment. Tribal areas are characterised by (1) difficult terrain, often isolated for months, and (2) backwardness due to long neglect by colonial administration. The tribal people have one thing in common, and that is that they are, by and large, economically, and socially backward. But ethnically, linguistically, and culturally they are not only different from the general population but there is a lot of diversity even amongst themselves. Therefore, the personnel dealing with them need special training to understand and appreciate their problems before they embark on formulation and implementation of plans for their development.

By the end of Second Plan period, it became evident that the personnel working in tribal areas require a good understanding of the tribal life and culture, and their needs and problems. They also require adequate training in evolving an appropriate approach and suitable measures for tackling these problems. It was noted by the Elwin Committee that, personnel working in Special Multipurpose Tribal (SMPT) Blocks who came from a different cultural and socio-economic background were unable to appreciate tribal ways of life and could not understand the specific problem that tribals faced in different areas. Although training in community development work in C.D. Blocks recognised the importance of relating schemes to the local needs, but in practice stereotyped schemes tended to be implemented on the basis of schematic budget. Some of the field workers themselves felt the need for adapting the schemes to suit the requirements of the tribals, but these workers did not possess necessary knowledge of tribal background to do so.

Training programmes for personnel working in tribal areas especially in SMPT and later Tribal Development (TD) Blocks, were started in a modest way during Third Five Year Plan. The Tribal Research Institutes established were required to initiate training programmes for all types of personnel working in tribal area. With the acceptance of the concept of integrated development of tribals and tribal areas and formulation of sub-plans, training of personnel at all levels of administration dealing with tribal development becomes more imperative. Tribal development now covers nearly every sector of development. Each sector of the economy is responsible for the programme under the sub-plans. Awareness of tribal problems and their specific needs has, therefore, assumed greater importance both at policy formulation level and implementation level. It is necessary that orientation of all those connected with tribal development and its different sectors should be undertaken urgently. The Working Group on Tribal Development constituted by the Planning Commission in connection with the preparation of the Sixth Plan, has emphasised the urgent need for such orientation training and added that the need for such reorientation would become more so with heavier financial investments and growing administrative structure in tribal areas.

Organisation of training programme for personnel dealing with tribal development will require to take the following factors into consideration :

(a) Type of personnel,
(b) Type of training to be imparted to different levels, i.e. syllabus ;
(c) Duration of training courses ; and
(d) Methods and techniques of training.

Evidently the training and orientation will have to vary in content, structure and length for different echelons of the administration and the different types of personnel ; for the top level, the middle level and the field level.

The top level officers at the Central and State headquarters are concerned mainly with policy formulation, monitoring and evaluation. These are officers of the All-India and State Civil Services as also specialised services at the All-India and State levels. The need for providing orientation training in tribal way of life and culture to such officers is obvious since they are at the decision making level, whether it is on policy frame, budgetary arrangement or changing the pattern or programmes. The orientation for such group of officers would have to be of a different type and duration, mostly on the lines of seminars or discussions combined with field visits.

The middle level group, comprising officers at the district and project level, is the backbone for the success of any tribal development programme. At the district level, technical officers and other officers dealing with agriculture, animal husbandry, forestry, village and small industries, public health, education, revenue and excise etc. need special orientation course besides training in their own disciplines. A clear understanding of tribal way of life and tribal pattern of economic activity is essential to enable them to formulate, adapt or modify the schemes under their respective sectors to make them acceptable to the tribals and effective in upgrading the level of their socio-economic life. At the project level, training of project officers, B.D.Os, Registrars of Co-operatives etc. require intensive training in not only tribal life and culture but in project formulation, and general management of the projects/blocks. These officers play the crucial role in the success of sub-plan programmes. They not only have to be trained in general tribal life and culture but have to know the different tribal groups thoroughly in a project/block area, their specific problems and needs, and the resource potential of these areas in terms of physical and manpower resources. A lot will depend on the knowledge of the people and the area to draw up a proper project plan and get them implemented.

Lastly, but equally important, come the field level functionaries of various departments, whose number is very large. The VLWs, the forest guards, the ancillary medical health workers, the primary school teachers and all others connected with the actual implementation of the various programmes at the grass-root level have to deal with tribals directly in their daily life. The need for their training is evidently an absolute necessity. They need to understand the tribal people thoroughly, their customs and their economic practices, the urges and their aspirations and also the dialects they speak. Only then will such personnel understand the problems that the tribals encounter and be able to help them and motivate them to accept the Plan programmes. This will also enable them to project the various issues correctly before the higher level functionaries.

To sum up, the need for basic training and orientation training for personnel at various levels is very urgent and cannot be over-emphasised. In this connection it may be mentioned that the Working Group for Tribal Development constituted for the purposes of preparation of the Sixth Plan has made an important recommendation that training in tribal development be made part of the general training programme at entry-point to various All-India, Central and State services dealing with tribal development or likely to come in touch with the tribal people, although the content and intensity of training may differ for different categories of personnel. The Working Group has further recommended that since forests and tribals are considerably co-extensive, tribal development should be an important part of the curriculum of forest officers training. In this connection, it may be noted that Bihar has already prescribed training for State Civil Service officers at entry point into service, while in-service orientation courses are held for other services.

The content of training courses in each category of personnel would have to be different but would generally include tribal ethnology, constitutional safeguards, government policy, approach and strategy in respect of tribal development, programmes under implementation under different sectors, financial investments and budgeting. The syllabi should be so devised that the trainees get a clear picture of the problems faced by the tribal population and the various aspects of their socio-economic conditions. The training content should also give a clear picture of the problems that the implementers have to face at the various levels, particularly at the project and field level, and also the approach to solution of these problems. The training programme should be broad-based and oriented to the duties of different officers and functionaries in the tribal areas. When the content of training is devised for any category of personnel, the organisers of the training would have to keep in mind the diversity of tribal people even within a State and the diverse problems that each tribal group faces. Stereotype courses with theoretical anthropology, sociology, economics, statistics or stereotype courses dealing with development programmes for the general people will not cover the regional or local problems the personnel will have to encounter in implementing any tribal development programme. The courses would have to be supplemented with practical bias oriented towards the target group, viz. socio-economic development of the tribal areas and the various tribal groups living in the various areas.

As has been mentioned earlier, apart from the in-service training to the members of the various services, those at the top level would need orientation training from time to time which may be in the form of short duration seminars or discussions extending for 7-10 days interspersed or followed by field visits. This short duration is considered adequate as officers at this level would already be trained in their respective disciplines. The middle personnel group at regional, district and project levels, including supervisory officers under technical departments, who implement programmes in tribal areas, would require more intensive training of about 2-4 weeks' duration. For the field level workers like VLWs, forest guards etc., the orientation programmes may be of two types. The first may be a universal programme to cover the entire personnel within a short time. Secondly, there may be an in-depth orientation training of selected persons covering a wider area, in their respective field of activity. A minimum of 4-6 weeks training for this type of intensive orientation would be needed as recommended by the Elwin Committee.

Before concluding, it is necessary to mention about the need for the training of tribal leaders as well and creating a sense of awareness amongst the tribal people in general. The Working Group on Tribal Development, referred to earlier has also emphasised this aspect and recommended that the seminars and other training programmes suggested for the Government personnel should also be extended to the tribal leaders at appropriate levels. It is also necessary to train the members of the Cooperative Societies in respect of the functioning of the Cooperative Societies, the credit and marketing aspects and such other allied matters that deal with the activities of the cooperatives.

FOURTEEN

G.S. Grewal

ORGANISATION OF TRAINING PROGRAMMES FOR TRIBAL DEVELOPMENT ADMINISTRATION

PUBLIC ADMINISTRATION in India in the pre-independence era was focussed on maintenance of law and order and collection of revenue. The emphasis shifted towards developmental activities in the mid-50s and the need for proper infra-structure including trained personnel for such activities was intensely felt. There still remained a wide gap between the accepted concepts of development administration and placing personnel for development activities. While the developed urban and suburban areas received most of the attention from the implementation agencies, the predominantly tribal regions received a rather raw deal. The outlay proposed for such areas was generally diverted towards the non-tribal regions. This created a sense of separatism between the tribal leaders and mainstream of the country. While the talk of "detribalisation" and bringing the tribals into the mainstream of the nation continued, the action plans began to be prepared only a few years ago. Separate autonomous authorities and special agencies were created for intensive development of tribal areas in the States and the North Eastern Region which received the pointed attention of the Planning Commission and the Ministry of Home Affairs.

Every training programme in development administration entails the matching of particular needs of personnel equipped with various competences, with the goals of national or sectoral development. Development administration is a continuous cycle of formulating, evaluating and implementing inter-related measures to reach established objective in a scheduled time-sequence. It, therefore, basically differs from the traditional functions of administration such as the maintenance of law and order and revenue collection. It is essentially concerned with planning and administering a social and economic change. The civil servants involved in the formulation of training programmes are quite logically termed as "change-agents". Attitudes towards training often reveal an inadequate understanding of this change process, its relation to the public administration working environment, and the nature of the trained "product". Some attitudes are clearly dangerous and misleading ; for example, the view that newly appointed civil servants who have completed a short formal course of training at some Academy or Institute are able to deal with live administration situations. On the other hand, it is commonly believed that competent administrators will contribute effectively to a training programme especially if they have some teaching experience. The worst attitude one comes across is that pre-entry University education is adequate for the civil servants and no formal training is necessary to make them efficient development officers. Some of the frustrations and underlying cynicism towards training in development administration is primarily based upon an inadequate and distorted concept of the training process itself.

Training in development administration not only aims at inducing charge in the person's attitude and behaviour towards life but also induces him to work with the purpose of creating a dynamic and progressive society through the application of modern technology and humane social relations. In short, such training programmes tend to envelope the entire spectrum of society and many different decisions and activities calling on many kinds of people are involved.

The development concepts in the areas where tribal way of life is predominant do not basically differ from those postulated in the development of underdeveloped non-tribal areas. When we perceive of a change in social organisation, the ethnic, linguistic and social factors play an important role in deciding upon the techniques and methodology to be adopted by development administrators in achieving the desired behaviour and performance objectives.

Before one thinks of organising a training programme the training needs for the system have to be fully established. There are some things that could be said about organisations. First, they exist ; second, they have a purpose ; third, they are interested in surviving. To survive, the organisation has to meet change. Every training programme looks at tomorrow (which would be different from today) and, accordingly, designed for the future. The question is often asked why don't the development plans get going, when the plan documents show that all the requirements for achieving the desired objectives have been fully met. The initial step of Plan formulation i.e. overview of the entire system gets diffused due to certain difficulties, handicaps and realities faced by development administration in every governmental set-up. These difficulties are primarily political and administrative, not economic ; they arise from numerous factors, inter alia, dispersed, diffused and duplicating functions, offices and responsibilities ; inadequate managerial facilities ; inadequate planning of administration ; political interference, and lack of skilful administration.

Most government officials charged with planning and administering development and most expert personnel do not have adequate experience or training to design and establish effective organisation, institutions, processes and operating systems.

Further, Government officials are generally dispersed amongst an excessive number of ministries, departments, authorities and agencies. More and more Agencies and Corporations to fulfil development objectives are superimposed upon traditionally oriented government departments without a prior review of the entire structure. The result is a multiplicity of organs and duplication of functions and diffusion of responsibility. Similarly, the offices needed for development administration functions are often inadequate or lacking in expertise in planning, programming, budgeting, personnel administration, and organisational methods. In the tribal regions, the preponderance of non-tribal development administrators creates a communication gap and the resultant poor response from tribal population defeats the purpose of every development activity. The tribals of one area vary in culture, work habits, social customs and level of development from another so widely that it is difficult to propose a common approach to their problems.

Another difficulty stemming from poor organisation and programming is a lack of coordination between the agencies responsible for planning and financing programmes and projects, and those responsible for executing them. It is a matter of common knowledge that funds, materials, personnel and other necessary resources may not be authorised or available when needed and where needed to carry out a project or activity. Similarly synchronisation amongst the departments in planning and implementing field projects is also lacking. For instance agricultural programmes may be initiated without planning highways for transporting and marketing facilities. Due to lack of training in project formulation, development programmes are often inoperable because the officials who prepare them seem to view them as self-executing and do not back them with operationally designed programmes and projects. The projects are described in vague terms and inadequately tested for economic viability or administrative feasibility; data of natural resources and manpower needs and availability are fragmentary; required manpower, equipment, and materials are not scheduled; or financing is not fully arranged. While every obstacle may be serious, the lack of trained manpower is of most immediate concern. In the tribal regions this deficiency is still more acutely felt. The educational system is not linked to the manpower requirements for development administration.

A large number of trainees coming to a development training programme do not have a clear idea as to why they have been sent for training or what their expectations or aspirations from the training programme are. What some of them are clear about is that they should be helped to perform as effectively as possible their present jobs. They relate the training programme not to the new skills or techniques they could learn about, but to optimising what they actually know. The problem for them is of using the present store-house of knowledge and experience with maximum advantage. Some of them are keen to understand the new control tools now becoming available. There are some who want an understanding of their role in the organisation while a few of them want understanding of the impacts of change and innovation. While designing the programme for development administration, it is important to understand that the training needs are essentially related to change. Therefore, the roles of the four identities connected with this concept of change and dynamics namely the individual administrator, his work team, the Govt. organisation and the trainer and their inter-relationship have a direct bearing on the training programme.

Having analysed the overall system, the present context requires that the training programme limits the field to tribal areas and their manpower requirements. The jobs and tasks as a part of the overall plan have to be defined and analysed. One has to live with the fact that analysing individual jobs is a long process, and performance appraisal systems have serious flaws. The detailed job description acts as a starting point for the Trainer to construct the objectives for the Programme, and to identify the knowledge areas, skills and attitudes, which can and should be reflected in the components of the Programme. This also points to the target population—"Who is to be trained"? For purposes of the present discussion, it appears that almost every one concerned with tribal development needs to be exposed to the concepts and techniques attendant upon the anticipated change

(i) Government leaders, political and administrative, who must know something about the strategy and process required to foster rapid change.

(ii) Personnel concerned with the formulation and implementation of development policies, plans and programme.

(iii) Administrators and supervisory officers in departments, States and districts/local bodies concerned with development in specific sectors.

(iv) Personnel in Ministries, public sector corporations, and regional or local authorities concerned with development in specific sectors.

(v) Professional and technical personnel (engineers, doctors, public health personnel, agronomists etc.) who have supervisory roles, but who need some training in management, institution building, programme development and operation, and administrative problem solving.

(vi) Community development and rural action programme personnel,

(vii) Statisticians, accountants, health technicians, agriculture extension workers, and many other categories of specialist staff whose improved skills are needed in development activities.

(viii) Instructors to train these various categories of personnel.

This process leads the programme formulator to state in specific terms the felt or perceived needs and anticipated needs; and relating them to the objectives of the programme in behavioural form. In other words, he has to put down in detail what type of trained personnel the society needs and would need in various sectors and in what manner would the ability of the trainee to perform would improve. The training programme should seek to—

(i) Produce an awareness that administration involves both technical and behavioural aspects of work and is the process by which the best answers to complex situational problems are produced,

(ii) Explain the relationship between administrator and government,

(iii) Help the administrator improve his understanding of himself and his role in development activity,

(iv) Establish concepts of administrative behaviour and function,

(v) Introduce and develop administrative techniques, both technical and behavioural.

The next phase is the construction of the course based on the inputs received from the above mentioned studies. It includes definition of syllabus, analysis and synthesis of the course contents, Determination of Teaching Strategy decision on means of presentation, and writing of Lesson sequences. These decisions would vary for each learning situation. The training in the first instance could be "Off job" or "On job". Both have their relative merits, but the initial training of a development administrator could best be carried out mainly

"Off job" i.e. in an Academy or Institute. It provides them the opportunity to :

(a) share the "language", and have an understanding of similar experiences; they can form a rich core around which the culture of the organisation can be built.

(b) develop an information sharing and problem solving attitudes, and

(c) remove the feeling of isolative, each one would consider himself to be a member of a large fraternity work for the same set of objectives.

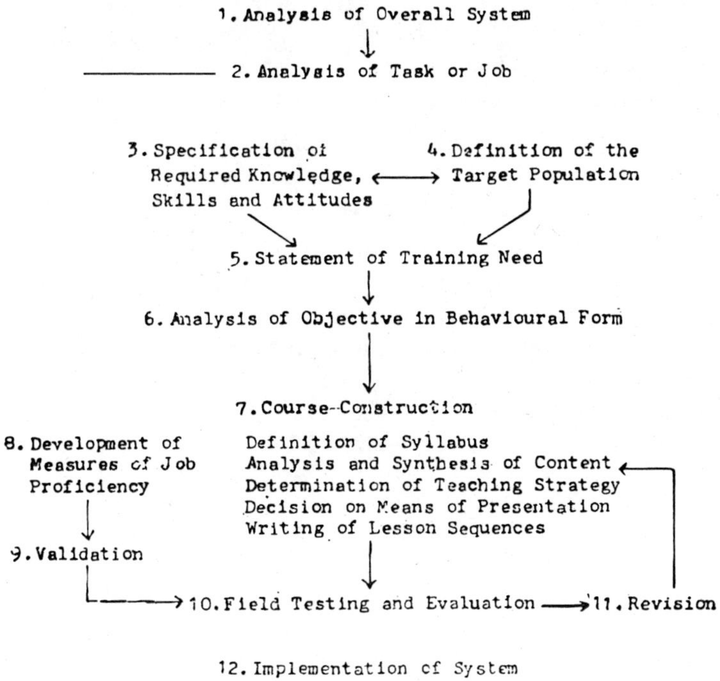

A follow-up by job-related training, i.e. "on job", would prepare the trainee to handle live situations by learning from the successes and failures of his superior. The real life problems and experience that the trainee goes through in this manner cannot be created for learning.

Hearing methods include lectures with or without aids, case studies, role playing, syndicates, structured exercises or management games, in-basket.

The role of the organisation and the work team is significant in optimising the terminal performance of the trainee. This terminal behaviour is expected to be improved, and if the organisation and the work team have not moved dynamically towards better performance while the trainee was undergoing the training process he is bound to find himself in alien environment, where his language and performance are not easily accepted. The organisational development should therefore be a simultaneous activity to achieve the optimum performance results. At the conclusion of each programme, evaluation and field testing has to be carried to relate the course with the objectives. Evaluation is carried out on the basis of information sought from the Course participants :

(i) Pre-Programme Questionnaires
(ii) Post-Session or Immediate Questionnaires
(iii) Post-Programme Questionnaires

The validation of such conclusions is further carried out by the trainer organisation by means of field studies. If any gap is perceived between the objectives and results of the Programmes, and it can be traced to deficiencies in the course contents or methodology then suitable steps should be taken to revise them. The system thus evolved can be implemented and the desired objectives would be hopefully achieved.

FIFTEEN

S.M. Shah

EVALUATION TECHNIQUES

EVALUATION TODAY has achieved a central place in the process of economic and social development in several countries. Plan formulation, plan implementation and plan evaluation are three integral parts of an organic whole process of economic development.

Evaluation works through its own "data gathering" and seeks this "information transfer" to the policy makers as a feedback mechanism. The greatest asset of evaluation is its credibility. Hence, an evaluation organisation should collect data first-hand through its own trained personnel who have reputation for objectivity and candour. Reports based on such information system are very valuable to the policy makers as also to the agencies engaged in financing either national programmes or overseas development efforts.

Evaluation helps improve the basic understanding of the programmes and seeks to answer why certain elements of the programme achieve significant successes whereas others result in failures. For example, in a programme to assist what John P. Lewis calls the unemployed "Low and poor", several governments in India launched in the year 1977 a programme of *Antyodaya* (poorest of the poor) upliftment. This programme has met with tremendous success in certain States whereas it has not picked up in the others. Furthermore, whereas the identification of the poorest of the poor through organised village assemblies did achieve a target of 90 per cent, the actual programme benefits viz. the delivery of services could reach only a target of 30 per cent of these identified families. Achievements significantly differ from state to state. This was largely on account of structural weaknesses, absence of a shelf of projects ready to go on steam or inadequate staff to handle the increased workload. In yet another programme called Integrated Child Development Services Scheme, the programme attracted children in the age group of 3 to 6 years but not the most vulnerable group below 3 years age, for, under the programme, their attendance in *anganwadi*, a nursery school, was compulsory. Take home food was not permitted. The evaluation study brought out these parameters and advised the Government of India to redesign the programme accordingly for the next years. Revised guidelines are issued by Government in respect of several programmes, based on a feedback from evaluation studies.

Evaluation thus provides an important information system to watch and improve the effectiveness of the programme in order to meet the desired objectives as enunciated. Evaluation may even question the very design of the programme and its parameters on the basis of the first-hand information collected by the evaluation personnel in the field through its own network. It may even question the Plan priorities and thus improve the effectiveness of investment, particularly for the poorer countries. But the utility of evaluation even for developed countries is considerable since evaluation indicates the directions of effective programmes for such countries. These may include international assistance also.

Evaluation provides important "data" to the policy-makers in making appropriate choices about the programmes. For example, if an irrigation system in which a country has invested as much as Rs. 400 million is not effective in the sense that it has failed to generate impact resulting in the benefits of increased yield, incomes and employment to materialise as compared to those in the "control" areas, would it not be worthwhile for the Government to use this money instead in constructing drinking water wells in all the villages throughout the country to meet the more basic needs of the population, namely, the clean drinking water supply. Or, would it not be useful to open health care centres dotted in every human settlement throughout the country for health improvement ?

Evaluation is, therefore, an important management tool in the hands of the planners to provide them with a systematic assessment of the past performance and to improve planning and implementation of both current and the new activities.

In an ideal State, "Programme Evaluation and Information System" should be built into every project or investment. Though there are internal evaluations for agencies working on private profits, such evaluation is not widespread in the public system where large amounts of money are involved. It is the duty of the Information System to provide a back up to the programme evaluation through a well organised information network.

In order that evaluation is objective, it is desirable that evaluation is best carried out by an outside agency which has creditability of collecting unbiased information, scientific interpretation and forthrightness in giving the results as are seen. Both evaluation and informatics believe that the surest way of success of any programme is to let others know how the programme is in actual operation and whether it has been able to achieve its objectives.

There are several techniques of evaluation of which the internal and external evaluation as mentioned above are the two main. Evaluation is not administrative reporting but goes beyond it. It just does not collect information but reads and interprets the information in the light of the programme objectives, the contents and the delivery of the scroices (programmes) to the target groups. It may even rank performance, based on certain scientific measurements as excellent, very good, good and poor. This information generation can be a good guide to the policy-makers in shooting the trouble spots.

Two well-known methods in evaluation are ex-ante and ex-post. A third method that has emerged in India in recent years is the method of "quick" evaluation going concurrently with the run of the programme to take mid course correction much before the completion of the projects.

Survey research is an important element in the techniques of evaluation. In order to do this, the various levels of information gathering are the (a) State (b) district, (c) development block, (d) village, and (e) the individual beneficiaries. Data collected at the State and the district level explain largely the organisation of the programme and its administration. The levels at the development "block" and the village explain at the micro-level the detailed mechanism of planning and the execution of the programme, e.g., the manner of identification of the beneficiaries such as through village assemblies, muster rolls and such other. Nevertheless, information collected from State to village level is largely qualitative in the sense that this information is sought from those who administer the programme. It is not 'weighed'. At the beneficiary level, data are collected by the trained investigators first-hand from the field by canvassing a specially designed schedule. The beneficiary schedule then is the most important instrument which reflects the success or failure of the programme. It is the mine of information on which judgments are based.

Another technique which is followed in evaluation is the case study method. Particularly when an evaluation organisation is called upon to assess the performance of pilot or exploratory projects, there is no past knowledge. Hence certain case studies are taken on hand not only to understand the problem but even to evolve a methodology of attack in respect of information gathering. Recently, in India, at the instance of the National Flood Commission, the Programme Evaluation Organisation of the Planning Commission, Government of India undertook two case studies of the Flood Embankment projects in the States of Bihar and Assam. The method of stratification for the selection of villages followed was that of watershed. Villages were selected from (a) the region where embankment was constructed, then (b) at the tail end of the embankment, then (c) within the 5 kms of the embankment which is prone to waterlogging, and (d) beyond 10 kms etc. In doing this, the main problem was protection against flood damage. This has now given a methodology for studying the flood embankment projects, a knowledge of which did not exist earlier. Case studies, however, require that the staff is well-trained and is equipped with analytical faculties of mind.

Besides the survey research and case studies, the participation observation method is also followed to get from the beneficiaries their own reactions about the programme. In a recent study (1979) connected with the evaluation of "Food for Work" Programme introduced in India in 1977, the beneficiaries were asked what was their staple food. The success of the programme depends very much on whether those employed on public works are given the food they normally consume; otherwise, either they will not be attracted towards the programme or they might sell away such food in the market for cash to buy food they are accustomed to which would result in mal-practices. Benefits to the workers might thus be "leaked" away.

There are several other techniques of evaluation. But the greatest need today for objective evaluation is the trained evaluation personnel in evaluation methodology, evaluation techniques and report writing. Evaluation studies are not the studies of field investigations; they go much beyond. Evaluation uses judgment and the field investigation is only a part to arrive such a judgment. The benefits of undertaking evaluation studies and training the staff engaged in evaluation work have to be kept under constant review.

It would be better for the governments to train a large number of evaluation personnel who could look at the effectiveness of the programmes at their own sites and geographical levels, for, it would be beyond the reach of any single agency to generate data on such a large scale. The information system must be built in the evaluation of the programmes itself. One way to spread the evaluation culture is to discuss continuously the evaluation methodology, the evaluation results and the evaluation techniques in workshops and seminars not only on past projects but with reference to projects on hand. The information gathered through such evaluation could be gigantic if geo-coding is followed. Such information system can answer considerably large number of questions which would assist any country in its effort in the field of social and economic development. The "rate of return" on evaluation is without doubt absolutely great, for, evaluation shows the policy-makers whether to stop sinking money on the bad adventures and indicate the fruitful way of future programmes to benefit its populations.

There are systems known as self-evaluation, cooperative (loaner and borrower) evaluation, joint (with centre : State) evaluation and multilateral (Centre : more than one State) evaluation. Each one has its role to play. A good information system should be able to reach each one of these different types of evaluation and further improve evaluation techniques themselves.

SIXTEEN

S. Patankar

PROJECT FORMULATION AND APPRAISAL OF TRIBAL DEVELOPMENT PROGRAMMES

THE PROJECTS in tribal development field differ from other Projects in certain respects. Owing to the specific characteristics of the tribal population, when the Projects are conceived to render benefit to the tribals, the needs and the environment have to be taken into consideration. Even when the projects are planned to benefit the national economy in general but they are physically located in the tribal areas, the project and the local tribals react with each other giving rise to many consequences unforeseen earlier. We shall revert to this subject in greater details at a later stage.

If we closely observe the functions and activities of any organization whether it being a part of Government or otherwise, we find that these activities can be divided into two broad categories. One group of activities serves to keep the operations of the organisation on a steady level. They maintain the organization. The organization survives at its normal level. The other group of activities is responsible for growth and development of the organization. We are concerned here with the latter type of activities.

The direction of growth and development is determined by the overall objectives of the organization. Sometimes these objectives may in course of time undergo a charge but generally these objectives are of a basic nature and have some permanency for the organization. Any change accompanying the organization will actually be viewed as growth or development if it is in tune with the organizational objectives. For the national economy, the objectives are enshrined in the national plans, short, medium and perspective. To attain these objectives, programmes are thought of. A particular programme of activities may be on the basis of the specific functions, technical knowledge required or on a particular resource being utilized. We talk therefore about sectoral programmes, like agricultural sector, power sector or transport sector. The programme on the other hand may be clientele oriented. It may be designed to cater to the needs of a particular section of the people. Such types of programmes are the Rural Development Programme, and Antyodaya Programme. Tribal Development Programme also falls in this category. The sub-objectives of a programme will be in line with the overall Plan objectives.

The programme needs to be divided into precise, concrete and identifiable plans of action. Such a unit of activity is called a Project. A Project has a definite starting point and a definite ending point. It serves a particular clientele group and covers a specific geographical area. In other words, a project has definite contour in space and time dimensions. Projects are the building blocks of a development programme. The Project will, no doubt, have its own objectives which will subscribe to the concerned programme objectives. In the sense that the plan objectives and programme objectives are attained through projects, the Projects are the effective tools of the national endeavour of development. They can be considered to be the cutting edge of the development effort. Herein lies the importance of the correct identification, formulation and appraisal of the Projects. The entire planning and development machinery has interface with the people through the Projects. In tribal development programme, this aspect attains added importance as the response of the tribal people cannot be presumed to follow a pattern which may be prevalent in case of other sections of the people.

Projects consume resources which are scarce in our economy. They involve investment of these resources to create an asset producing benefits which are desirable and which flow over a period of time after completion of the Project. The fact that project objectives subscribe to the programme objectives is not an adequate ground for taking up a project.

The most general justification for taking up a Project hinges on whether the events occurring with the Project are better than those occurring without the project by an extent exceeding the cost over the Project. This element of cost covers all such factors which involve a sacrifice on the part of the society. It may be financial or non-financial. This is also applicable when we decide whether certain events are better. The merit of the changed events will be assessed on the basis of the benefits that flow from these events. These are deemed to be benefits from point of view of desirability of the entire integrated society. It is obvious that these benefits may be capable of being quantified or not. They may be tangible or intangible. The benefits may appear to be benefits from the point of planners and the Government but not so from the point of the people for whose benefit the Project is taken up.

There is another point of considerable significance when we speak about tribal development. All types of development projects even though located in tribal areas do not have a direct bearing on tribal development. Projects in some sectorial programmes such as Power, Transport, Steel etc., do not impinge directly on tribal development. They have a place in total framework of development in the sense that without these projects, the society cannot set itself on the path of modernization and self-reliance. The tribal community is interested in these projects only remotely to the extent that it feels it is a part of the entire society, and without these projects, the development of the tribal community will be limited by the general stage of development of the entire society. The Projects in other sectors such as Agriculture, Education, Rural Industries and Health have a direct bearing and impact on the tribal community. It is obvious that these later type of Projects are close to the minds of people interested in tribal development.

A project goes through various stages during its life. It starts with the stage when it is conceived and goes to ultimate stage when after execution it is assessed. The assessment may lead to certain inferences pointing towards conception of new projects. Each stage grows naturally out of the previous stage and gives birth to the following stage. So the Project moves in a cycle which is termed as Project Cycle. Such a Project Cycle is shown in the following diagram. These stages in the cycle are

(1) Identification or Conception
(2) Formulation or Preparation
(3) Analysis or Appraisal
(4) Selection or Sanction
(5) Implementation or Execution
(6) Evaluation.

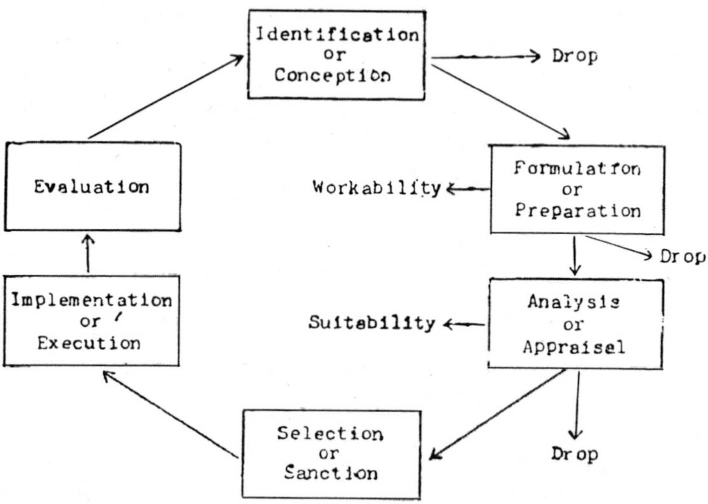

It is not essential that a Project which is conceived will pass through all these stages. It may meet with a premature death. Before it goes to the stage of Formulation, it may be considered on the basis of a number of criteria, that it is not worth pursuing and it may be dropped. Similar thing may happen after the stage of formulation or after the stage of appraisal. During the stage of formulation attention is riveted on the consideration of workability or feasibility of the Project. Overall factor under examination is whether the benefits outweigh the costs. During the stage of appraisal, thought is given to the suitability of the project. From the shelf of feasible Projects, a proper selection with a view to put the scarce resources to maximum benefit is done. Evaluation is a stage usually neglected. The evaluation may be done by the authority responsible for planning the project, or by one appraising the Project or by the authority executing the Project It may also be done by an independent authority. Obviously the last alternative will be preferable. The evaluation may give pointers for identifying a new project of the same type or a modified Project.

There will be a certain framework within which a Project will be identified. There should be availability of the particular types of resources in adequate measure necessary for the Project and the technology should be also at hand either local or imported. The Project should strive to conform to the general Development Objectives and also to the Programme Objectives. It should also be in tune with the environment in which the Project is to be executed. Apart from the physical environment, the more important aspect in Tribal Development Programme is the social environment. The Project has to be acceptable to the local people. Either the Project objectives are accepted as the desirable objectives by the local community or they at least are not against the community objectives. The Project objectives may be only partially desired by the community. In such a case it is important whether local community considers the potential partial benefits good enough against the cost to the local community. However in order that the Project is acceptable socially in the local community, the local people have to be convinced that the Project is desirable from the local point or the local community has to be enthused to adopt the broad national objectives as their own. This point will be given more attention at a later stage.

Along with broad identification of the Project, the project objectives have to be delineated. The objectives need to be firmly established as the subsequent edifice rests on these objectives. If there is a plurality of objectives, a clear priority or weightage should be assessed. This will come useful when the Project is formulated. The constraints on the Project have to be identified. The constraints may be of different kinds. They may relate to time, funds, natural resources, available technology, location etc. Within the framework of constraints and the potential availability of resources, various alternatives are to be considered. These alternatives will be only broad project ideas keeping in view the project objectives. A tentative priority among these possible alternatives has to be examined in order to decide which project ideas should be taken up first for formulation of the Project. In case there are interchangeable types of resources to be consumed in the Project, the policy decisions regarding selection of one type in preference to another will have to be kept in mind in giving shape to the Project idea. For instance indigenous technology may be preferable to imported technology. Labour intensive technology may take precedence over capital intensive technology. A particular type of fuel may be desirable to be used. Urbanization may have to be avoided. All such considerations will narrow down the choice among the different alternatives.

Next step in the formulation of the Project is preparation of the Feasibility Report. It is to be examined whether the project is feasible technically and financially. In tribal development programme, the Project has to be feasible also from the social angle. The Project has to be acceptable socially by the tribal community.

Various alternatives on different decision points are to be conceived and weighed. There can be no fool-proof method for identifying the available alternatives. The authority in charge of formulation of the project has to familiarize itself and acquire insight into the technical and social aspects of the Project. These decision points will vary from Project to Project. But some of the common areas for decision will be regarding the size of the Project and its location. There may be points for decision on technical and engineering aspects, regarding the choice of manufacturing process, specification of equipment, size, type and layout of buildings and the technical characteristics of the product and service. An assessment will have to be made regarding the market or demand for the product or service. Next comes the important aspect of financial consideration. What should be the size of the investment outlay both in terms of fixed and working capital, profitability and the break even analysis, will be discussed in details. The financial statements will be projected. Assessment regarding the requirement of personnel will be done and availability looked into.

An important feasibility aspect in Tribal Development Programme is the social feasibility or social acceptability. A close analysis of the socio-cultural aspect of the local tribal community and its beliefs and practices will provide a background to assess the acceptability of the project. A study will have to be made whether the different ramifications of the Project either during execution or thereafter have any relevance to the local cultural traits, beliefs and practices. Firstly, some aspects of the Project may be in tune with the cultural traits and may draw support from the local people; secondly, some may be just neutral while the third category may be opposed to the local beliefs and practices. Wherever the third category dominates, there will be considerable local resistance and it will be difficult to take up the Project. An identification and assessment of these factors will help to judge the extent of the opposition if any, of the local people to the Project.

When we have come to the conclusion that a set of projects is feasible after the Projects are formulated or prepared, we have to develop a method to help us to select the best Projects. Considering that the resources at our disposal are going to be scarce, we cannot plan on the basis of taking up all feasible Projects. Within the available Projects, we have to select those Projects which will give us maximum satisfaction. In order to do this we have to identify the Project benefits and costs. Adverse effects may be taken as negative benefits. After identification we have to quantify these costs and benefits so that an objective measurement of these costs and benefits can be done. This may pose a number of difficulties. But at present we are not going into these details. In order that the different types of costs and benefits can be compared and added/subtracted, they have to be converted into a common measuring rod. Obviously the most suitable even though not ideal such common yardstick is money. So money value is to be given to these costs and benefits. To give proper and correct money value is also bristled with a number of problems. These we are ignoring for the present.

Adding up the costs and benefits involves one more concept. Easy approach will be to treat the costs and benefits in terms of their money value for manipulation without any consideration for the time element. Certain methods based on such an easy approach are the Pay Back Method and Accounting Rate of Return. Obviously such an approach is not faithful to our experience. Money that is available right now and which is available at a future date do not have the same value for us. Generally we value money immediately available more than when it is available at a future date. From this arises the concept of interest and discount. When we calculate the value at a future date we add the increase in value by way of interest. When we deduct value to assess present value of money available at a future date we discount.

There are a number of relationships connecting values of money at different timings. We will state the relationships only in a few cases without going into their proof.

Let us presume that i, the rate of discount per rupee per year is constant. P is the present value. F is the value after n years.

$$P = \frac{F}{(1+i)^n}\ ; \quad F = P\,(1+i)^n$$

Let A_r be the amount available at the end of the rth year. As a simple case, let us suppose that all these amounts are equal.

$$P = A.\ \frac{(1+i)^n}{1(1+i)^n} \qquad F = A\frac{(1+i)^{n-1}}{i}$$

Therefore in order to compare costs and benefits with different time dimensions, we convert all of them to the present value, so that they can be subjected to addition On cost stream side, all the costs are brought to present value, and totalling up gives us the present value of costs, say C: Similarly. The present value of benefits are calculated say, B.

There are two other concepts which are relevant, they are salvage value and sunk cost. If a Project which is valued at any point of time in the sense that so much money we get for the assets of the project it is called salvage value. To calculate the total benefits, we have to take into account the salvage value among others. Salvage value may be based on assessment of the value of recoverable assets or it may be calculated on the basis of the unexpired period of the Project. The sunk cost is the cost over a project before it is being considered for being taken up. It is possible that some cost has been already incurred. But we are not expected to take this account for our cost stream as it is something prior to the Project.

One more point that is important is that whenever we are assessing costs and benefits, we have to consider the incremental costs and benefits. As we have discussed earlier, we have to compare for justification of the Project the difference between events with the project and events without the project with the cost. Hence we are interested in finding out the difference. Hence the increment in costs and benefits is relevant for our purpose.

Our objective is to compare the worth of different feasible Projects to help us select the best Project. The worth will depend on the present value of benefits and present value of costs. One point needs to be kept in mind. When a number of projects are being compared, the period of analysis of these projects should be the same. Suppose there are two projects P_1 and P_2 with life L_1 and L_2. We can either have projects of type P_1 one after another so that the total life of these projects equals L_2. Then we can compare the set of projects P_1 on one side and P_2 on the other. In the alternative, if $L_2 > L_1$ we can find out the salvage value of Project P_2 after time L_1 and then compare the two projects.

We have two types or preferably two stages of project appraisal, one is Financial Appraisal and the other is Economic Appraisal. Financial Appraisal is assessment of the comparative worth of the project from the point of view of the project authority. The costs and benefits are costs and benefits to the project authority. Economic Appraisal is the analysis of the comparative worth of the Project in terms of its contribution to the national economy. It is obvious that in public sector activities we will be interested in Economic Appraisal rather than the Financial Appraisal.

However for a project in Tribal Development Programmes, it is necessary to consider the third dimension. A project may compete in its worth for the Project authority or for the national economy. But only on this basis, it is difficult to convince the concerned tribal community regarding its worth. Considering the present gap in credibility and the sensitivity of the tribals, they will be extremely reluctant to incur cost (in their view) to earn benefits for the national economy. We cannot blame them if they assess the worth of a project through their own values. We also do the same thing. We only claim, with doubtful justification, that we are better equipped to judge our values. It will be proper to provide the tribals the wherewithals and capacity to analyse and assess value concepts with better knowledge and sharper tools. Hence we should keep both the economic appraisal and appraisal from tribal view in mind while making the selection. For want of any better term, we may call this Tribal-oriented Appraisal.

The prevalent methods of the Appraisal are the Net Present Worth Method, Benefit Cost Ratio Method and Internal Rate of Return Method. If we take the difference in the present value of benefits and the present value of costs, it is the Net Present Worth (NPW). Therefore

Net Present Worth = B—C

If for a Project NPW is larger it competes for selection. However the point regarding proportion of NPW to the investment of scarce resources is ignored in this method and to that extent it is defective.

Benefit Cost Ratio (BC Ratio) is the ratio of the Present Value of the Benefits to the Present Value Costs. Therefore

$$B : C \text{ Ratio} = \frac{B}{C}$$

If for a project the BC ratio is higher it stakes its claim for selection. However there is one snag. A particular item can be considered as positive cost or negative benefit. Either choice has no effect on NPW but it affects BC ratio.

Internal rate of return (IRR) is the value of discounting rate (i) which makes the NPW nil.

So IRR = i

Such that NPW = 0

B—C=0

∴ B=C

The equation B—C=0 will be generally an equation with n^{th} power for the unknown i. It is not susceptible of easy mathematical solution. Hence value of i is found by graphical method. Generally we have a unique real positive value for i but multi-value positive solutions cannot be ruled out.

The method of IRR is widely acceptable method as this method disposes of the element of value of i for comparing projects. One is clear regarding the rate of return on the investment. Generally we accept a particular value, so that if IRR for a Project exceeds this value, the Project is selected.

In Financial Analysis, the measurement of costs and benefits is easier as they can be taken to be the same as their apparent money value. However for the economic analysis the value of Costs and Benefits as is significant to the national economy cannot be taken as their apparent money value. Elaborate theories have been evolved to calculate the correct value of the costs and benefits. The corresponding money value is called the shadow prices or the accounting prices. It is not proposed to discuss these theories in this paper.

For tribal development programme, what we have called the tribal-oriented appraisal is important. Here the benefits and costs to the local tribal community are to be identified as a first stage. These should be based on the value judgment of the local tribe. The cultural factors, beliefs, practices and customs need to be taken into account. Suppose for instance we have a small water reservoir project in a tribal area where the tribals as a custom do not catch, sell or eat fish. In normal appraisal, income from rearing fish will be identified as a benefit but from the tribal-oriented appraisal it is not a benefit. Even after identification is done, the valuation of the benefits and costs may differ from that in economic analysis. The usual shadow prices will not be tenable. We will have to evolve a different technique to calculate the appropriate prices from the tribal view, we may call these as "social" prices. Here we can describe only the rationale and the broad basis for calculation of the "social" prices.

Let us consider the land cost for a project in a tribal development programme. In Financial Appraisal we shall consider the actual price paid for the land or otherwise the market price of the land. In Economic Appraisal we will take the opportunity cost of the land. This will be based on the net benefit from this land if the land is put to the best alternative use. Generally this opportunity cost will be less than the market price of the land. In tribal-oriented appraisal, the values of the land in both these methods will not be applicable. The reason is that a tribal has particular attachment to the land and even if he is paid the market price, he has a feeling of deprivation and sacrifice which is not adequately compensated by the payment of market price. He feels that he has been uprooted in the set up of the local tribal community. Moreover, it is more likely that the tribal will not be in a position to invest the amount because of various constraints in a productive endeavour to give him proper return. In reality, the tribal pays much more price than the market price when he is deprived of his land. This price will be the social price and the cost on this item should be based on this social price in analysing the project in the tribal-oriented approach. It is extremely difficult to evolve a formula to arrive at the figure of social prices for calculation of the costs and benefits. In absence of such a formula we have to assess the value of the conversion factor based on the tribal culture beliefs and practices for particular items of costs and benefits. Let us assume that we are in a position to calculate the net present worth under this system of tribal-oriented appraisal.

For selecting projects in the Tribal Development Programme, the normal methods of economic appraisal will be applied. Only one more condition may be imposed that for the selected projects the net present worth under the tribal-oriented appraisal is non-negative. This will ensure as far as is practicable that there is no opposition to the Project by the local tribe and that the local community does not consider the Project harmful for their interest according to their values.

The Identification, Formulation and Appraisal of Projects in Tribal Development Programme deserves special consideration in view of the nature of problems specific to the development administration for the tribal areas. The most important factor in tribal development is to bridge the gulf between the viewpoints of the tribals and administrators. The tribal beliefs cannot be changed overnight even if it is desirable to bring about such a change. The tribal themselves should be allowed to decide change and the development administration should only help the tribals to develop ability to grasp the implication of change. The methodology of identification, formulation and appraisal of projects need to be modified from this point of view.

PART IV

INSTITUTIONS, IMPLEMENTATION AND CASE STUDIES

SEVENTEEN

Sudesh Kumar Sharma

TRIBAL UNDERDEVELOPMENT IN INDIA
Some Administrative Issues

THE BROAD development goals of nations differ in strategies and emphases depending upon particular given conditions. At the time of independence, the Indian government inherited a large tribal population and area. According to the latest census figures available (1971 data), there are 38 million tribals 'scheduled' by the government, over 200 tribes and over 30 principal language groups. There is a very low level of literacy, 11.5 per cent as compared to 29.5 per cent for the nation as a whole, with some tribes under 2 per cent. The Government of India has made a number of plans to protect the rights of the tribals and to integrate them into national development planning. In the Constitution of India, the rights of the tribals were explicitly recognized and clauses were included to permit positive discrimination in their favour. The evaluation reports and a number of study teams and task forces in the past many years point out that these special provisions have so far failed to bring any positive gains to the tribals. Tribal areas contain over half of the country's mineral and forest resources but still much outcome of the efforts has not been possible. In the words of the Planning Commission Document (1973), "Reviewing the policies and programmes of the preceding five year plans we are of the opinion that the efforts so far made for social and economic development of the Scheduled Tribes have not brought an appreciable change in their condition"

There can be a number of explanations for the failure of the government programmes for tribal development. Some serious foreign observers maintain that Government of India has not only failed to encourage the development of the tribals but has actively maintained their underdevelopment.[1] This thesis is based on three grounds : (a) funds allocated to tribal development by successive governments since independence have both been meagre and greatly outweighed by the value of the resources extracted from tribal areas; (b) Government supported exploitation of the tribals' traditional environments involving heavy social costs ; (c) the tribals had been prevented from acquiring any real political power. The Eastern belt is split up into small units so that the tribals never form more than a small minority. There are other studies[2] which point out that the laws and programmes have failed because of the power of the non-tribal landlords and the non-involvement of the tribals in the development process. If all these factors are taken into consideration, an unfortunate impression is bound to be created that no new programmes have been implemented to successfully overcome these problems. This is not so looking at the number of schemes and projects initiated by the government for a number of years. In this paper, an alternative for the reason why the government's efforts to bring about development have failed, will be proposed. A corollary of this exercise will be that other social and cultural factors are no doubt responsible partly for the present state of affairs but that is not enough. The most crucial prerequisite for tribal development is a sound administrative structure so that whatever plans and programmes are initiated for the tribal population are effectively delivered. Three decades of planned national development have brought into existence a network of public service delivery systems but a look at the tribal landscape shows that these delivery systems have not adequately serviced the people to enhance their capability for increased production and productivity. This paper critically examines salient administrative issues which are fundamental in tribal development administration. The field studies had been conducted in Himachal Pradesh for a period of over two years and issues have been discussed with many knowledgeable officials and non-officials. Not much has been written in this field except some documents published by the government from time to time. The following pages present a critique in depth and in a dispassionate way so that the tracks of underdevelopment may disappear by adopting those methods which are within the administrative reach.

Developmental Capacities

Tribal development is a challenge where a restructuring and modernization of the traditional society has to begin. However, no care is taken to give any special attention to tribal areas and development effort is looked after like any other subject—a departmental hierarchy run on traditional lines. Bureaucracy, in order to be responsive to social change, has to provide for organisational flexibility and adoption of administrative policies which encourage experiments with new organisational forms. This has four policy implications : (a) Implementation through deconcentration, planned and financed by the central government, implemented by central field officials in the region, mainly for sectoral projects; (b) Implementation through decentralization, planned, financed and implemented by local government officials, for local government projects; (c) Implementation through co-action, planned and financed by the central government and implemented by the local government apparatus; (d) Implementation through the process of community initiative, planned and financed by the rural community with additional funds from the central government, if necessary.[3] There are, however, two constraints, first the structure of administration as at present is rational, impersonal, ensuring a career with fixed tenure and sufficient security which makes it underdeveloped and unintegrated because it does not encourage full delegation and decentralization of authority. In this long process of decision-making, the task of implementation becomes ritualistic. Second, due to multiplicity of services, cadres and ranks, there is a type of conflict of tension within the administrative organisation encouraging status and rank consciousness. Rank is seldom associated with responsibility which results in a type of class and caste structure which has a tendency towards the diffusion of responsibilility. The targets and objectives are side-tracked and become less important.

Tribals' Participation under Conditions of Inequality

The major task in tribal development is to develop standards and sensitivity in the society which helps to identify leadership poten tial in these terms. Tribal development efforts and programmes face numerous impediments that spring from organisational and financial constraints. There are many parties whose vested interests are disturbed by the radical changes and some obstacles may be created. By proper involvement of the people at the local level, at least three objectives of tribal development strategy can be better achieved: viz., (a) laying down maximum standards of productivity or efficiency for those who own or use precious natural resources; (b) minimum standards of performance by public agencies by asking them to be accountable to local people; and (c) creating a scientific temper which implies a changing of the mind and old habits of thought and action.[4] In most of the tribal development programmes, not enough care was taken to involve the local Tribal Councils. It is strange that development is something done to tribals by non-tribals, not a process in which the tribals are actively involved and can control.

Financial Constraints

Mostly tribal development is paying lip service and one would expect the per capita allocation to tribal programmes to be at least equal to and probably greater than those allocated to other sectors. Tribal people are supposed to benefit from general funds as are applicable elsewhere in India as well as from special extra funds for tribal welfare and development. Compared to the rising prices and other financial allocations, there has been a continual decline in the proportion of the total Plan expenditure allocated to the Special Scheduled Tribes Programme. In addition, bank and open market borrowing available elsewhere is conspicuous by its absence. The cost-benefit analysis, if made would indicate that funds spent by the government in tribal aress are considerably less than the value of the minerals and timber extracted from these areas. There are also deleterious effects that the huge forestry, mining, irrigation dam schemes have made on traditional vocations of tribals. There are many laws controlling sale of tribal agricultural land to non-tribals, but large amounts of tribal land have been alienated.[5] Some writers even go to the extent to conjecture that the amount of tribal land taken by individual non-tribals is dwarfed by the amount of local government and para-statal organisations take from tribals for big projects.[6]

Institutional Change and Organisation of the Tribals

Poverty, underdevelopment and unemployment are consequences of a social and economic process. The type of institutional support will depend on the functions, skills and support level involved in the development of crafts and other avenues of production. Studies have pointed out that because of various pulls and pressures, the facilities and inputs intended for the tribals are largely siphoned off along the way. Due to the absence of viable organisations at the local level, there is hardly any check. It is believed that innovations can be introduced in tribal areas through proper extension services and activities over a period of time by utilizing established local leaders, influential people and progressive thinkers. It is true that a large majority may not participate in this innovation-introduction programme, but through democratic influence, demonstration and percolation effects, the majority can be mobilized to support the programme. There are others who favour the conscientisation approach which assumes that tribals can be mobilized only when they are sufficiently discontented about any concrete event or a situation signifying the potentiality of an acute conflict. This is another extreme but the necessity to have well organized, articulate tribal organisations is recognized. Unless such groups exercise pressure and play a decisive role in the planning and the implementation process, the path of implementation and also of planners may not be helped.[7]

Problems of Inter-institutional Linkages

The establishment of a multi-tier structure of decentralized tribal development management immediately creates problems of inter-institutional linkages. In tribal areas, the existing administrative systems in most situations were based upon the concept of a single-line administrative hierarchy, but the development programmes for trible are as involved simultaneous action at so many points that administrative integration of the field projects was no longer possible. Historically there was a tendency to operate a centralized administrative structure with only a minimum of penetration into tribal areas, but the new challenges led to the establishment of a network of administrative institutions operating far away in the field. This shift in the focus had its implications for personnel administration. A proper feedback system is also a must with suitable formats to assess the progress of work vis-a-vis targets in respect of each scheme or project. Behind institutional, administrative and bureaucratic obstacles, is the outmoded system of financial sanctions and obsolescent system of realising funds. The tight method of administrative control would have to give way to corporate management, bringing officers from various professions and departments to adopt plans jointly and accepting common responsibility for their implementation.[8]

Strengthening the Delivery Systems

Adaptation of administration to suit the particular needs requires great effort and attention. The first priority is the formulation of policies in the right direction and normally this is a political function. Another equally important issue in area-level planning is the problem of reducing the planning-politics gap. It was necessary to devise an organisational structure which would suit the democratic aspirations of the elected representatives, give them an executive role and at the same time give a supervisory and guiding role to the administrator.[9] In short, attempts have to be made to (a) review the major lessons of experience of the adequacy and effectiveness of the administrative systems for greater production and productivity, (b) redefine the concepts, approaches and methodologies of the delivery systems for the tribals in terms of contemporary needs, (c) explore new directions and methods for greater participation in and control of the delivery systems by the poorer population and (d) identify concretely the main bottlenecks in the planning, organizing and management of the administrative organisations and to prepare a set of guidelines for their improvement.

Some Correctives

In the preceding pages, new organisational forms have been suggested, far reaching changes in the personnel policies recommended, greater and greater devolution and decentralisation emphasized, considerable allocation of funds pleaded, cooperation and reception from the tribal people emphasized, but still some concrete suggestions where specific action can be taken are given below. A prerequisite of course is that no one can hope to explain the underdevelopment of any one group in society by looking at that community in isolation. A wider perspective linking the community to the political and economic power structure of the state must be adopted. No amount of administrative reforms can succeed if the environment is not conducive to change.[10] It may, therefore, be cheaper and quicker to refashion existing organisations and instruments and to go in for new ones where clearly unavoidable. Some of the correctives suggested are :

1. A certain amount of flexibility and variety in the organisational arrangements should be recognized as necessary. Regional disparities in India are such that a uniform approach may not be feasible.

2. The local community which has mostly been playing a passive role needs to be activated by proper and effective participation in decision making and implementation.

3. As far as possible the number of agencies and departments which deal with different aspects of development programmes should be strengthened and the number of contact points with which the target group has to deal must be cut down to the minimum.

4. With a view to make the planning exercises realistic and manageable, a system of communication has to operate and be made fully effective so as to provide the required feedback.

5. Information, monitoring and current evaluation should be done internally. This should be beyond the routine reporting merely of physical and financial progress for measuring the efficiency.

6. A high degree of professionalisation of the field level staff of specialized skills is absolutely necessary. Special purpose training programmes specially geared to them need to be formulated.

7. To allow field organisations to operate effectively, decentralization of authority within a broad policy frame is an absolute necessity. In planning basic services, the objective should be to establish them on an integrated basis so that they would be mutually supportive.

8. There has been much failure of micro-coordination. Whereas greater coordination is needed at every level, but it has to be assured at the implementational level. Horizontal as well as vertical coordination must be improved. Modern management techniques and information systems must be fully utilized.

9. The non-official organisations should be actively involved with the tribal development programmes. They should be helpful in motivating the local people to participate as well as act as strong pressure groups to check any lapse or callousness.

10. The delivery systems meant to bring distributive justice would necessitate measures which have to be built into the whole spectrum of production, distribution and employment policies of the government.

In short, tribal development cannot be administered from above; it has to be organised from below. Development as contrasted with more growth, is a long drawn out process and it has to be viewed on a long-term perspective from various vantage points—legal, social, cultural, economic. While the realization of these issues has grown considerably, institutional arrangements have, however, not been developed adequately. Thus, there is an increasing need for special policy orientation and developed administrative capabilities to break the isolation and bring the tribals in the main stream of the development process.

REFERENCES

1. Steve Jones, "Tribal Underdevelopment in India", *Development and Change*, Vol. IX, No. 1, January 1978, p. 42.
2. Annual Reports of Commissioner for Scheduled Castes and Scheduled Tribes, Report of the Committee on Special Purpose Tribal Blocks, 1960, Report of the Committee on Tribal Economy in Forest Area; 1967, Report of the Study Team for Tribal Labour, 1969; Report of Study Team on Tribal Development Programmes, 1969, Report of the Task Force on Development of Tribal Areas, 1973. etc.
3. United Nations, *Rural Development Administration in India : Some Emerging Policy Issues*, Bangkok, 1979.
4. Michael Lipton, "Urban Bias and Rural Planning—Strategy for Agriculture" in P. Streeten and M. Lipton (Eds.) : *The Crisis of Madhya Pradesh*, Bhopal, 1975.

5. R.S. Srivastava, "Problems of Land Alienation Among the Tribals (District Bastar)", *Bulletin of The Tribal Research and Development Institute* (Bhopal, Madhya Pradesh, Vol. 10, 1972), pp. 59-75.
6. M.L. Patel, *Changing Land Problems of Tribal India* (Bhopal, Progress Publishers, 1974).
7. Keith Griffith and Azizar Rahman Khan, "Poverty in the Third World: Ugly Facts and Fancy Models", *World Development*, March, 1978.
8. B.D. Sharma, "Tribal Development Administration", in S.K. Sharma (ed.) *Dynamics of Development : An International Perspective*, Delhi, Concept, 1978).
9. L.P. Vidyarthi, "Socio-Cultural Implications of Industrialization in India : A Case Study of Tribal Bihar", (Research Programmes Committee. Planning Commission, 1970).
10. Perspective Planning Division, Planning Commission, *Studies on the Structure of Indian Economy and Planning for Development*, New Delhi, 1977.

EIGHTEEN

L. M. Prasad

A SURVEY OF ADMINISTRATION IN TRIBAL AREAS

With Special Reference to Bihar

THE ADMINISTRATION of our tribal population has acquired a new significance after Independence. The Republic of India has decided to do justice to the hitherto exploited Scheduled Tribes.[1] It would not be an exaggeration to say that what India planned to do after Independence was more audacious and more idealistic than what she had attained through struggle for independence. No other non-communist under-developed country had ever planned to do so much for its down-trodden and underdeveloped people with the limited resources it had at its disposal.[2] We have crossed 33 years of our Independence. If it is not too long span a time it is also not a short one. It has, therefore, become our prime duty to examine, a few questions. Are our adivasi brethren being benefited by the government's activities and programme? Or does the Programme benefit the officials more than the people ? What is their present status and condition ? Have we been able to associate our Adivasi brethren in governance of the country so reasonably that we may call India a government of the people, by the people, and for the people ? What is their future in this democratic country ? All these and a number of other questions have cropped up with acute poignancy during the post-independence period.

At the very outset the question arises, what is meant by "tribe" ? and, what is meant by "Administration"? Andre

Beteille[3] says,

> In general, it was applied to people who were considered primitive, lived in backward areas, and did know the use of writing. Sometimes, it was considered synonymous with the term race, which in scientific usage has an entirely different meaning. . . . . By and large, this was the case in Australia, in Melanesia and in North America, the regions which were first studied by the anthropologists.

He further says, "Finally, we come to the definition of a tribe as a collection of individual sharing a common culture". He opines that the second definition has been accepted either explicitly or implicitly by a wide range of anthropologists.[4] For our purpose also this definition suits most. It hardly needs to be mentioned that the term culture is used in its widest anthropological sense to denote those traditional beliefs, arts and practices which an individual acquires as a member of a particular society.

Having defined the term tribe, we now turn to the concept of Administration. Here, the term, "Administration" constantly refers to Public Administration as opposed to variety of administrative activity run by private individual or a group of individuals. That is to say Public Administration or its brief use as administration here refers to that aspect of administration, which is "Co-extensive with the organized government", and therefore, it has to be treated as that branch of Political Science which deals with "the art and science of management applied to the affairs of the state".[5] The term, "Administration" here, in short, embraces all those processes that in India have lead to "the fulfilment or enforcement of public policy". In simplest term Public Administration is, "co-operative human action with a high degree of rationality".[6]

Relation between Culture and Administration

Our next immediate task would be to establish the necessary link that exists between culture and Administration. The question arises is there anything like Tribal Administration ?, or Tribal Administration is a myth ? Here one is very well reminded by the famous statement of F.M. Marx—"Administration is culture bound". If culture changes administration, then definitely Adivasi should have different Administration. Because, Adivasi have well-knit categorical different culture. Differences between tribal and more advanced societies are apparent even to the casual observer.[7]

As a matter of fact there had been different administrations in the plains and hills since British days. The British thought that the complicated procedure adopted for the administration of the plains was unsuitable for the hills. In the hills and forests, the administration of justice was simple and direct. Simple taxes like the toll tax, house tax and hoe tax were levied. Rural policing and the maintenance of law and order were left to the local chiefs.[8]

Free India has also allowed that simplicity in various fields. But one is tempted to say that while in British days these distinctions were quite categorical, in the present day these are becoming more so hazy. Red-tapism is the nature of our administration both in Civil and Tribal areas. If we want that tribal people should get maximum benefit from the administration, administration will have to be moulded according to their culture. We should not feel shy if we have to adopt altogether a different administration in tribal areas.

Waldo Dwight rightly opines, "There are important difference between administrative systems, depending upon the location, the tasks, the environment, and the inhabitants of the system". He further says, "administration is a part of the cultural complex; and it not only is acted upon, it acts. Indeed, by definition a system of rational co-operative action, it inaugurates and controls much change. Administration may be thought of as the major invention and device by which they seek simultaneously to achieve—within the limitations of their wit and knowledge—the goals of stability and the goals of change".[9]

"Traditions die hard", this is also an old maxim.[10] Without going in details we can take one very simple and glaring example of difference in administration in two countries where culture are quite different. Just think of one crime adultery and see its punishments in India and in Britain. In India, in a crime like adultery only male is supposed to be a party. Woman herein is exempted from all punishments. However, researches of Pramila Kapoor reveal that in such crimes women are more active partners. Still, women have been regarded as the weaker sex and been exempted from punishments, according to our culture and tradition. The position is quite different in Britain. Here man and woman are considered equally guilty in this crime and it is a good cause for divorce.

We could, however, look at some of the cultural facets of our tribal administrative life and view the variety of changes that have overtaken both at the cultural and administrative complex of the Tribal Society.

II

TRIBAL DEVELOPMENT AFTER INDEPENDENCE

After Independence a plethora of governmental programmes were launched by various departments for the welfare of the tribals. Side by side various non-official organizations also came into the field of tribal welfare. They include Bhartiya Adimjati Gramodyog Sangh, Adimjati Seva Mandal, Ramkrishna Mission, Bharat Sevashram Sangh, Srimamta Shankar Mission and a few others.[11]

The Indian National Congress—as the majority party—has, from the time it framed the Constitution of the Indian Union, adopted various measures to handle the tribal problem. Special clauses have been incorporated in the constitution for the creation of Scheduled Areas and their intensive development. Further, they are provided with special representation in Parliament, in legislative assemblies, and special privileges in the form of reservation of a certain percentage of posts in government services, and seats in educational institutions.[12]

Christian missionaries and Hindu social reformers have also intensified their efforts to study and reform the conditions of the tribes. Academicians—anthropologists, sociologists and others—have all launched a vigorous drive to study scientifically the situations and problems of the tribal populations[13]. Among anthropologists Dr. L. P. Vidyarthi and Dr. Sachchidananda, are among the few who have done an excellent job to highlight the tribal life in different perspectives in India and abroad.

A Tribal Research Institute was established at Ranchi in 1954 to explore methodically and examine the conditions and the problems of the tribal communities. Further, various political parties have been extending their activity to tribal areas. They have created numerous organisations in the tribal areas and even launched various movements to redress the grievances of the tribal population.[14]

Students of political science are aware that pressure groups have to be there in modern power politics. It is not possible for any society, to be free from the influence of pressure groups. Pressure groups may function in different ways: ideological pressure groups, economic pressure groups, caste-ist or sectarian or tribal pressure groups.[15] The "local" educated and richer sections of the tribes in various parts of the country have also started independent organisations of the tribal population to secure concessions which they feel will be beneficial to the tribes.

Some of the important projects launched by the Govt. of India and Bihar for tribal welfare are as follows :

(i) A number of multipurpose blocks for the tribals for their intensive development.

(ii) Training-cum-production centres and subsidies for the development of cottage and village industries in tribal areas to provide employment.

(iii) Colonisation of the tribals (settling of the tribals who are practising shifting cultivation on land) and the introduction of improved methods of shifting cultivation which may bring more yield without doing harm to the soil.

(iv) Educational facilities—scholarships, free studentships and other educational aids.

(v) Establishment of tribal cultural institutes for studying the vorious cultural problems effecting tribal life.

(vi) Reservation of posts in government services for the tribals.

(vii) Enactment of Regulation Acts to counteract exhorbitant rates of interest charged by money-lenders.

(viii) Establishment of the office of the Commissioner of

Scheduled Tribes and Castes to enforce safeguards.

It would be worthwhile to study the findings of the reports of the Commissioner for the Scheduled Castes and the Scheduled Tribes as well as the published Report of the Study Team on the Social Welfare of the Backward Classes. These reports were published in the beginning of the sixties. The salient points of these Reports are as follows:

(i) The achievements during the First Five Year Plan cannot be properly assessed because progress during the first two years was meagre and during the subsequent three years they could not be assessed as many State Govts. has failed to submit progress reports.

(ii) The benefits of the schemes mostly accrued to the vocal section of the population only.

(iii) The employment exchanges failed to provide jobs to a large number of educated and un-educated tribes enrolled in the register.

(iv) The tribal research institutes failed to play a functional role in bringing about the coordination of research with the formulation of welfare planning.

(v) The exploitation of the tribals by money lenders and contractors persisted.

(vi) The training-cum-production centres were a total failure (in either providing successful training or even functioning as production units) and much money was wasted.

(vii) The provision of cultivable land and other facilities to settle the tribals was meagre.

(viii) Red-tapism and lack of co-ordination among different departments resulted in the lapse of grants and the untimely supply of materials etc.

The above observations reveal for themselves the superficial and uncoordinated nature of the aid provided to the tribal population. It has rightly been pointed out that it creates acute frustration which is exploited by the 'vocal section' of the tribal population for its sectional interests.[16]

Special Multipurpose Tribal Blocks

On the 2nd October, 1956, forty three special Multipurpose Tribal Blocks were opened in different States of the country to speed up the process of development in the areas of the greatest tribal concentration. These Blocks were jointly sponsored by the Ministries of Home Affairs and Community Development. As usual the State Govts. were given charge of implementation of this programme as well. These Multipurpose Blocks differed basically from the normal blocks on the following points :

(i) Development Programmes to be implemented were more intensive in character.

(ii) The population and area coverage was to be much less than normal Block.

(iii) People's contribution had to be kept to the minimum and limited only to supply the unskilled labour at a lower rate.

(iv) 'Loan Funds' were tc be diverted as subsidies.

(v) Personnel appointed for these areas had to be suitably trained.

After operation of this scheme for some time, there was apprehension at the highest level that the programme was not moving in the right direction. And therefore on 1 May 1959, by a resolution of the Ministry of Home Affairs, a committee was framed to :

(i) study the working of the special Multipurpose Tribal Blocks; and

(ii) to advise the Government of India on how to implement the intensive development programme of the Blocks more effectively and give the programme a proper tribal bias.

The committee was presided over by no less a person than Dr. Verrier Elwin who had hold the widest experience in the field since 1931.

This committee went into the various aspects of the programme in detail and made the following main observations and recommendations.

(i) Though the programme suffered from the defects of all pilot projects, it was sufficiently successful to justify its extension.

(ii) In tribal areas top priority should be given to agriculture and allied subjects like irrigation, reclamation and soil conservation and not less than Rs. 10 lakhs should be spent under these heads.

(iii) There should be really serious attempt to relate the programme and the ways of doing things to the tribal background etc.

In the time of the above and many other recommendations, the programme for tribal development was further revised during the Third Five Year Plan. The C.D. Programme was extended to more tribal areas and 450 Tribal Development Blocks were started.

Tribal Development Blocks

During the third Five Year Plan, in the line of the recommendations of the Committee on special Multipurpose Tribal Blocks, it was decided to extend the programme of tribal development in more areas with concentration of tribals population up to the minimum of 66 per cent of the total population. If necessary, this was to be done by carving out areas of some of the existing blocks irrespective of the scheduled and non-scheduled areas. Other criteria that were laid down for location of T.D. Blocks were :

(i) The area should not ordinarily exceed 200 square miles.

(ii) The total population should not normally exceed 25,000 and if any particular area is more densely populated, the area may proportionately be reduced to 150 square, miles, or so.

(iii) In areas however where the concentration of population is less, the area may be increased proportionately and the minimum scheduled tribe population in such areas should be kept at 10,000.

Following the above criteria, up to the 30th June, 1965, it was possible to select 450 T.D. Blocks for implementation for the T.D. Blocks Programme.

Like the S.M.P.T. Blocks, these blocks also are nothing but a normal C.D. Block of one stage or the other plus a block having additional funds of Rs. 10 lakhs in the stage I and Rs. 5 lakhs in stage II for more intensive efforts of development.

Further, instructions were issued to plan the programmes for the tribal areas in such a way as to promote their growth by their own efforts, and by the efforts of the extension of workers, recognising—

(i) the totality of the community life of the tribals, (ii) the integrated life of the individual within the community, and (iii) culture and traditions of the tribals and their adaptability to change.

From this, it naturally followed that development programmes for the tribal areas were to be planned after a study of the culture, tradition, and practices of the tribals. To fulfil this requirement three types of surveys viz. (i) Preliminary survey, (ii) Basic survey, and (iii) Special surveys, were to be conducted.

On completion of these preliminary stage, the following programmes were planned and implemented according to the priorities prescribed.

Agriculture

Emphasis on change in pattern of agriculture from shifting cultivation to settled cultivation were to be continued. Apart from that, establishment of agricultural supplies; stores in conjunction with existing village organisation; establishment of grain gola for supplying fruit plants, grafts, vegetable seeds and seedlings; provision of a set of agricultural implements to each tribal organisation; provision of loans and grants to tribals for soil conservation, minor irrigation etc. and setting up demonstration farms to introduce improved agricultural practices etc. were taken care of.

Animal Husbandry

Piggery, poultry keeping and sheep breeding were promoted with vigour.

Cottage and Small Industries

It was to be promoted on the basis of availability of raw materials.

Social Education

Promotion of the existing village institution like Dhumkuria into community centre were aimed at.

Women and Children's Programme

Emphasis on teaching of Health and sanitation, through 'Demonstration' were planned. Children's education were also promoted through the women. The approach to this programme was possibly made through recreational and cultural programmes among the tribal women.

Thus with emphasis on understanding of "Tribal life and culture" it is proposed to promote economic development, facilities of communication and provision of social services in tribal areas, ultimately paving paths for a good and prosperous life for the tribals.[17]

The impact of the tribal development programmes undertaken during the First, Second and Third Plan periods has been studied by several special committees. The study team on Tribal Development Programmes (1969) evaluated the progress achieved in regard to tribal welfare and development. The Committee opined that the programme had fallen short of expectations although it succeeded in bringing about a change in the outlook of the tribals, particularly in the fields of education and agriculture. The tribal development blocks succeeded in making only a limited impact due to certain basic problems such as subsistence level of living underdeveloped infra-structure and high percentage of illiteracy among the tribal population. It was also observed that the problems of land alienation and shifting cultivation hindered development in these blocks. Among other problems noted were shortage of technical staff and their frequent transfers. Some of the general criticisms of the programmes related to the following :

(i) Schemes drawn up for more developed regions were applied to the tribal areas without change.

(ii) Preparatory steps were not taken to settle land disputes.

(iii) Bulk of the developmental outlay was used up by construction programme.

(iv) Employment aspect of development was not given due consideration.

(v) Co-operatives were started without adequate preparation or orientation of the tribals.

Again it was found that there was a tendency among block authorities to concentrate schemes in easily accessible areas and the needs of the people inhabiting the more inaccessible and backward areas remained unattended. The next problem was that the better off among the tribals appropriated the bulk of the benefits following from the various programmes taken up for implementation. The working of both the tribal development blocks and the tribal development agencies has shown that development of the tribal people so far have had a limited coverage.

Fifth Plan Approach

The Planning Commission appointed a Task Force on Development of Backward Classes which considered the problem in its numerous facts. The Task Force appointed a number of working groups notably the one on Personnel policies. The Task Force suggested a three-tier developmental structure at micro, meso and macro levels. The meso unit was suggested to be the main building block of this strategy.

The Central Co-ordination Committee[18] for Welfare of Backward Classes has been set up in the wake of the new strategy for development of tribal areas in the Fifth Plan for ensuring the flow of sectoral funds for tribal development, for watching the progress of schemes in tribal areas and for suggesting measures for effective implementation of the programmes. This committee decided to constitute a working group under the Chairmanship of Sri B.R. Patel to work out the details of integration of various sectoral programmes in the tribal development projects.

These working Groups and Committee evolved a new strategy for Tribal development and that new strategy is called the Sub-Plan approach. The Sub-Plan is not a scheme, it represents a new approach. The strategy clearly spells out the problem of tribal development into two parts—(a) that of areas of having more than 50 per cent tribal concentration, and the Scheduled Areas, and (b) that of areas with dispersed tribal population. Besides these two categories, primitive tribal Communities at pre-agricultural level of technology were identified as a special group.

The strategy for areas of tribal concentration culminated in the concept of Sub-Plan for these areas. States and Union territories have been grouped into three categories for this purpose :

(i) States and Union Territories having more than 50 per cent tribal population—Meghalaya, Nagaland, Arunachal Pradesh and Dadra and Nagar Haveli, L. M. & A. Island.

(ii) States and Union Territories having large tribal population—Andhra Pradesh, Assam, Bihar, Gujarat Himachal Pradesh, Madhya Pradesh, Maharashtra, Manipur, Orissa, Rajasthan and Tripura.

(iii) States and Union Territories having scattered tribal population, i.e. Kerala, Mysore, Tamil Nadu, Uttar Pradesh, West Bengal, A. and N. Islands, Goa, Daman and Diu.

The State Plans of State/Union Territories in category (i) above are really Tribal Development Plans and, therefore, necessary in their case.

The long-term objectives of the Sub-Plan are :

(i) to narrow the gap between the levels of development of tribal and other areas, and
(ii) to improve the quality of the tribal communities of life.

The immediate objectives will be to eliminate exploitation in all forms, speed up the process for social and economic development and improve the organisational capabilities.[19] It was agreed that a general strategy for achieving these objectives has to be evolved, reviewing the entire local administrative and institutional frame, as also the inter-sectoral and intra-sectoral priorities, keeping the primary focus on the welfare and development of the people. In relation to the developmental programmes, the tribal Sub-Plans represent the totality of public sector effort in that area. The resources comprise the following elements :

(a) State Plan Outlays;
(b) Sectoral Outlay in the Central Ministries;
(c) Special Central Assistance; and
(d) Institutional Finance.

Essential Features of the Sub-Plan

The following are the essential features :

(i) Total as against sectoral approach to the problems of tribal area;
(ii) Evolving a suitable frame for development of these areas;
(iii) Accepting the uniqueness of the problem of each viable area and community and formulation of programmes with reference to it;
(iv) Major thrust of development to be provided by the general sector;
(v) Substantial supplementation of State's effort by the Union Govt.
(vi) Reconstructing the Administrative and Institutional Frame.

The scope of the sub-plans, thus, is much wider than that of the State Plans. In this case, a 'problem solving' approach has been accepted for the first time not only in principle but with adequate provision for policy review in all important matters and financial support for any action necessary.[20] The guidelines for preparation of Sub-Plans have set this frame in very clear terms. It is stipulated :

At the development of the people has to be the central point of attention of the Sub-Plan, in many cases, it may be necessary to look at the problem unfettered by the existing formal, procedural or legal frame. The final course may be defined only after fully examining the impact of all the factors on the tribal life. The States may bring up these issues, where necessary to the Union Govt. level so that they can be considered at the highest level before any thing is allowed to stand in the way of fast development of these people.[21]

Integrated Tribal Development Projects

The Sub-Plan area in each State is to be divided into various project areas taking into consideration administrative boundaries, topography level of economic development, ethnic composition, natural resources and potential for development. As the tribal development block was too small a unit for

Planning and Co-ordination, it was decided to constitute a project comprising a group of development blocks. Therefore the entire tribal Sub-Plan area has been divided into a number of viable integrated tribal development projects (I.T.D.P.). As the situation varied from one State to another and from one area to another, in the same State, the project size was decided keeping in view the specific situation in a particular case. As project has, on an average, about three to four lakh population and about six to seven blocks; 178 integrated tribal development projects have been carved out. Some of the projects are co-terminus with the district in the case of small district. In most cases, the projects are co-terminus with sub-division/tehsils. There are some projects which are one block units, because there are no adjoining areas of tribal concentration. In some cases, the project cover an area smaller than a block for the same reason.

The project represents the total developmental effort in that area and has to accept the problem solving approach, covering a large spectrum from protection to welfare, it has been conceived as comprising the totality of the existing administrative apparatus in the concerned area. The I.T.D.P. is expected to gradually subsume functions of all the diverse agencies in the concerned area.

Annual Sub-Plan for Tribal Areas of Bihar (1980-81)

The area of the Tribal Sub-Plan in Bihar has already been delineated during the Fifth Plan period and the same is being continued during the Sixth Plan as well. It consists of the whole of Ranchi and Singhbhum districts, Latehar Sub-division and Bhandaria block of Garhwa sub-division of Palamau district, Dumka, Pakur, Rajmahal and Jamtara. Sub-divisions and Sundarpahari and Bansjore blocks of Godda Sub-division of Santhal Parganas district. In all, 112 blocks have been included in the Sub-Plan covering an area of 43,792 sq. kms. and total population of about 74.93 lakhs out of which 37 86 lakhs or 50.1 per cent are tribals. Thus 77 per cent out of the total tribal population of 49.33 lakhs of the State are residing within the Sub-Plan area. The entire Sub-Plan area has been divided into 14 Integral Tribal Development Projects, all of which except Chaibasa and Chakradharpur are co-terminus with the concerned administrative Sub-divisions. Chaibasa Sadar Sub-division has been bifurcated into two I.T.D.Ps. viz. Chaibasa and Chakradharpur.

Pockets of Dispersed Tribals

In addition to the area covered under the Sub-Plan, pockets outside the Sub-Plan where there is concentration of tribals, are also being brought under the Modified Area Plan during the Sixth Plan period. This is being done with a view to bring in as many tribals as possible within the fold of special development programmes viz, the Sub-Plan and the Modified Area Plan.

The tribal population living outside the Sub-Plan area is about 11.47 lakhs. They are mainly distributed in the following districts :

(1) Palamau (in the non-Sub-Plan area), (2) Santhal Parganas (in the non-Sub-Plan area), (3) Hazaribagh, (4) Giridih, (5) Dhanbad, (6) Monghyr, (7) Bhagalpur, (8) Katihar, (9) Purnea, (10) Saharsa, (11) Rohtas, (12) Bhojpur, (13) West Champaran.

In order to look after the dispersed tribals under the Modified Area Development Approach (M.A.D.A.), the Planning Commission and the Ministry of Home Affairs had suggested to identify compact pockets of 10,000 population which should contain at least 50 per cent tribals. Taking into account the guidelines given for the purpose, 43 pockets of tribal concentration spread over in 41 blocks (one each in 39 blocks and 2 each in 2 blocks) have been identified. Excepting Purnea, Saharsa and Bhojpur districts these areas are found in all the above mentioned districts.

With the identification of these 43 pockets, about 4.69 lakhs of tribals are proposed to be brought under the programme of M.A.D.A. out of a tribal population of 11.47 lakhs residing outside the Sub-Plan area. Thus the total tribal population under some kind of special programme would add to 42.55 lakhs (37.86 lakhs of the Sub-Plan plus 4.69 lakhs of M.A.D.A.), which would cover about 86.3 per cent of the total tribal population of the State.*

*For details see Annual Sub-Plan for Tribal Areas of Bihar.

There are altogether 30 scheduled tribes in the State. Taking into account the level of literacy and economic condition, 9 tribes have been identified as the most backward and primitive and special programmes for their economic uplift were initiated during the Fifth Plan period. These primitive tribes are Asur, Birhor, Birjia, Hill-Kharia, Korwa, Parahiya, Sauria-Paharia, Mal-Pahariya and Savar and their number as per 1971 Census is about 1.68 lakhs. Special programmes for the development of identified families belonging to these tribes are under implementation during the Sixth Plan as well.[22]

Protective Measures

In order to protect the tribals from various kinds of exploitation particularly at the hands of money-lenders, traders and other middlemen, a number of protective measures have been taken by the State Govt. The measures relate particularly to land alienation, forest, excise, credit and marketing, administrative structure etc. These measures are providing sufficient relief to the tribals and they can expect to enjoy the fruits of their own labour and the Govt. efforts towards their development which has hitherto been usurped largely by the exploitative elements.

Chotanagpur Tenancy Act (1908) and Santhal Parganas Tenancy (Supplementary Provisions) Act

These acts contain provisions for banning illegal alienation. Section 46 of Chotanagpur Tenancy Act prohibits transfer by raiyats of their rights in land. The law permits tribal raiyat to transfer his right by sale but only with the permission of the Deputy Commissioner. Santhal Parganas Tenancy Act contains far more restrictive provisions in respect of transfer of land by a raiyat tribal or non-tribal. Transfer can be exercised only to the extent to which it has been conferred and only in favour of other tribal who is a resident of the same pargana.

Scheduled Area Regulation (1969)

This Regulation deals more effectively with the problem of land alienation. It empowers the Deputy Commissioner to enquire into any case of illegal alienation having taken place within 30 years (as compared to the period of 12 years under the Limitation Act) set it aside and restore the land to the original raiyat. This regulation is applicable to entire scheduled area, new co-terminus with the Sub-Plan area.

Since the introduction of the Regulation and until March 1978 about 22,000 cases were filed out of which 11,000 cases were dispensed with in favour of the affected parties restoring thereby an area of 14 thousand acres. A simple survey is being conducted to assess the extent of land alienation in the Sub-Plan area. The magnitude differs from place to place.

Debt Relief Act

In December 1974, the State Govt. had promulgated the Bihar Scheduled Caste, Scheduled Tribes, Backward Classes (Annexure I) and Denotified Tribes, Debt Relief Act and the Bihar Money Lenders Act, 1974. But the Debt Relief Act, provision was made to grant relief to the Scheduled Castes/Tribes and Backward Classes who owned not more than one acre of land. The debts of all such persons belonging to the above classes were liquidated with the exception of Governmental and institutional loan.

The Debt Relief Act has no doubt put some curb on the activities of private money-lenders but there are still many unknown transactions going on unabated in the area particularly in the absence of easy availability of credit from Govt. and other sources for the pressing needs of the people for agriculture or other purposes.

Bonded Labour

In the Sub-Plan area, bonded labour system has been identified in the district of Palamau. With the promulgation of the Bonded Labour System (Abolition) Ordinance, 1975 by the Centre, the bonded labourers have been freed and their mortgaged lands restored to them. According to the Government figures 1800 bonded labourers have been freed in the district of Palamau; a sum of Rs. 61,211 on account of their debt-money has been liquidated and 34.14 acres of land which were mortgaged have been restored to them.

Administrative Structure

The administrative structure has undergone considerable change in the tribal areas. The Chotanagpur and Santhal Parganas Autonomous Development Authority was constituted in 1971 by an Act for the speedy development of the tribal region of the State. By an amendment, the Chotanagpur and Santhal Parganas Development Authority, which became the focal institution in the Sub-Plan area, was trifurcated into three Authorities namely the South Chotanagpur, the North Chotanagpur and the Santhal Parganas Development Authorities. Each Authority is expected to prepare perspective and short-term (five year and annual) plan for the all-round development of the respective region. The new Authorities have yet to take up the role in full measure. For implementation of the Sub-Plan a unified chain of administrative command has been conceived from the State down to the Project level.

State Level

At the State level the Planning Department handles administration of the Sub-Plan. The Development Commissioner, as the Co-ordinator of all the development activities of the State, Superintendents and Co-ordinates the activities of the Sub-Plan as well.

Regional Level

At the regional level, the State Govt. has appointed a Regional Development Commissioner with headquarters at Ranchi. He has been placed in overall charge of all the development programmes of the region with powers of supervision, control and co-ordination of all the development works in the same manner as the Development Commissioner does for the State as a whole. In essence he is the chief representative of the State Government in the area with powers of Principal Secretary to Government in all the Development Departments. However, many Departments of the Secretariat at Patna have not yet decentralised the work of formulation of plans and schemes at the regional level. Plans and schemes continue to be formulated in the Patna Secretariat. The purpose of a separate tribal Sub-Plan, a local Secretariat with adequate delegation of powers and an implementation hierarchy has not yet been fully achieved.

Project level

At the Project level, the project authority comprises of a Project Officer in the rank of Additional District Magistrate and a Project Implementation Committee consisting of the Deputy Commissioner of the district as Chairman and the concerned district technical heads as members. The Project Officer has been made fully responsible for the implementation of the Integrated Tribal Development Projects (I.T.D.P.) in his Meso area under the guidance and control of the Deputy Commissioner of the district. He is assisted by the Sub-Divisional Officer of the concerned Sub-division who acts as Additional Project Officer of the I.T.D.P. The Project Officer is expected to exercise administrative, operational and disciplinary control over all the development functionaries at the Sub-divisional level. He is the Secretary of the Project Implementation Committee at the district level of which Deputy Commissioner is the Chairman. The Project Officer has to make use of the existing infra-structure at the Sub-divisional and blocks levels for formulation of Project Plans and implementation of schemes. But this arrangement has not become fully effective and as a result plan formulation and implementation of schemes often run into difficulties.

III

CONSTITUTIONAL SAFEGUARDS

The Constitution makers were guided by the history of the Indian Administration and had thought out well-defined safeguards for the welfare of these people which have been incorporated in the constitution. When we read the Indian Constitution, we come across the word, "special" when there is a reference to the scheduled castes or scheduled tribes. These special provisions are incorporated in Part III on Fundamental Rights, Part IV on Directive Principles of State Policy. Part X on the scheduled and tribal Areas, Part XII on Finance, Property etc., Part XVI on special provisions relating to certain classes and lastly the schedules Fifth and Sixth.[23]

Due to lack of space we can narrate only some of the important provisions.

Tribes got a concession under article 164(i) proviso that there should be a Minister in charge of Tribal Welfare in Orissa, Bihar and Madhya Pradesh though it does not necessarily mean that the Minister should himself belong to the tribes.[24] There is provision for the appointment of a special officer for them, called commissioner, at the centre, who is to be appointed by the President with special duties of investigating all matter relating to the safeguards provided for the Scheduled Castes and Scheduled Tribes and reporting to the President upon the working of the constitutional safeguards. This Commissioner submits his reports annually detailing all that has been observed by him personally and through his Assistant Commissioners in the matter of working of these safeguards. It has also framed special welfare schemes exclusively for them with the objective of bringing these tribes on par with the rest of the Indian people. The President is also empowered to issue directions and to appoint a Committee of the Constitution to investigate their conditions in the States (Art. 359). Under this provision the President appointed Dhebar Committee in 1960 which made its report by the end of 1961. This Committee had unanimously held that while the constitutional provisions for safeguarding their interests were adequate, the hope that these would be effectively followed had not materialised. Its recommendations included inter alia the creation of a separate ministry at the centre. A similar suggestion was earlier made by the All-India convention of Scheduled Caste and Scheduled Tribes legislators held in Hyderabad in February, 1961, inaugurated by Prime Minister Nehru.

Right to freedom guaranteed under Article 19, has been restricted under clause (5). This restriction has considerably stopped the transfer of property from the Scheduled Tribes to non-tribals. It is under this provision that tribal people here in Chotanagpur, are holding land unlike their brethren elsewhere thanks to the Chotanagpur Tenancy Act which restricted the transfer of land from the tribals.

Provisions for administration and control of the Scheduled Areas and Scheduled Tribes have been incorporated in the Fifth

Schedule. Under it the Governor of each State having the Scheduled Areas therein is required to submit to the President a report regarding the administration of the Scheduled Areas. Tribes Advisory Councils have been empowered to issue notifications about application or non-application of Acts to the Scheduled Areas and make regulations for peace and good for government of the Scheduled Areas. In fact, the Constitution divided these tribes into three classes—into those living in the Plains, those living in compact areas with the administrative jurisdiction of the States, and those living in the Assam Hill States. The first kind get no special safeguards except, a tacit recognition that an "Adibasi carries his law with him where he goes". The second are treated on the same footing as those of the 'partially excluded' and 'excluded areas' of the 1935 Act, and their problem is tackled by Schedule V which gives them exemption from the operation of certain laws made by the Parliament and the State Legislatures. The problem of Assam Hill Tribes is a special one, and they are given the greatest autonomy possible both in social and administrative matters, by the VI Schedule.

The major forces that have been released through the constitutional provisions relating to reservation of seats for the Scheduled Tribes in the House of the People and the State Legislative Assembly have left an indeliable imprint upon the Scheduled Tribes particularly in respect of political rights. An Asur in the most inaccessible area in Bihar has got one vote while the Prime Minister has also one vote. Researches on tribal political behaviour by Vidyarthi and Sachchidananda reveal that tribals are very much conscious of their voting rights.

IV

SOME RECENT PROBLEMS

Though tribals have protested several times against Britishers in the past and several great rebellions are in the recorded history of tribals, they have been peaceful by and large since Independence. This peace may be due to many reasons. This may be just a lull before a whirlwind. Or, this may be due to many programmes of Indian or Bihar Government in amelioration of the living conditions of the tribals.

But in 1973 in southern part of Bihar, an uncommon and unprecedented rebellion was seen under the leadership of Sibhu Soren and Binod Bihari Mahto. The prelude to the rebellion was seen in butchering a Sub-Inspector of Police named Ghatak of Topchanchi Thana, Distt. Dhanbad. This Inspector of Police was not a regular recruit but a promotee from the D.I.G. office, where he was probably a stenō of the D.I.G. Ghatak proceeded in a tribal area to capture a criminal. By this time Tribals of Dhanbad, Hazaribagh, Giridih and Santhal Pargana were wanted in several forceful harvesting cases. Ghatak was captured by an unruly mob of Adivasis and butchered mercilessly. It is said that his body was cut into a thousand pieces and thrown to crows and vultures. Others say that as supreme revenge the Adivasi themselves chewed every part of his flesh. However, whatever may be the case one thing is quite clear; the corpse of the Sub-Inspector of Police remained traceless to the entire police force. Binod Bihari Mahto was arrested as he was accused in several cases and government had a premonition that he had some hand in instigating the murderer. Binod Bihari Mahto remained in confinement for a long time. When tribals felt that Binod Bihari would not be set free by government they became ready to procure him by force under the leadership of Sibbu Soren. They learned that Mahto was confined at Giridih Jail. In December of 1974 Santhals and Tribals from Giridih, Hazaribagh, Dhanbad Distt. and Santhal Pargana came on foot at P.W.D. ground, Giridih which is situated in front of Giridih Jail. More than ten thousand Adivasis took part in this show of strength. They were remarkably peaceful and disciplined. There was a rumour that they would attack the sentry of the jail to procure Mahto. The Administrator took vent of this and light machine gun was ordered to take position on the Jail's gate. The slogan of the Santhal was *Jail ka Tala Tutega Binod Bihari Chutega*. (The lock of the jail would be broken Mahto would be free). The position became quite tense and anything could happen. However, the Deputy Commissioner of Giridih handled the challenge tactfully and became successful in convincing them that the disputed prisoner had been transferred to Bhagalpur Jail. Then they decided to withdraw. Santhal and tribes returned to their houses seeming well satisfied. When I asked some of the adivasis returning from the procession, what had happened in their meeting, they did not know the above mentioned things. Surprisingly they replied, "Indira Ne Mafi Mang Liya". (Indira Gandhi apologised to our leaders).

One more important case occurred at Giridih Distt., Pirtand Thana, in village Beldiha. Adivasis had forcefully harvested the grain from the local Mahajan's fields, which brought court cases on their heads. It was in 1974 B.M.P. and C.R.P. along with a magistrate Sri Sastri proceeded to arrest the wanted criminals. Adivasis by this time had tasted blood. Again they attacked the police force. Before attacking they beat Dugdugia. When Police force was attacked the B.M.P. and C.R.P. fired several rounds in their self defence wounding a couple of Adivasis and arresting 36 of them. All India Radio reported that in the firing 3 Adivasis had died. Sibbhu Soren in an interview with the correspondent of the *Illustrated Weekly* published on 8 April, 1979 has accused the police of rape and the weekly came out with the photograph of the raped women. Since no judicial enquiry has been ordered the reality still hangs in mystery.

In 1974 and 1975, a large number of Adivasis came out in procession armed with axes and *farsas*. Their women folk used to cut the paddy and they used to be by the side of the field. If the owner would prevent them they would cut him into pieces. These fields used to be the fields of the Adivasis long sold either by the forceful harvester himself or by his father. Their cry was that the above mentioned land was theirs and it had been fraudulently taken away by the *dikkus*. When the administrator became strict in emergency this was stopped. It has not occurred again. However, cases and counter-cases are still going on in the court of law.

V

PEOPLE'S RESPONSE TO DEVELOPMENT PROGRAMMES

An analysis of the various programmes for development of rural and tribal areas from the point of view of people's participation reveals that since their inception they have gone through for different phases. They started in the year 1952 as government programmes. This was the official phase. With the establishment of Block Advisory Committees people were associated with the programme to a certain extent. This could be termed as the advisory phase.

Following the recommendations of the Balwantray Mehta Committee report, these advisory committees were converted into Panchayat Samities under Panchayati Raj legislation enacted in various States. There came into being a hierarchy of Panchayati Raj institutions from the village level to the district consisting of a three-tier system—the Gram Panchayat, the Panchayat Samiti and Zila Parishad. This phase of the community development programme has come to be known as Panchayati Raj phase.

Third phase may be called the Community Development phase. From the very beginning it has been essentially a programme of education. Its overall aim has been to assist in the building of a modern nation, bringing all its potential resources into line with modern, political, economic and social standards as established in the majority of democratic countries.[25] The significance of our programme of community development lies in our effort to arouse the rural community to democratic action so that it will function like a healthy community. Which takes initiative in utilising the resources which are available and in procuring and creating new resources which may not be easily forthcoming.[26]

The fourth phase can be called the Sub-Plan and Antodaya phase in which poorest of Adivasis are being given some capital to start their living. Various other loans are also being distributed by Nationalised banks. Let us see what our authorities on tribal administration feel about these governmental measures and how far they are successful.

L. P. Vidyarthi says,

"Our study suggests that changes in outlook and economic activities are more influenced by urban centres and much less by Community Development Programmes. It appears that in isolated tribal village Community Development schemes are not accepted enthusiastically for want of adequate awareness and because of the predominance of tradition orientation of the illiterate tribal people. The isolation of the villages and the tradition orientation of the people are usually broken with the establishment of certain modern institutions run by some educated and urbanised individuals like village schools (In Senaguta, Bhandra and Chaghra); Health centre and co-operative societies in Fhudi; Graingola in Kumharia; Weaver Co-operative Society in Sevagutu. These urban institutions, wherever present, become clearing houses of the respective villages which also serve as isolated models of urban influences in and around the villages".[27]

"This pattern of change may be looked at from many angles. When we idealise the traditional Adivasi culture, we record numerous traits of Adivasi style of life—simplicity. homogeneity, honesty, co-operation, group identification optimism etc. Then we note that these values of tribal life are being fast replaced by heterogeneity, individualisation secularisation, hypocracy etc., and emotionally feels disturbed".[28]

Similar reports have been received from tribal villages in Chotanagpur studied by Sachchidananda. He goes on to explain the reasons also. He says, "The failure to make an impact was also due to cumbersome administrative machinery, the kind of checks and balances which we inherited from British days. The general assumption was that all persons below are dishonest. So efficient administration was made synonymous with ever increasing inspections. Finding faults and discovering lacunae in the works of the subordinate was the main objective of the inspection. The V L.W. was inspected by the Extension Supervisor, the Extension Supervisors were inspected by the B.D.O. and the Distt. and Sub-divisional level officers, the B.D.O. was constantly subjected to inspection by the S.D.O., Collector, District Level Officer, District Development Officer etc. and so on. There was a general atmosphere of fear, suspicion and distrust instead of encouragement, sound technical guidance and suggestions for improvement. The rules of procedure, financial powers and too much of centralization also led to enormous delays in the execution of the programmes. All these rules were made for those days, when development was not in the air, they have become long out of dates".[29]

The U.N. mission made a special study of the development programme in relation to scheduled tribes. The mission made study in the Chotanagpur Division of Bihar where they visited a few Multipurpose Blocks. The mission also held discussions with the individuals and groups in M.P., Orissa and Bombay. While the mission has not made any specific observations regarding the attitudinal change and other social changes in the tribal community, it does mention some obstacles which were working in the progress of development work in tribal areas. These relate to geographical isolation, health conditions, educational backwardness and the low economic condition of living due to a poor subsistence economy. Some people are not convinced about its necessity and utility and believe that it has been thrust by government on the people. Some believe that the programme benefits the officials more than the people.

However, there is a brighter side also. Carl Tangler observed that villagers were no longer lethargic and that they were eager for any change that meant progress in their production, in their amenities and in their levels of living. He thought that the villagers had changed more rapidly than the concepts of some national leaders about the villagers.[30] An opinon survey of rural leaders and officials conducted by the Indian Institute of Public Opinion in June 1964 brings out that there is an appreciable degree of awareness of the responsibilities and duties by the leaders. They are however more aware of the development programmes but not so much of the social aspects like uplift of the weaker section. Leadership in the rural areas is progressing towards the younger and more educated. The people feel that the benefits have been in the form of agricultural amenities, communication and educational facilities, but they hardly feel that the people have become "more co-operative" and less "faction minded". Surprisingly the survey shows that a majority of those who think that some sections have got more than they deserve, hold that it is Harijans and Scheduled Castes/Tribes who have benefited more than others from development programmes.[31]

The P.E.O's, report of 1957 in its Chapter "Some Aspects

of Social Change" mentions that even though the project programmes did not provided adequately for improvement of the economic and social condition of the under-privileged groups, changes had however taken place under the impact of the project and other development programmes. The development programmes brought an increase in employment, irrigation facilities were extended and there was some increase in agricultural production. The facilities of drinking water wells and schools were extended which helped in narrowing the social distance. Generally speaking the P.E.O. observed that in the majority of the cases to traditional leaders were from receptive to the new opportunities. They participated in the programme and helped in mobilising the requisite effort. Emergence of new leadership was noticed in a number of villages.[32]

VI

CONCLUSION AND SUGGESTIONS

The tribal problem is a problem which raises the fundamental issue—the issue of the establishment of a social order founded on equality of opportunities and the elimination of exploitation. Thus the fundamental problems of the tribal population are economic-political. There are problems such as the security of job, a decent standard of living, easy accessibility to the resources of the civilised life, the acquisition of education which can enable them to decide what customs, what rituals and what aesthetic cultural elements they should retain, eliminate or absorb from their culture and various others.[33] The Development programmes of the government have done many things. Yet there are many things which are yet to be done. There is no need to be complacent. We can summarise our aims for improvement in tribal areas under the following heads.

A Change in the Orientation of Civil Service

Among the developing countries of the Third World, India enjoys the comparative advantage of being equipped with an administrative "Steelframe" which has served its diverse politico-economic needs over several decades. In the wake of launching of a number of programmes of rural development, however, its forms as well as norms need to be re-aligned in order to cope with the emerging challenges of administering a large number of projects and schemes scattered over a large area unto which its penetration was hitherto minimal.[34]

The first characteristic of the Indian Administrative system which would inescapably strike any observer is its orientation towards revenue functions, viz., collection of taxes and non-tax demands of the Government. Even after the attainment of India's independence this basic functional orientation has not been replaced by an alternative ethos.[35] India, in fact, has launched upon a wide-ranging portfolio or rural development projects and programmes without having to de novo fabricate state-village delivery systems. It has been further noticed that the same person gets a more respectful audience when he visits a village in his capacity as collector than when he goes around as a development administrator trying to push through programmes of agricultural development or adult education. We feel that it is high time that we should reorganise our "Steelframe" in such a manner that it can match with the challenging task of development administration with great care and precision with beneficial results. Another area in which significant realignment is needed is the steady erosion of the status and authority of the field-staff and functional Directorates while the State level Secretariats are increasingly taking on the responsibility for issuing detailed executive orders leaving very little discretion to the functionaries actually engaged in development administration.[36] Sachchidananda was also pointing the same thing when he criticized vehemently the system of inspection, supervision and checks and balances, which has been discussed in the previous pages. The only solution that can work in this regard is to decentralize the development works. The administrative case for administrative decentralization is, in fact, far stronger than the political arguments in favour of "democratic decentralization" which were given an enthusiastic reception upon the publication of Balwantrai Mehta Study Teams report in November 1957 but were either indifferently implemented or gradually ignored.

The new Public Administration is openly anti-bureaucratic. Its advocates want to debureaucratise the government and replace the bureau with a more flexible, humane, democratic form of organisation.[37] Our scheduled tribe brethren also seem to be anti-bureaucratic. Unless tribals feel that Bureaucracy is not their masters but their servant, we cannot expect co-operation and participation from them. We can change their attitude by making Bureaucracy, "a representative bureaucracy". Now, what is "representative bureaucracy" ? "Briefly stated, the theory of representative bureaucracy advocates that the socio-economic composition of bureaucracy should resemble the society as a whole and every social group should have its own spokesman in the bureaucracy to 'guard' the group interest".[38] No doubt there are reservations for them in the central and in the State Government services. But their representation in the Indian bureaucracy has not been scientifically studied by the scholars. Writing in the Indian Journal of Public Administration Sri Jha rightly suggests, "It would be worthwhile to study the scheduled caste and other minority entrants into Indian bureaucracy, not only from the point of view of the specific sections within these minority groups from which the recruits come. But also their value congruence. Do such recruits 'actively' represent the minority groups ? This present an extremely important and interesting area of research on Indian bureaucracy.[39]

One of our major problems of C.D. Programme in tribal area, as mentioned in the report of the Government of India, is the lack of suitable trained personnel to serve as village level workers and Block Officers. Living conditions are hard, amenities such as education for the children are poor, the personnel do not know the language and they cannot communicate to the tribal groups.[40] Sri Jha says, "Bureaucracy is recruited from a restricted social category and retains its "elitist" character".[41] Bhabhari also supports this thesis.[42] He adds "of 273 I.A.S. recruited in two years 1966-67 and 1968-69 over 70 per cent came from an urban background . . ." One of the most frequently mentioned criticism of the programmes of development in India has been that it has relied entirely on the urban middle class bureaucracy, whereas the programmes are to be implemented mostly in the rural areas, affecting the poor and illiterate peasants.[43] We suggest that tribals should be given due share in Civil Service and other services too, so that the entire tribal mass should not feel alienated.

Understanding Tribal Culture

We have already discussed that there is an integral relationship between culture and administration. Unfortunately, we try to administer Adivasis without understanding their culture. If one cannot possibly drive a car only because one has one and know only how to press the accelerator, how can an administrator administer a people without understanding them ? Sri Bage has rightly said, "As an administrator and as a man among the masses, I know why a government machinery of planning fails. It fails mostly due to lack of proper understanding of the people and their problems. And a greater danger is the fact that they think that they know the people.[44] If one goes to Bishunpur Block one finds the houses built by government for adivasis. In Beti areas, Birhors have made huts adjacent to their houses. They are sentimentally and traditionally attached to a hut. This may look preposterous. But a Birhor is used to it. At the same time they dislike a spacious house. Some Birhors have abandoned ventilated houses and have shifted to smaller and dark house. At many places government houses are abandoned. Adivasis do not live there due to one pretext or the other. Though the government's initiative is praiseworthy it all fails due to ignorance of understanding the culture of these Adivasis by the bureaucrats.

We, therefore, sincerely feel that only those bureaucrats should be posted at tribal areas who know their culture. In fact, Anthropology should be introduced as a compulsory subject at the time of training of the personnels. Those personnel who learn tribal language should be awarded with extra-increments.

Reasonable Constitutional Protection

The founding fathers of the Indian Constitution have given several protection to Scheduled Tribes. But there are also some inimical provisions. K.V. Rao, rightly says, "By far the most inimical are the provisions contained in article 44 and items 1 and 2 of the concurrent list in the VII Schedule regarding uniform civil and criminal code. Culture and law cannot easily be separated in the case of the Tribes; and it will take a long time before these people can be educated in this so called civilised law of ours".[45]

We can cite an example to make this case clear. An aboriginal girl was married by a reforming society to a tribal boy against her wish. In the nuptial chamber she killed him because he 'violated her modesty'. A caste Panchayat held in the tribal area exonerated her as it was allowed by their custom. But the police charged her for murder. And a jury consisting of plains-men found her guilty and she was sentenced to death by a process of law and procedure which she could never understand.

It is barbarous to impose a system of law which under-developed people cannot understand. Either law should be made very simple in tribal areas or tribals should be developed to that a stage where they can cope with other people. If there can be a separate "Muslim law", why cannot be there a separate "Adiwasi law"?

Giving Due Share in Finance

Bihar as a whole is a deficit State in food. Tribal areas are more a deficit zone. But they are very rich in minerals. Recent researches reveal that yet vast minerals are still to be exploited by the government. But the provisions of the constitutions are so unsatisfactory and deficient that the income accrued by the minerals are snatched away by the centre. Here there is no Ganga in Chotanagpur and no Bhakhra. We cannot match in agriculture with Punjab and Haryana. We can beat and we actually beat all the provinces in minerals. But it is all Central share. In tribal areas, the central has become, "the banker and the collecting agent for the States".

Recently the N.D.C. set up a committee to consider the question of transfer of larger resources to the States and for a revision of the Gadgil formula. The N.D.C. committee which comprised mostly of the Chief Ministers was unanimous in its demand for a larger transfer of fiscal resources to the states.[46]

We feel that Centre-State financial relations are quite unsatisfactory more so in tribal areas of Bihar. In tribal areas a number of development programmes and project are yet to be started. We depend mostly on the central assistance. We have already seen that in a game of power-politics mostly the vocal sections get benefits. It is common experience that the States, particularly the deficit ones, are facing numerous difficulties in getting central assistance. A hostile central government may not be eager in sanctioning central assistance. Tribals still have not learnt the game of power politics. So they lose their dues. Government, generally listens when there is strong demonstration. Our suggestion is, in Tribal areas Centre must share the income collected from that areas either from minerals or by central taxes. Our tribals are proud people. They want their share and not gift.

The Tribal areas are not mandates but trusts and the trust administration is to be carried on with the active participation of the Tribals themselves. Let the tribals feel that the Administration is for them, of them and by them.

REFERENCES

1. Nirmal Kumar Bose, "India's Eastern Tribes" *Tribe, Caste and Religion*, Macmillan, 1977, p. 57.
2. B.M. Pandey. "Development Schemes as Factors of Change in Tribal Areas," *Journal of Social Research*, (Deptt. of Anthropology, Ranchi University), Vol. XI; No. 2, September 1968, p. 35.
3. Andre Beteille, "The Definition of Tribe", *Tribe, Caste and Religion*, (Macmillan, India), p. 7.
4. Ibid, p. 10.
5. L.D. White, "Public Administrators" *New York Encyclopaedia of the Social Sciences* (Vol. 1, 1954 Ed), p. 440.
6. Dwight Waldo, *The Study of Public Administration* (New York, Random House, 1961), p. 11.
7. Andre Beteille, "Definition of Tribe", *Tribe, Caste and Religion, 77*, p. 11.
8. Venkat Rao, *A Century of Tribal Politics*, (S. Chand, 1976), p. 45.
9. Dwight Waldo, *The Study of Public Administration*, p. 11.
10. N.K. Bose, "Traditions Die Hard", *Journal of Social Research*, (Anthropology, Ranchi University), Vol. VII, No. 1-2 March-September 1964, p. 29.
11. B.M. Pandey, "Development Schemes as Factors of Change in Rural Areas": *Journal of Social Research*, Vol. XI, No. 2, September 1968, p. 45.
12. A.R. Desai, "Tribes in Transition", *Tribe, Caste and Religion*, 1977, p. 16.
13. Ibid.
14. Ibid.

15. Sachin Sen, "Impact of Modern Forces on Caste in India", *Journal of Social Research*, Vol. VII, No. 1-2, March-September 1964, p. 117.
16. A.R. Desai, "Tribes in Transition," *Tribe, Caste and Religion*, p. 27.
17. B.M. Pandey. "Development Schemes as Factors of Change in Rural Areas," *Journal of Social Research*, (September 1968), p. 49.
18. (a) The Planning Commission set up Task Force on "Development of Tribal Areas", 1972.
    (b) Working Group on Identification of Tribal Development Area and Less Developed Tribal Communities (Chairman Dr. L.P. Vidyarthi).
    (c) Working Group on Legislative and Administrative Set-up (Chairman Dr. B.K. Roy Burman).
    (d) Working Group on General Programmes and Area-wise Programmes on Infrastructure and Social Services in Tribal Areas. (Chairman Sri K.V. Natarajan).
    (e) Personnel Policy in Tribal Areas (Chairman Sri R.N. Haldipur).
19. K. Shanmugavelayuthan, A Sub-Plan Approach to Tribal Development, *The Indian Journal of Social Work*, Vol. XL, No. 2, July, 1979, Tata Institute of Social Sciences, Deonar.
20. B.D. Sharma "Administration for Tribal Development," *The Indian Journal of Public Administration*, Vol. XXIII No. 3, July-September 1977.
21. Preparation of Sub-Plans for Tribal Regions (Guidelines issued by the Planning Commission), Govt. of India, Ministry of Home Affairs, New Delhi, 1975, pp. 9-10.
22. For details see, "Annual Sub-Plan for Tribal Areas of Bihar" 1980-81 (Draft) Govt. of Bihar, p. 4.
23. K.K. Leuva, "Impact of the Constitutional Safeguard on the Scheduled Tribes", *Journal of Social Research*, September 1964 and K.V. Rao, Parliamentary Democracy of India (World Press, Calcutta), 1965, p. 209.
24. K.V. Rao, reports in his book (page 215) that the present practice mostly is to select him from Scheduled Tribes Members only.
25. Govt. of India, Ministry of C.D. & C. Report of a Community Development Evaluation Mission in India, p. 47.
26. Report of the Teams for the Study of Community Project and National Extension Service, Vol. II, p. 96.
27. L.P. Vidyarthi, "The Changing Face of Tribal Bihar", *Journal of Social Research*, September 1964, p. 59.
28. Ibid.
29. Sachchidananda, 'Community Development and the Tribals", *Journal of Social Research*, September 1964, p. 74.
30. Carl Taylor, "A Critical Analysis of India's Community Development Programme," p. 57.
31. Indian Institute of Public Opinion, Public Opinion Surveys, October and November 1964, p. 55.

32. Govt. of India, P.E.D. Evaluation, Report of the Working of C.D. Projects, April p. 64.
33. A.R. Desai, "Tribes in Transition", *Tribe, Caste and Religion*, 77 p. 28.
34. P.C. Mathur, "Administrative Re-alignments for Rural Development : Some Policy Issues in the Context of India", *Indian Journal of Political Science*, Volume 40, No. 1, March 1979, p. 66.
35. Ibid., p. 68.
36. Ibid., p. 72.
37. T. Golembiewski, "Public Administration as a Developing Discipline" New York 1977, Review Article by Jain, R.B. in, *The Indian Journal of Public Administration*, Vol. XXV, No. 1, Jan-March 1979.
38. S.N. Jha, "Representative Bureaucracy : An Indicator of Political Development," *The Indian Journal of Public Administration*, Vol. XXV, No. 2, 1979, p. 327.
39. Ibid., p. 329.
40. B.M. Pandey, *Development Schemes as Factors of Change in Tribal Areas*, p. 55.
41. S.N. Jha, "Representative Bureaucracy", *Journal of Public Administration*, Vol. XXV, No. 2, June 1979, p. 330.
42. Bhabhari, "The Indian Administrative Service, Milieu Challenges and Response", *Administrators in a Changing Society* (National-Delhi) 1972, p. 43.
43. Haridwari Rai, and S.P. Singh, "Indian Bureaucracy : A Care for Representativeness", *Indian Journal of Public Administration*, Vol. XIX, No. 1, January-March 1973.
44. S.K. Bage, "Anthropologist and Tribal Administration," *Journal of Social Research*, Vol. VIII, No. 1, March 1965, p. 13.
45. K.V. Rao, *Parliamentary Democracy of India*, p. 230.
46. *The Times of India*, August, 23, 1978.

NINETEEN

A. C. Sinha

ETHNIC IDEOLOGY AND RURAL VIOLENCE IN INDIA

IN THE early anthropological literature little distinction was made between cultural, racial and ethnic phenomenon. This resulted in a bio-cultural conception of ethnicity. Among such efforts one of the most important may be identified with M.G. Smith's definition of ethnicity in pre-colonial Africa as

> . . . . common provenance and distinctiveness as a unit internal uniformities and external distinctiveness of biological stock, perhaps of language, kinship, culture, cult and other institutions.
>
> (*Smith, M.G. 1969 : 104-05*)

Theoretical and methodological implications of this definition are so grave that no serious researches have been made keeping this in view. In this context, Frederick Barth's analysis must be mentioned. For him an ethnic group in anthropological literature is generally understood to designate a population which (i) is largely biologically self-perpetuating; (ii) shares fundamental cultural values realised in overt unity in cultural forms; (iii) makes up a field of communication and interaction; (iv) has a membership which identifies itself, and is identified by others, as constituting a category, distinguishable from other categories of the same order.

After enumerating the above points of view, he rejects the "traditional proposition" that race=culture=language=

(nation) as removed from the empirical situation. He suggests "no simple one-to-one" relationship between ethnic units and cultural similarities and differences. For him ethnicity is ". . . . in terms of his (person's basic most general identity presumptively determined by this origin and background. To the extent that actors use ethnic identities to categorise themselves and others for the purpose of interactions, they form ethnic groups". He further clarifies his concept :

> Since belonging to an ethnic basic identity, it also implies being a certain kind of person, having that basic identity, it also implies a claim to be judged, and to judge one self, by those standards that are relevant to that identified.
>
> (*Barth, F. 1969* : *14*)

In this way, he rejects the first three formulations put forth by him in favour of the fourth one. It is to be noted here that for Barth ethnicity is one of a poly-ethnic type of statuses.

Undoubtedly ethnicity persists in those societies that have been levelled as complex, multiple, multi-ethnic segmented, heterogeneous, urban, industrial, pre-industrial or plural. An ethnic group in such a larger society discovers its culture different from the latter. Members of such an ethnic group feel themselves, are considered to be, and are bound together by a common bond of race, nationality or culture. Thus, Schermerhorn identifies an ethnic group :

> . . . collectivity within a larger society having real or putative common ancestry, memories of a shared historical past, and a cultural focus on one or more symbolic elements defined as the epitome of their peoplehood. . . . A necessary accompaniment is some consciousness of kind among members of the group.
>
> (*Schermenhorn, R.A., 1970* : *12*)

If added to this the economic dimension, ethnic complexity may clearly be discerned. Thus, Whitten means by ethnicity those

> patterns of human interaction, which form the basis for categorical social relations with observable, or projected economic consequences. (Such) categorical social relations are characterized by stereo-typical criteria as distinct from structural relations which are characterized by extent exchange patterns between interacting individuals. Land access is intimately tied to the economic consequences of ethnic status.
>
> (*Whitten, N.E., 1976 : 60*).

From socio-economic dimension emerges a concern for maintenance of ethnic identities and boundaries. For that ethnicity is used as an ideology "... ethnicity is an ideology of and for value dissensus and disengagement from an inclusive socio-political arena, that is, for pursuing major values deemed not shared by others in the arena. I distinguish economic ideologies first from class ideologies, which... assume or call for value consensus, which demand the achievement of values and scarce goods deemed SHARED by the total arena... To the contrary, an ethnic ideology says in effect that we do not agree on the intimate values (or goals, or ends) of this system, and we want to be left alone (perhaps with enough resources) to pursue" own ends, whatever you may be doing. Applied to others, it says,

> we will treat you as if you are pursuing different values for those we have.
>
> (*Aronson, Dan R., 1976 : 14-15*)

Such ethnic identities have been used for political and cultural mobilization as a tool to gain a larger share of what is to be gained from a plural system . In this case, "ethnicity may save as the ideological basis for political mobilization, if the ethnic participants co-ordinate their activities for the pursuit of goods that are not commonly held by non-ethnics in the wider system.... Ethnicity as a means of cultural mobilization has structural properties when viewed from the perspective of social organisation and interaction. Thus, the researcher moves from the cultural cognitive domain of abstraction into the social domain when he focuses on the processes by which individual actors manipulate their ethnic identity for the purposes of social interaction and group formation" (Holzberg, C.S., 1976: 142). This leads to the conflict between "the needs of the ethnic groups as perceived by its leadership on the one hand and the conceptual and analytical pattern to which sociologists and anthropologists are socialized on the other" (Provinzano, James, 1976 : 385). Naturally, the ethnic groups continue to concern themselves with the development of ethnic consciousness and as adjunct to their organization.

Approaches to the Study of Ethnicity

A glance at the various definitions put forth by the individual scholars suggests that specific definitions were conceived mainly keeping in view the particular community being studied. In other words, there is no effort to conceive the ethnic phenomenon conceptually for universal or almost universal application. No doubt it is too difficult a task because of the ambiguity, complexity and lack of enough reliable data on ethnogenesis. That is why Despres finds "a theoretical framework capable of informing comparative ethnic studies" yet to emerge. However, some broad approaches for uncovering the ethnic complexities may be identified.

Subjective or Interactional Approach

No ethnic studies in the contemporary social sciences is complete without reference to Barth's study of Pathans and his theoretical formulations. He rejects the ambiguous and uncritical aspects of ethnicity and emphasizes the limits of interaction within a territorial boundary. Within a given locality where poly-ethnic complexity is confronted, there is a competition for limited resources. Who gets what and how depends on the relevant identity of the members vis-a-vis the community in question. For such identification of the membership to the ethnic communities, he adopts a subjective criteria, when he opines that a population "identifies itself, and is identified by others, as constituting a category distinguishable from other category". In his scheme of things ethnic groups are formed to the extent that actors use ethnic identities themselves and others for purpose of interaction. It also presupposes a set of rules governing situations of inter-ethnic contacts. Thus, he seems to have elected to conceptualize ethnicity as one of a poly-ethnic type.

> The presentation of this thesis remains couched in troublesome conceptual and epistemological ambiguities and, . . . research is too limited to sort out and model all of the variables that may be involved. Still, the data presented in support of this view have been sufficiently persuasive to warrant its further consideration.
>
> (*Despres, Leo, 1975* : *3*)

Objective or Cultural Approach to Multi-Ethnic Societies

As against Barth's subjectivist conception of ethnicity, objective criteria were suggested for identification of ethnic groups. At the same time, an exclusively objectivist or cultural conception of ethnicity was being considered equally unserviceable. This led to uncovering of the complex societies known as multi-ethnics. Furnivall, an economist and an administrator, may be termed as the pioneer of the study on pluralism. It was he who coined the term plural society to conceive the social and cultural divisions characteristic of South-East Asian societies (Furnivall, J.S., 1939 and 1948). Among the anthropologists, M.G. Smith emerged as the chief exponent of this approach in his study of the West Indies (Smith, S.G., 1956). In a similar way, Benedict studied the multi-ethnic society of Mauritius (Benedict, B., 1965) ; Kunstadter uncovered tribal minorities in South East Asia (Kunstadter, p. 1967) ; and Kuper and Smith analysed the pre-colonial and emergent post-colonial African socio-cultural scene (Kuper, Leo and M.G. Smith, 1969). In these studies, emphasis has been placed on the cultural differentiation of population units within an overall system of a multi-ethnic unit. This approach seems to have blurred the political factors that determine the functioning of complex societies.

> It emphasizes the importance of the values and institutions of the various groups in the society and the value

> consensus that exists between them. It also belittles the role that actual or potential force plays in arriving at the value consensus that permits societies to exist, even in the face of unequal distribution of their resources. There is little appreciation of the dissatisfaction of social groups with their societies. Conflict is ignored or minimized because groups are viewed as getting what they want out of their societies.
>
> (*Kuper, Leo, 1971 : 183*)

The above approach was also criticized not because of its emphasis on plural societies, but for impossibility of dissociating ethnicity from class status. There was also a methodological problem involved in it.

> Ethnicity is both an objective and a subjective phenomenon, the interrelation between these two aspects being, once again, an empirical question. Any conception of ethnicity which reduces either the objective or subjective side of it to an insignificant role distorts reality.... (Thus) ethnic groups are defined both by objective culture modalities of their behaviour (including most importantly their linguistic behaviour) and by their subjective views of themselves and each other.
>
> (*Van Den Berghe, PL. 1975 : 72*)

Ideological or Sociology of Dependence Approach

Operational difficulties with the first two approaches led to further conceptual exploration to establish ethnic identity. The most sophisticated attempt to account for the complex interplay of class and ethnicity is found in the "sociology of dependence" approach, which was applied to uncover Peruvian social milieu. This approach rejects the concept of plural society in the Peruvian context because it presupposes fairly well-drawn ethnic boundaries.

> The approach interprets Peruvian social structure in terms of multiple and interrelated chains of dependence between persons or groups of unequal power, wealth and status. These chains converge at the apex into the national and,

> beyond it, the international ruling oligarchy, as the structure of control is extremely centralized. Peruvian social structure is conceived as a multitude of binary relations of dependence and domination based on half a dozen or so interrelated dimensions.
>
> Besides centralization and inequality, these relations of dependence and domination are characterized by the fact that the closer one approaches the bottom of the pyramid, the more atomized and marginalized people are to national life; and, conversely, as one approaches the apex, the better interconnected and integrated the organs of domination.
>
> (*Van Den Berghe, P.L., 1975 : 73-74*).

Van Den Berghe gives four arguments in favour of accepting this approach to ethnicity as the most fruitful. Firstly, it anchors the study of ethnicity squarely in the matrix of relations of power and relations of production. Secondly, it rejects the cultural determinist approach that the Indian" are the heirs of the pre-Columbian civilizations and the *Mestizos* the carriers of Spanish culture. Thirdly, the concept by relating ethnicity to class, allows for a flexible description of a fluid and complex situation. And lastly, by avoiding the extreme subjectivism (which reduces ethnicity almost purely to the mutual perceptions and definitions of the situation by the members of the groups present), this approach links ethnicity to objective relations of power and of production.

The above approach goes closer to the Marxist bipolar class concept. However, there are suggestions to consider ethnicity as an ideology of and for value dissensus and disengagement from an inclusive socio-political arena. Aronson, who suggests this approach, views ideology of ethnicity distinct from the class ideology in which the latter presupposes pursuing major values deemed not shared by others in the arena.

> If ethnicity is an ideology for disengagement, then we need to give priority in the study of ethnicity not to boundaries once established, or to mechanisms of maintenance, but instead to independent variables which make or deepen the appeal of such ideologies, and the

> consequences of such ideologies for the arenas in which they arise. We must look harder than we have at the 'ethnic entrepreneurs' who formulate and manage the ideologies, and how situations are defined or reinforced to their advantage . . . This approach asks why and when ethnic groups come to be, and not how they, like all kinds of groups, build institutions elaborate an internal culture, define 'outsiders' and struggle to maintain themselves.
>
> (*Aronson, Dan R., 1975 : 17-18*)

James Provinzano, who studied the Chicano migrant farm workers in south-western United States of America, poses the same issue :

> If consciousness of deprivation and concomitant organization are not sufficient to unite the migrants in a labour organization, what other factor is available to an organizer ? The answer to that question is ideology. In this case, specifically, ethnic ideology or pride in one's ethnic identity.
>
> (*Provinzano, James, 1976 : 395*)

He pleads to the social scientists for making every effort to comprehend and incorporate the use of ideology by particular groups into the analytical tools devised to deal with the observed phenomena.

The Traditional Indian Social Structure

The Indian social structure is based on an innate social inequality. A person's location in the hierarchy is determined by his birth. It is divided into four *Varnas* and thousands of *Jatis*. So far as occupations are concerned they are identified very broadly at the level of Varnas. On the other hand for regulation of sex life the reference group is the Jatis. In this way while one comes across as the all India phenomenon of the Varnas, Jatis are regional in character. Some scholars such as M.N. Srinivas, Oscar Lewis, MacKim Marriott etc. have found distinct life styles pursued by various caste Jatis. So much so that not only their food habits, work specialisations and dresses vary, castes have their particular caste duties also. In certain parts of Karnataka and Andhra, in their villages various castes have their own religious shrines. It is common knowledge that various dominant castes had the privilege to use umbrellas, shoes, silken cloth, golden ornaments, riding horses, palanquins etc. These dominant caste groups made it a point to deny the use of the above articles by the members of lower caste groups. In certain parts of Tamil Nadu, Brahmins who inhabited parts of the villages were not even to be crossed in their paths by the members of the untouchable castes. In this way, one finds a more or less clear picture in which ritual and social status invariably went with economic prosperity. On the other hand, lower social status and ritual inferiority was further strengthened by denial of economic status to the lower castes. In this hierarchical structure, many occupations were privileges of various caste groups. These caste occupations had a loose religious ranking which is known as *Jajmani* system. This Jajmani system was evolved around ownership of landed property. There were owner cultivators and service castes such as the priests, barbers, carpenters, washermen, blacksmith, goldsmith, gardener cobbler and so on. The land ownership was basically feudal and even in social relations people were differentially treated. Such was the stable traditional social structure in which every centre had a secured occupation and they were happy to pursue their vocation.

Factors Responsible for Disturbing the Traditional Social Equilibrium

The picture of stable social structure presented above is inferred on the basis of secondary informations from the past. India is such a vast country in which social change had not occurred all over at the same rate and with the same speed everywhere. Even today one may find certain pockets of traditional Indian societies. However, it is more appropriate to term the Indian society as a transitional one. This transmission from the traditional to the present one has been caused because of the following factors :

(i) *Mass Media* : Availability of radio, television, microwave system, printing press, newspapers have made it possible to disseminate information quickly.

(ii) *Mass transportation* : Unlike in the past all weather metal roads, extensive railway system, airways and even waterways have made distance immaterial.

(iii) *Mass education system*: Unlike in the past when education was a caste occupation, the technique of education was oral and education was restricted. These days education has been made universal, easily available to any person with requisite qualification. Moreover, education has been liberated from any religious study.

(iv) *Demographic explosion* : Population in traditional India was stable because birth rates and death rates were both high. By the end of the 19th century because of the various steps taken by the Government the death rate was reduced, while the birth rate continued to be high. Thus one finds that during the last five decades, India's population has grown very high. This additional increase within two generations cannot be provided within the traditional rural peasant—feudal-villages. Thus the traditional social structure had to undergo some strain.

(v) *Emergence of the metropolitan cities* : Bombay, Calcutta, Delhi, Madras, Kanpur, Bangalore, Ahmedabad and Hyderabad have emerged as highly westernised, industrialised and metropolitan windows which attract people from the villages in search of new opportunity.

(vi) *Legal/Constitutional provisions* : Various provisions relating to providing facilities to the weaker sections of the society also go against the traditional social behaviour.

Dimension of Rural Violence

It is obvious from the above that the Indian society is passing through the phase of transition. The traditional caste roles are no more accepted now. Many of the caste occupations specially those which are of a dirty nature or of a polluting character, are now resented by the service castes. Many of the caste disabilities are no more tolerated. Religious sanctions to the social inequalities are being challenged by specially the lower status groups. On the other hand, cash privileges enjoyed by the higher social ritual status groups are not being surrendered. Thus, there is a heightened expectation from the least privileged groups. Thus there is a confrontation between the privileged and those who are denied these.

The constitutional/legal provisions made in favour of the weaker sections of the population have aroused new expectations, new awareness and a novel urge to change their age-old disabilities. Because of the above mentioned factors, these weaker sections are in a position to free themselves from the traditional sanctions. They may not have the ritual and social status, but they may have stable economic sources to buy a new status. But this new status may not be acceptable to the traditionally privileged dominant social groups. Thus, there is every likelihood of confrontation between those privileged and those who are denied it. So long as this confrontation is in existence in our transitioned society, caste conflict will continue. And the administrators have to take the problems of rural violence with foresight and tact.

SUGGESTED READINGS

Barth, F., *Ethnic Groups and Boundaries : The Social Organisation of Cultural Difference*, George Allen & Unwin, London 1969.

Despres, L., (ed), *Ethnicity and Resource Competition in Plural Societies*, Mouton, 1975.

Henry, *Ethnicity in America*, Mouton, Paris, 1975.

Sachchidananda, *The Harijan Elite*, Thompson Press, Delhi, 1976.

Singh, Y., *Modernisation of Indian Tradition*, Thompson Press, New Delhi, 1973.

Smith, M.G., *Social and Cultural Pluralism in Africa : Social Problem of Change and Conflict* (ed), R.L. van Den Berghe, Chandler, San Francisco, 1965.

Srinivas, M.N., *Social Change in Modern India*, 1966.

Srinivas, M.N., *Caste and Other Essays*, Asia Publishing House, Bombay 1962.

Vidyarthi, L.P. and Mishra, N., *Harijan Today*, Delhi, 1976.

TWENTY

A. R. N. Srivastava

ON THE SIGNIFICANCE OF TRIBAL ECONOMIC INSTITUTIONS IN DEVELOPMENT PROGRAMMES

THE AUTHOR aims in this module to assess the significance of an anthropological study of tribal economic institutions in development programmes. In so doing, he has assumed that the participants have a layman's acquaintance with social anthropology, and shall, therefore, refrain from explaining the way in which trained anthropologists set out their field study among the small rural/tribal groups. It is, however, important to state that even though a social anthropologist is interested in a particular aspect or institution of a society such as economy or kinship he tries *to view it in relation to the total system in which all aspects are constantly interacting.*

According to the problem at hand, in Part I of this module various units of the economic institution with reference to Indian tribes have been briefly discussed in elementary terms; in Part II a model of directed change has been outlined, and in the end, attempts have been made to "factor out" potential sources of resistance to desired/purposive change *and on the other, inhibit it.* In other words, the concluding part of the module may be viewed as practical conclusions one can arrive at the level of treatment.

I

UNITS OF ECONOMIC INSTITUTION DEFINED

Broadly speaking, the economic institution consists of the cultural knowledge people use to provide goods and services to meet biological and social wants (a word we will use to indicate both what people have to have as well as what they desire).

The heart of economic organization lies in the provision of *goods* and *services*. But, these two automatically do not apply themselves to the fulfilment of people's wants. There must be some organised way which allows individuals to obtain these things and use them effectively. The economic system provides this organization by defining two basic areas of activity, viz. a system of *production* and a system of *distribution*.

Aspects of Production

Aspects of production of any society are the rules which allocate resources, define a technology and organize labour.

People everywhere depend for their survival on a number of material resources (foodstuffs and raw materials) for manufacture of tools, shelters, etc. By allocating resources we mean the knowledge people use to assign rights to ownership and use of resources.

In the tribal world resources are held jointly by a group of people who exercise only partial rights over their disposition. However, in some cases private ownership also exists as in cases of personal belongings (material objects such as tools, etc.).

People in every society have a technology which consists of the cultural knowledge, the information that people possess about manufacture and use of tools. It also includes extraction and refinements of raw material.

The need to organize people's labour is felt in every society. No single person can carry on all tasks necessary to his biological and social life. These people everywhere organize their work by making a division of labour and forming units of production.

The Division of Labour

It refers to the rule that regulates the assignment of jobs to the people. Associated with division of labour are a number of attributes such as age, sex, physique, skill and wealth (status). Among the tribal people age and sex are the most important attributes governing economic tasks. In almost every society, from the Birhor, a forest-hunting tribe of Chotanagpur to the sub-urbanites of Ranchi, men and women perform some tasks exclusively.

Units of Production

It refers to the size and organization of the group of people responsible for producing something. The unit of production may include one person or a small group. In the tribal world this small production group is basically kinship-oriented, i.e. all the members of a nuclear or extended family work together under the direction of an elderly or experienced person who is usually the head of that kinship (family) group.

Distribution

In all societies the output of production are dispersed among the people. To facilitate this a set of strategies (for apportioning goods and services among the members of a group) is followed. We often call it economic exchange or transaction modes. These important media of economic exchange are reciprocity, market exchange and redistribution. While reciprocity is found in all societies the other two may or may not exist in the same society. In some economic systems all three exist concurrently.

Reciprocal Exchange

Based on the principle of reciprocity, it refers to the transfer of goods or services between two persons/groups based on their role obligations. Usually these two persons/groups are known to each other. Further, it is not dictated by maximization. Another important point associated with reciprocal exchange is that in some cases exchange of items is delayed by one party. It is called delayed reciprocal exchange.

Market Exchange

This mode of exchange refers to the transfer of goods and services based on price, supply and demand. Traditional tribal economy is not regulated by these market principles, however, in modern times, with the introduction of modern money whose operation is governed by the Central Agency (government), tribals have come to know the operation of market exchange though in a limited way.

Redistribution

It refers to the transfer of goods or services between a group of people and a central collecting source based on role obligation.

A crude type of redistribution system may be seen in our daily life itself. Imagine a joint family in which five adult sons are engaged in different works. At the end of the week each contributes something to the head (father) of the family. The latter distributes the collected items (cash, items etc.) among all the members of his family including the four sons. In cases such as this there is no requirement that people get back precisely the same amount of cash or items they contribute to the head (central agency). Modern state taxation is a good example of a redistributive system. Among the traditional people it works on occasions like birth, marriage and death ceremonies. For example, among the Oraon of Ranchi, every Oraon householder contributes rice and drink to the family of a person who has died. The bereaved family redistributes these things at a memorial feast to those who contributed them and also to the invited guests.

TRIBAL ECONOMY OF INDIA

The tribal people in India (numbering a little over 38 million in the latest census record) form 7 per cent of the total population of the country. They have remained a weaker section in the population throughout historical times. Tribes of India are classifiable under various headings: geography, physical characters, language, social organization, economy and religion.

A classification by the types of economic activities and arrangements according to their primary modes of living will be of our immediate concern. We may refer to Vidyarthi's scheme (1976) since it also takes care of the recent change-over among the tribals to industrial occupations ond white-collar jobs. It must, however, be noted that no two tribes possess precisely the same means of economic activities, and further, within a single tribe a number of secondary economic activities may coexist.

Hunters and Gatherers

In this are included those societies in which people employ techniques and tools to hunt and collect wild, naturally occurring foods. The Birhors of Chotanagpur subsist in this manner.

Pastoralism

It is a form of food procuring that depends on the maintenance and control of large herds of animals. In India, pastoral tribes are few in number. The Gujjars of H.P. are migratory cattle keepers. They migrate seasonally from the plains of U.P. to the hilly regions of western U.P. and H.P. The Toda of Nilgiri Hill (south India) are a classic example of a pastoral economy.

Hill Cultivators

This includes swidden cultivators, i.e. people in shifting agriculture, who burn off a patch of land, plant it with aid of a digging stick, and move on to clear another patch of ground when brush and weeds make the original piece of land difficult to cultivate. Sauria Paharia of S.P. (Bihar) and some sections of the Gond of Bastar (M.P.) still practise this primitive form of agriculture.

Folk Artisans

This includes scattered societies which have specialized in making articles for domestic consumptions by means of crude technology. Lohra, Asur and Mahali of Chotanagpur are good examples of this type of economy.

Plain Cultivation

In this specialized method farming is followed in which draft animals, ploughs, fertilizer and, if necessary, irrigation are commonly used. The Oraon and Munda are good cultivators.

Industrial and Argicultural Workers

In this members of societies are usually landless who work on a wage basis. Tribals living close to industrial and mining areas work as wage labourers in neighbouring factories and agricultural communities.

Due to paucity of data it is not possible to quantify the correlation of geographic (territorial), economic and social factors with the occupational gradation of Indian tribes. The available records contained in the Census of 1971 reveal the following statistics. Nearly 65 per cent tribal population depend on agriculture (as against 56 per cent for the country as a whole), the number of agricultural labourers is 28 per cent (as against 25 per cent for general population). The rest 7 per cent are distributed in other sectors.

Some other general features of tribal economy in India are as follows :

Subsistence Economy

Production-consumption level of the most of the tribes is of the bare minimum type. In traditional villages where agriculture is the mainstay people still use the age-old technology. In progressive tribal villages modern irrigation and other farming facilities are available to the families which have a sound economy base.

Marketless Economy

Although markets are regularly held in the heart of tribal areas this does not mean that tribals exhibit a market economy. The traditional market (*Haat*) satisfies social, economic, religious and political needs of the tribals; in economic terms, it does not regulate the economic affairs of the people. Money as a medium of exchange, store and measurement of value does not play an important role in the tribal economy. The notion of property is closely related to the display and expenditure of wealth rather than to accumulation. Intra - and inter-tribal relations are generally based on barter exchange. It must, however, be noted that in these days tribals living in the remotest parts of the areas have come to know about modern money and they use them in some cases especially when they deal with non-tribals. Modern banking and credit facilities are known to only a few progressive members.

Surplus and Profit

As we use these terms in modern economics, tribal economy does not display surplus and profit motive characters. What we get is a sense of mutual obligation.

Economic Activities are Cooperative in Nature

Cooperation on various occasions are reflected differently in different tribes. Beyond the family level (see above, section on division of labour, productive units) cooperation is seen with lineage, clan and village level. In certain cases economic cooperation is observed at the inter-tribal level.

Economic Artifacts are Traditional and Quasi-Modern Type

Artifacts are things (objects) people make or shape from natural resources. People everywhere surround themselves with artifacts such as bow and arrow, rope, trap, wooden stick, axe as seen among the hunting-gathering tribes; and plough, spade, sickle digging, stick, soil scraper, basket as among the agricultural tribes. It is to be noted that not all artifacts are made by the tribals themselves; in some cases, they are obtained from the neighbouring communities by paying cash or harvest produce. Judging by any standard tools used for getting food are of traditional or quasi-modern type. Modern tools powered by gasoline and electricity are used only in a few cases.

Role of Non-Tribals (Traders, Moneylenders, etc.) in Tribal Economy

Tribal economy is influenced by certain members who generally come from neighbouring areas and play the role of traders and money-lenders. These outsiders have been influencing the tribals for the past few hundred years.

II

ECONOMIC INSTITUTIONS VIS-A-VIS DEVELOPMENT

Development is a concept loaded with value judgments. Without going into much detail about its concept building we may work out an operational definition, which, by the way, is accepted by the social anthropologists engaged in micro-research. Development is "a process by which poverty is alleviated, inequally reduced, and the opportunities for the self-fulfilment of *all individuals* are increased" Epste in 1977: 91, emphasis added). Development is usually associated with planned or directed change. It is also called *purposive change.*

Any planned change involves four major steps : Innovation, social acceptance, performance and integration. A model of planned change involves five elements :

1. Existing conditions
2. The goal

3. Research
4. The innovation blue print (statement of what is needed and how to achieve it)
5. Implementation

Its working order goes like this :

Existing Conditions → Research → Innovation Blue Print → Implementation → Goal

To illustrate the above, an agency (the government) wishes to provide the people with drinking wells (goal) and approaches the development specialists who do their work i.e. what is needed to construct the wells in a particular village (research). The specialists (change agents) must know a number of things : site, people, etc. (existing conditions). On the basis of the knowledge a plan is chalked out (innovation blue print). Someone must set to work on the basis of plan (implementation). Finally, the project is completed (goal).

Whenever a change is attempted, resistance is likely to appear especially during the implementation phase. It is the task of specialists to work out and overcome the potential sources of resistance. This can be done through action research, a phrase very popular among the development anthropologists, which means use of anthropological knowledge for purposive change by the target cultural group itself.* It is worthwhile to mention some potential sources of resistance.

Potential Source of Resistance to Planned Change

Resistance is any conduct that goes against a motion or thing. Focusing on planned change in health care systems Irwin Rubin observes : "By resisting, actively or passively, an organization is communicating a message—it is providing data. . . . it is telling us something about 'who it is'—its major and change, its important internal norms and values, and the nature of its relationship to other systems in the environment" (quoted in Zaltman and Duncon 1977 : 62).

Potential sources of resistance are from both sides, i.e.

*See for example, L.P. Vidyarthi, A.N. Sandhwar and A.R.N. Srivastava's report on *Action and Research Programmes among the Birhor of Chotanagpur*, Ranchi University, 1978-79. See also Sandhwar, 1979.

from target group (client) as well as from innovator group (change-agent). What important for us is to know the sources of resistance occurring among the members of a target group since resistance from the change agent group can be minimized to a great extent, if not all. We will briefly note important sources under the headings of cultural, social, organizational and psychological barriers to change. A point, however, must be noted that these sources are mutually inclusive, i.e. overlapping and these vary from situation to situation and innovation to innovation within a given context. Here we are separating them only to facilitate their presentation.

Cultural Barriers

Under this can be enumerated a number of factors such as cultural values and beliefs, cultural ethnocentricism, incompatibility of a cultural trait with change, etc.

In the context of community development programmes in rural villages Dube (1958) has cited a number of case studies how cultural values play a dominant role in a change programme. One such barrier coming from people's values is a lack of a work ethic. Discussing economic development Rostow notes the absence of entrepreneurship. According to Foster (1969), fatalism is another source of resistance to change.

By ethnocentrism we mean the belief that one's culture is superior to another. Different cultural perspectives held by clients and change agents cause different perceptions of what problem is.

Incompatibility of a cultural trait with a proposed change is one of the most frequent causes of resistance to change. Hunting-gathering groups will have more difficulties in accepting permanent agriculture; likewise, for the adoption of Christianity polytheistic people, as compared to the practitioners of monotheistic religions, may show limited resistance in embracing Christianity.

Social Barriers

Group solidarity, rejection of outsiders, conformity to norms, conflict, group insight are, among others, important social barriers to change.

Simple societies such as the tribals are formed of group-oriented people. In economic affairs they exhibit reciprocity or mutual obligation and inter-dependence. These may be a strong force for resistance. For people having high degree in group identification rejection of outsiders is another source of resistance to change. Norms are essential rules for the conduct of any social behaviour. Therefore, any change that is incompatible with prevailing norms will tend to be resisted by many.

Organizational Barriers to Change

One of the most vital sources of resistance is that an innovation may be seen as a threat to the power or influence of various facets of the organization. In order to have a successful change programme it is also important that the structure of the organization in terms of authority including hierarchical patterns, channel of communication, division of labour etc. be compatible or supportive of the change.

For a proposed change there must exist a climate for change. In development terminology, climate for change in organization means *need* for change, *openness* to change and *potential* for change (Zaltman and Duncon 1977 : 78-80).

Psychological Barriers

A number of psychological traits are responsible for individual and group personality. Proponents of change should be aware of the personality characteristics such as dogmatism, low tolerance for ambiguity, low risk-taking propensity, etc. of the members of the change group. Specialists on development programmes have found that rejection through ignorance or through default (knowledge of an innovation but not interested in it), erroneous logic and unsuccessful experience with the change are some of the important sources of resistance to change (For details, see Foster, 1962).

Above I have simply enumerated various factors which form the potential sources of resistance in any proposed change. Since the economy is embedded in society many of the above barriers may be confronted by development workers even though some of them do not fall under economic institutions.

To recapitulate our discussion we may note the following

facets of economic institution as crucial variables in development programmes :

1. Primary and secondary nature of economic tasks.
2. Work and its pattern (Organizational aspect of productions especially role of females and preadult children).
3. Work-technology, tools (artifacts) used.
4. Ownership and rights over resources.
5. System of distribution including market transaction.
6. Role of outsiders (including neighbouring tribal/non-tribal communities).

SUGGESTED READINGS

Belshaw, C.S., *Traditional Exchange and Modern Markets*, Prentice Hall, New Jersey and New Delhi, 1965.

Dalton, George, *Economic Development and Social Change* : The Modernization of Village Communities, Garden City, N.Y., 1971 (ed.).

Dube, S.C., *India's Changing Village* : Human Factors in Community Development, Cornell University Press, Ithaca, 1958.

Epstein, T.S., *Economic Development and Social Change in South India*, University of Manchester Press, Manchester, 1962.

Epstein, T.S., "The Role of Social Anthropology in Development Studies." In Mathur, 1977, pp. 88-103.

Foster, George M., *Traditional Cultures and the Impact of Technological Change*, Harper and Row, New York. New and Revised Edition published in 1973 as *Traditional Societies and Technological Change*, Harper, New York, 1962.

Mathur, H.M., *Anthropology in the Development Process*, Vikas Publishing House, Bombay, 1977 (ed).
This edited volume contains twenty seven articles written by specialists including anthropologists over a period of past two decades.
See specially articles by Belshaw, Dube, Epstein, Mathur and Mayer.

Mayer, Albert and others, *Pilot Project, India* : *The Story of Rural Development at Etwa.*, U.P. University of California Press, Berkeley, 1958.

Mead, Margaret, *Cultural Patterns and Technological Change*, UNESCO, Mentor Books, 1955 (ed.).

Nash, Manning, *Primitive and Peasant Economic Systems* Chandler. San Francisco, 1966.

Sahay, B.N., *Pragmatism in Development* : *Application of Anthropology*. Book Hive, New Delhi, 1969. (Hindi edition is also available).

Sandhwar, A.N., "Applied Anthropology and Action in India with Special Reference to the Birhor of Hazari Bagh", in *Social Anthropology in India: Contemporary Perspectives.* Editor, Ratish Srivastava. Books Today, New Delhi, 1979, pp. 195-205.

Spicer, Edward H., *Human Problems in Technological Change A Case Book.* Russell Sage Foundation, New York 1952 (ed).

Srivastava, A. Ratish N., "Studies on Culture Change in the Tribes of Bihar," *Journal of Secial Research* 21, (2) 1978, pp. 71-104.

Vidyarthi, L.P. and Rai, B.K., *Tribal Culture of India.* Concept Publishing House, New Delhi, 1977.

Zaltman, G. and Duncon, R., *Strategies for Planned Change.* John Wiley, New York, 1977.

TWENTY ONE

S. P. Sinha

TRIBAL MOVEMENTS AND AGRARIAN REFORMS

If you desire peace, cultivate justice, but at the same time cultivate the fields to produce more bread, otherwise there will be no peace.

—*Dr. Norman, E. Borlaugh while accepting the Nobel Award in his famous Oslo lecture on 10 December, 1970.*

WHILE WE are talking of making India a "Grain power"[1] after the completion of the "first phase" of agriculture development which had ended food imports ; the peace is hardly the "crop being harvested in the fields of India".[2] Clifton R. Wharton Jr. calls the Green Revolution, on the one hand, a cornucopia which is believed to have lifted the spectre of famine in the immediate future and to have postponed the prospect of Malthusian Population disaster, and on the other, a Pandora's Box whose very success will produce a number of new problems which are far more subtle and difficult than those faced during the development of technology.[3] The problematic aspect of Green Revolution convinces many that the Green Revolution is sooner turning in to Red, for new conflicts are emerging along class lines in a new style in the Indian villages. It is unmistakable distinguished by its massive scale and militant overtones. The unrest took various forms. It took the form of a Naxalite outburst in parts of West Bengal, Bihar, Orissa. It took the form of Gandhian satyagraha, though in some form militant, in Maharashtra, Gujarat, Andhra Pradesh. Mass land grab marches, forceful seizure of harvested crop, unionised demands for higher wages and increasingly physical annihilation of landlords, and in retaliation burning of Harijan and tribal labour etc. became the order of the day. The Green Revolution has definitely accentuated the circumstances that led to the politicization of the peasantry.

And yet we talk of agrarian reforms to effect the transfer of land to the tillers. It is not the intention here to go into the details of the agrarian reforms which were undertaken in the wake of one rebellion or other to ease the situation ; but in this short paper an attempt is being made to assess the efforts of various political parties in enunciating the agrarian reforms in time perspective from Gandhi to the present time and thus try to understand as to what is going to be the fate of agrarian reforms to effect transfer of land from rich to poor tillers.

II

The story of agrarian reforms in India is more than two hundred years old. Its history dates from the passing of the Regulation of 1793 (popularly known as Permanent Settlement) and it is replete with twists and turns, ranging from the early attempts to protect the cultivator's rights in the land to "the land to the tiller" idea to "cooperativization" of agriculture and back to such fundamentals as security of tenure and controlled rents. The archives are full with reports and materials which certainly can give kudos to the early revenue administrators thinking specially in protecting and safeguarding the rights of tribals in particular and rayats in general. So much so that in British India we have practically in all the states having a sizable tribal population a separate tenancy system. Wol Ladejinsky,[4] the U.N. expert on land reforms, broadly viewed agrarian reforms as re-distribution of land among the landless ; the creation of individual proprietorships, security of tenure, and controlled rents, favourable financial arrangements for land purchases, better methods of cultivation through technical assistance ; land consolidation of fragmented holdings ; adequate credit, cooperative marketing facilities, farm price schemes to stimulate agricultural production, and so forth. Though agrarian reform is a combination of a great many things, "security of tenure" becomes a paramount issue. The security of tenure is seen as calling for a set of conditions which tend to stimulate agriculture production, improve the economic conditions of the tenants and preclude social unrest.

But agrarian reforms are difficult to attain because legislative assemblies are still dominated by land propertied classes, and both the enactment of appropriate legislation and its enforcement present formidable problems. It may be concluded that "land reform has not only powerful economic implications but commences essentially as a political question, running head on into a fundamental conflict of interest, between the "haves" and the "havenots". The conflict of interest takes place in a setting of which India is a classic example. The "havenots" in India more made up of "pure" tenants, tenants with some land of their own, and a rest among of landless agriculture. There is unequal distribution of land ownership, area cultivated, and the size of the holdings. While generally speaking 53 per cent of the rural households of India own 16 per cent of the land, at the other end of the scale only 7 per cent of the households own 52 per cent of land, 22 per cent own no land at all. The same kind of disparity can be focused in the data on operation of area. 70 per cent of the households operate 16 per cent of the land and on the other extreme 9 per cent operate 51 per cent of the area. Again 78 per cent of the holdings are up to 10 acres but they cover only 33 per cent of the cultivated average at the other extreme 6 per cent of the holdings account for 35 per cent of the area. These figures are from the reports of the Planning Commission.[5] Recent figures in these regards are difficult to get, but this can give us same impression on our agrarian front.

A study of the structural and tenurial aspect of rural economy in the light of the 1961 census[6] gives that in the country as a whole the percentage of pure tenants in terms of households and acreage held was 8 and 4 per cent respectively, the respective figures for mixed tenancy were 15 and 18 per cent. Of course, this position is an underestimation of the situation because two decades have elapsed since the study was made and in this analysis there is generally no inclusion of the common practice of oral agreements and there is a rise of unrecorded share-cropping type of tenancy. In tribal areas the poor landless tribals create tenancy like *Korkar* and *Utakar* and make clearings in the forest for cultivation. They are invariably not included in our records and yet these poor tribals are rejected from such tenancy by better resource groups. Khusro[7] opined that recent researches permit the statement that while the total acreage under open tenancy in India might be about 12 per cent of all acreage, the acreage under camouflaged share-cropping tenure of an exploitative type is likely to be at least so much as that under open tenancy.

In spite of the fact that zamindari or equivalents have been abolished, ceiling of ownership of land has been claimed to have been applied to avoid fragmentation and unequal distribution of land ownership, land distribution to landless has been feebly attempted, but by and large the Indian tenantry have only changed their horses in mid-stream. The reforms have been subverted and there is an anti-reformism shared by landlords and their lobby leaving the tenantry and the landless agricultural labour high and dry.

At the political level we have done precious little leaving much scope for improvement. True that India had not the same situation which Russia and China had, the situation which ultimately led to the two momentous Revolutions. Until the end of the First World War the nationalist movement in India stood isolated from the potent force of peasantry although there had been such peasant unrest and occasional risings. The radicalisation of the nationalist movement in India with the coming of Gandhi increasingly began to draw the masses into movement. May be Gandhi played a vital role in mobilising their support for the Indian struggle of freedom through his emulation of the simple life of a peasant speaking their language, and calling forth his supporters to go to the villages, his enunciation of social and economic philosophy, his villagism and Trusteeship concept etc.[8] "But if he made the peasant speak for the Congress, he did little to make the Congress speak for the peasant".[9] Alavi may be right for his remark only to some extent because Gandhi's Champaran Satyagraha, Bardoli Satyagraha, Pardi Satyagraha, Kapus Bench Satyagraha and other such movements can refute the above remarks. But this is certain that Gandhi cried a halt in 1921 when the peasants began to extend the struggle against British imperialism into a struggle against the landlords and usurious money-lenders. Gandhi, it appears was not prepared to arouse class consciousness on the issue of class exploitation in the villages (might be he thought to fight the British first) rather his most powerful appeal to the peasantry was through the millenial concept of *Ram Rajya* (God's Kingdom) and styled the poor as Daridranarayan, and the object of veneration. It was Gandhian ingenuity that the abominated Dubbes became Halpati and the Untouchables as Harijan. Some of the middle class intellectuals at the call of Gandhi went to the village and tried to imbibe the spirit. Marxism had strong influence on them but Gandhi's terminating the Civil Disobedience movement of 1921 and 1930 each time precisely when the movement was gathering momentum and getting initial success and thus caused many middle class intellectuals in 1934 to join the Congress Socialist Party, of course, within the Congress organisation. But instead of mobilising the peasants themselves to fight for their demands, they concentrated on fighting within the Congress for recognition of peasants' demands and thus a class organisation of the peasantry could not be built up in spite of a very fine set of intellectual giants like Acharya Narendra Dev, Jayaprakash Narayan, Ram Manohar Lohia, Yusuf Meher Ali and others. No doubt they ultimately left the Congress and formed the Praja Socialist Party after severing their connections from the Congress Party and what happened to this afterward is well known to all.

The Communist Party of India also remained aloof from the peasant struggle either because the Comintern line at that time did not permit its participation in a movement by the Indian bourgeoisie or due to the fact that the main leadership was in prison due to the Meerut Conspiracy Case. In 1936 Socialists admitted some Communists in their party and were responsible for the setting up in 1936 of the All India Kisan Congress later renamed as the All India Kisan Sabha. But unfortunately thinking remained that instead of starting a struggle for the special demands of the poor peasants they should carry the whole peasantry with them. Prof. Ranga[10] spoke of "a common front to be put up by both the landed and landless Kisan". Thus to Acharya Narendra Dev[11] in 1938, "the postponement of struggle for the poor peasants was a matter of political expediency because of the primacy of the anti-imperialist struggle".

To Ashok Mehta[12] (once Chairman of the Praja Socialist Party after independence) it was to use the wide array of tactics developed from Lenin to Mao Tse tung, to use one section against the another. It (peasant struggle) was against the survival of democratic rights and socialist value, and also the organic needs of the village community cannot be met by sharpening class conflicts or party rivalries, opined Mehta. Himza Alavi[13] rightly remarked that such an outlook "acquiesces in and perpetrates the exploitation of the poor peasant by the rich peasant".

But in spite of this the Communists through the Kisan Sabha concentrated on agitation on broad peasant demands, specially for security of tenure, debt relief, and cheaper credit facilities, etc. and sought to influence government policy rather than to bring about direct peasant action. They led some of the local struggles like Tal Satyagraha in Bihar like Tebhaga movement in West Bengal and Telangana movement in Andhra Pradesh some of which assumed proportions of major uprisings. After the Communist Party Congress of 1948, the party was committed to launching of insurrectionary forms of struggle, but was not able to organise any movement even on the scale of the Telengana movement. The party members were subjected to severe repressions in different states and many of them were jailed and remained underground between 1948-1952.

After 1952 the Kisan Sabha and the Communist Party unfortunately moved away from the idea of direct peasant action except for demonstration and agitation. In Amritsar the Congress of the Communist Party in 1958 adopted "a programme of peaceful road to socialism". At the Congress in 1961 at Vijayawada it proposed the "concept of national democracy is the most suitable form to solve the problems of national regeneration and social progress along the non-capitalist path of development". This shows that Communist Party of India believed in replacing the present Government of bourgeois democracy in which the leadership of the national bourgeoisie is decisive by a government of national democracy. The latter is to be distinguished also from people's democracy in which the leadership of the working class is decisive, the leadership having won the support of overwhelming majority of the people. The proletariat could share power with the national bourgeoisie a concept, which looks as acceptable to Communists and to Praja Socialists alike.

The Communist Party of India after the Great Schism of 1969 in the Congress Party stood as a solid rock in support of Congress (ruling) and with this realignment the last hope of direct peasant action by C.P.I. receded, rather the C.P.I. confined its energy vainly in exerting pressure on the Congress Government for implementing effective land reforms. The result is that both Communists and the Socialists are largely in agreement with the principles of land reforms adopted by the Congress, their main criticism remained directed at the manner of its implementation only.

This aspect was very nicely brought out in the Eastern Zone Seminar[14] on Land Reforms held in February, 1973 at Patna under the joint auspices of the Lal Bahadur Shastri National Institute of Administration, Mussoorie and the A.N. Sinha Institute of Social Science. That seminar was attended by Jayaprakash and the three different stalwarts who had been Revenue Ministers of their respective states enunciating their ideas and ideals of implementation of land reforms measures of course exposing their own way of achieving the goal. While Hare Krishna Konar, former CPI Revenue Minister of West Bengal termed land reforms policy as "landlords' policy", felt that much depends upon the political will and determination of the party in power, in implementing the programme as his Government had done. According to him the police must be kept on the side of the rural poor instead of performing the traditional role of lording over and terrorising them and taking the side of rich proprietors of land. Chandrasekhar Singh, one time Congress Revenue Minister of Bihar agreed that the implementation lacked a clear sense of direction, firm and determined approach, but all could be done through peaceful means. Indradeep Singh former C.P.I. Revenue Minister of Bihar opined that right of resumption and concept of personal cultivation be abolished and landlords be excluded from all land committees which may be set up for implementation of land reforms.

The C.P.I. itself got fragmented in 1964 in the wake of the Sino-Indian border war of 1962 and in 1980 when Dange group proclaimed the opening of his own party steering away from the C.P.I. Dange claimed Russian support for his party, and presently it comprises parties like the pro-Moscow Communist Party of India, or C.P.I. and the Independent Communist Party of India, Marxist or C.P.I.(M), a Maoist Party. The Communist Party of India (Marxist-Leninist) or C.P.I. (ML) and several Maoist groups which are not recognised as parties as yet. The difference between the C.P.I. (M) and C.P.I. (ML) covers the entire range of issues regarding revolution—its stage, strategy and tactics. The C.P.I. (M) holds that the Indian State is a bourgeois landlord state led by a big bourgeoisie which pursues a capitalist path while both collaborating and bargaining with foreign monopoly capital. The C.P.I. (ML) which generally follows the Chinese view holds that India is a semi-feudal and neo-colonial country, that is to say, its obsolete semi-feudal social system serves as a base for the United States imperialism and Soviet social imperialism and facilitates exploitation by a class of big comparador bureaucrat capitalists who are simple pawns of imperialism. Working of the Maoist tactical line dates from the Naxalbari peasant struggle in 1967. Indian Maoists set up revolutionary bases (Guerilla Zone) The C.P.I. (ML). leadership started anihilating the class economy in the countryside, but the failure of C.P.I. (ML) tactical line in the countryside is evident from the severe setbacks the party has received in Srikakulam in Andhra Pradesh and in Debra Yopivallavpore and other rural areas of West Bengal and in some parts of Bihar. Repression has since been greatly intensified but in spite of it the Maoist movement has registered extensive growth and there is a growing conviction in C.P.I. (M) leadership that the party cannot achieve anything significant within the framework of the bourgeois constitution. Thus revolutionary potential has existed in India but it is for the different parties to exploit it during the serious economic crisis.

REFERENCES

1. Rao Birendra Singh, Agriculture Minister in his address on the occasion of the XIXth Convocation of the Indian Agricultural Research Institute, New Delhi.
2. Hari P. Sharma, "The Green Revolution in India, Preclude to Red One", in *Imperialism and Revolution in South Asia*, Edited by Kathlean Gough and H.P. Sharma. Monthly Review Press, New York and London 1973 & 1977.
3. Clifton R. Wharton Jr., "The Green Revolution, Cornucopia or Pandora's Box" in *The Foreign Affairs*, April 1969, p. 464.
4. Luis J Walinsky (Edited), *Agrarian Reform as Unfinished Business*, Oxford, 1977, p. 369.
5. Planning Commission Report of the Committee of the Panel on Land Reforms, 1959, p. 3 table 4.
6. P. Sharma, *A Study of the Structural and Tenurial Aspects of Rural Economy in the light of 1961 Census*, table 7.
7. A.M. Khusro, *Rural Development* (monographed), p. 12.
8. Savitri Sinha, "Gandhian Impact on the Tribe of India", (unpublished Ph. D. thesis), 1980.
9. Hamza Alavi, *Peasants and Revolution in Imperialism and Revolution in South Asia*, New York, 1973, p. 316.
10. N.G. Ranga, *Revolutionary Peasants*, New Delhi, 1948, p. 89.
11. Acharya Narendra Dev, *Socialism and the National Revolution*, Bombay, 1946, p. 46.
12. Ashok Mehta, *Studies in Asian Socialism*, Bombay, 1959, pp. 213-215.
13. Hamza Alvi, "Peasants and Revolution" in *Imperialism and Revolution in South Asia*, New York, 1973, p. 319.
14. Proceedings of the Seminar on the Implementation of Land Reforms in Eastern Region, National Academy of Administration, Mussoorie, 1973.

TWENTY TWO

B. N. Sahay

POLITICAL INSTITUTIONS AND TRIBAL DEVELOPMENT

NO SOCIETY can exist without a framework of social regulation, to provide an order by which men live in groups and by which individuals are regulated. Order, as we all know, is the essence of social living and society, the natural habitat of man. Social control in any society is necessary to protect the individual against himself and to save the society from chaos. Social control is the process by which social order is established and maintained (by informal training habit). In any type of social control, the role of social sanction becomes very important.

Social Sanctions

In any community there are certain modes of behaviour (or the manner of acting in a given situation) which characterise that particular society. These are called usages. All social usages, have behind them the authority of the society, but among them some are sanctioned and others are not. Social sanction is the reaction on the part of a society or a considerable number of its members to a mode of behaviour which is thereby approved or disapproved.[1] The approved and disapproved behaviour are also known as positive and negative sanctions respectively. Again, the society may express the approved or disapproved behaviour either spontaneously (diffused) or positive and negative social sanctions may be carried out according to the traditional and recognised procedures (organised). Social sanctions can be broadly divided into

Refer the author's *Pragmatism in Development—Application of Anthropology*, Bookhive, New Delhi-110008.

two categories : (1) Primary and (2) Secondary. The primary social sanctions will be explained more clearly with the help of the following chart :

Social Sanctions

- Primary
  - Positive (approved behaviour)
    - Diffused
      - (a) Praise
    - Organised
      - (a) Honours
      - (b) Decorations
      - (c) Title
  - Negative (disapproved behaviour—more definite)
    - Diffused
      - (a) Moral or ethical
      - (b) Satire or ridicule
      - (c) Religious or supernatural
    - Organised
      - (a) Penal law (in modern states)
      - (b) Confinement
      - (c) Exclusion from the community
      - (d) Loss of rights, social rank
      - (e) Degradation fine
      - (f) Infliction of bodily pain
- Secondary

Secondary sanctions are concerned with actions of persons or groups in their effects on other persons or groups. They consist of procedures carried out by a community, generally through its representatives or by individuals with the approval of the community when recognised rights have been infringed. It is based on the principle that any person who has suffered an injury is entitled to satisfaction and the satisfaction should be proportionate to the extent of an injury. Such examples are : (a) Retaliation or self-help (socially approved—controlled and limited act of revenge), (b) Duel, and (c) Indemnification.

Social sanctions play an important role in regulating the behaviour of an individual in a society. The individual's conduct is regulated in conformity with the usages. It has greater effects on the person on whom it is applied. This is mainly due to the fact that every individual has a desire for being praised and avoids hatred of his fellow. Generally speaking, there is always a desire (by an individual) to win reward and avoid punishment that a community offers or threatens. One does not want to be unworthy, disreputable, dishonourable, discourteous, etcetera. Ultimately, it has a general effect on the community at large as it helps restoring the equilibrium by giving collective expression of social disapproval. Negative sanctions in a primitive community have also ethical and supernatural forces because certain acts displeasing to God make the accused also a sinner.

The Traditional Political System

The traditional political system in any community has grown in terms of time to regulate the individual's conduct and has a history of its own. The pattern of the political structure is determined by the total mode of living and the result of the interaction among the 'nature-man-spirit' complex.

E.A. Hoebel has tried to study the various stages of the traditional political system and has opined, that this institution has also evolved from the simple to the present complex form. For this purpose he has selected five contemporary communities[2] which are as follows :

(1) *The Eskimo* : The Eskimo are at the lowest level of cultural development and law is served well. Their group, does not normally exceed more than hundred persons. This group is led by a headman who is first among the equals. He simply lends direction to the people's activity but does not direct. His leadership status is achieved on his superior hunting skill and capacity to steal others' wives.

(2) *The Comanche* (*North America*) : The political system among the Comanche is the development on the plan of the Eskimo. They have regional chiefs over a much larger group than that of the Eskimo. The chief has both civil and military powers. Property and status are considered by the number of horses one possesses. Public opinion and morality play an important role in stopping absconding with others' wives.

(3) *The Ifugao* (*Philippines, North America*) : They have a more mature and well organised political system than

that of the Comanche. Their political system can control over 100,000 individuals.

(4) *The Cheyenne Indian*: Their political system is very well organised and more mature in relation to the Ifugao. They have organised states having a tribal council of chiefs with ten years of office tenure.

(5) *The Ashanti* (*West Africa*): Their political system provides a link with that of the one we find with the so-called civilised modern political system. They have a powerful monarchy and the criminals are brought to the royal courts.

The Traditional Political System

The Village Headman

By and large, in every tribal village there is a village headman who is either a secular or both secular and sacred head of the village. He, either with the help of the elected, or selected village elders, is responsible for the maintenance of law and order in the village. He sees that those violating customary laws are punished. He has both executive and judiciary powers. He is locally known by different names among the different tribes. The tribes, who are divided into a number of totemic clans, get their disputes adjudicated at the clan level (with the help of clan elders) first. In case of dissatisfaction with the decision made by the clan elders, the case is brought to the village headman.

The Regional Headman

Over a number of village headmen, there is a regional headman whose court (in some cases) is the highest court of appeal. When a party is aggrieved with the decision of the village headman, he appeals to the regional headman for better justice. Similarly, whenever there is a dispute between the two or amongst a number of villages and the concerned village headmen fail to adjudicate between or amongst (as the case may be) themselves, the case is heard and disposed of by the regional headman assisted by his councillors.

The Supreme Authority at the Tribal Level are the Tribal Chiefs

In some of the tribal communities, we find an authority at the tribal level who does not only look after and fight for the cause of his community, but is also a supreme judicial authority so far as the political structure of his community is concerned. His decisions in any case are final and sacrosanct.

Like the above, in almost all the tribes of India we find village and regional authorities who have the authority and power of decision-making and who maintain law and justice in their respective jurisdiction. Let us now examine the procedure with regard to administration of justice, generally followed in tribal societies.

Customary Law and Justice

The study of primitive law, in its widest sense, is perhaps the most general and difficult task of the social anthropologist. Legal institutions take on a fundamentally different form in primitive communities as opposed to modern ones and law cannot be considered apart from the whole normative system, the body of moral codes, aesthetic standards, rules of good behaviour and the like—of which institutionalised methods of legal procedure are but a part, albeit, an important part.

The anthropologist who sets out to study law in its entirety is not merely interested in the comparative few instances in which the law is broken, he must also consider the vast majority of cases in which it is kept. He must study all the forces of social conformity, including those primitive inducements which ensure that, generally speaking, honesty is the best policy. But he must not ignore the fact that cases of breach do occur, and that, in such instances, legal mechanisms are brought into play. Law cannot be considered apart from other forces of social conformity but its existence as a specific element in culture must also be recognised. The study of primitive law and custom has two aspects; the forces which induce people to conform in a vast majority of cases, and the procedure adopted in cases of evasion and breach of normative standards.[3] Law consists of a set of principles which permit the use of force to maintain political and social organisation within a territory. Where there are no legal sanctions, are matters of customs and conventions and not of law. The growth of law is a slow and gradual process of customs being given the sanction of law with time and force. There is an absence of legislation.

Nature of Primitive Law—Concept of Crime and Punishment

(1) It is based on kinship bond and therefore, clan elders are found playing important roles in the decision-making in many of our contemporary tribal societies. (2) It is backed by public opinion and morality which are based on common sentiments shared by all and the community's conception of 'good' and 'bad'. (3) It does not distinguish between the crime and torts, i.e., private and public wrongs. A private wrong may bring calamity for the entire community. Thus, collective responsibility plays an important role in primitive law. (4) Breach of public opinion (which originates from moral and ethical notions) and moral laws amounts to sin, the sinner has also to face supernatural punishment. It is, therefore, that we find strong public opinion against incest, adultery, etcetera. (5) There is limited civil law and more criminal law because of the lesser pressure on land and the customs are clear with regard to the inheritance of property. (6) Intention has no importance in primitive law because of the concept of sin and the fear of supernatural punishment which may come as a visitation on the whole group. Even provocation is accepted as a partial excuse for the commission of a crime.

Adjudication of Disputes

Evidence: In the administration of justice importance is attached to the establishment of guilt. In the primitive law it is mainly established in two ways—oath and ordeal, administered when the accused denies a particular charge against him and cannot establish his innocence through concrete evidence.

Oath and Ordeal: Oath is administered in the presence of the village headman and his council. The sacred head or specialist is also present on such an occasion. The culprit is asked to take an oath in the name of God and then say whether he is guilty or not. Among the Maler, the accused while taking an oath touches the sacred axe[4] and utters "I will die if I tell a lie " and among the Santhal the accused utters "Dharam Dharm". The result of perjury is greatly feared since it is considered to be a supernatural wrath.

If by the statement of an oath, the village headman and other members of his council are not satisfied, the accused among the Santhal is asked to take cow-dung in his hand and speak out the truth again. It is believed that even after doing so if an accused conceals the truth, he is bound to meet supernatural anger. But among the Maler it is also believed that a person's sin may invite calamity on the entire village including the sinner and hence they have a system of ordeal to establish the guilt. Authorities. (sacred and secular) go near the sacred stream where the sacred axeis made red-hot and the accused is asked to lick it with his tongue thrice. If he comes out without an injury he is held not guilty, otherwise he is held guilty and doubly punished. This is locally known as the process of undergoing *Saveli.* In some Maler villages, in place of undergoing Saveli, the accused undergoes *Kriya* process in which he is asked to take salt besmeared with cock's blood. It is believed that if an accused person has actually committed an offence and is trying to hide it to avoid punishment, he is bound to incur divine anger which would result in physical ailment and other family troubles.[5]

Punishment

A study of the customary laws among a number of tribes of India indicates that cases relating to Inter - and Intra-family and village disputes, assault, disputes over immovable property, theft, divorce, moral and sexual offences, etcetera, are tried and disposed of by the traditional Panchayats. Cases of murder, however, are now reported to the police station having jurisdiction over the area.

The amount of fine which may be in cash and in kind or both depends upon the seriousness of the crime and the capacity of the culprit to pay it. In cases relating to incest there may be ex-communication (like *Bitlaha* among the Santhal) and the accused can be accepted back in the community only when he gives a community feast.

Whatever may be the amount and kind of fine and nature of its realisation, it remains a fact that the concept behind a punishment is : (1) to compensate the party which has incurred a loss, (2) to purify the soul of the wrong doer, and (3) to bring the enemies together.

Thus, we find that in a primitive community there is an automatic submission to law. It is obeyed because of the fear from divine punishment. From another sociological angle, it is obeyed because people have to depend on each other and oblige each other.

II

Theories of Leadership

Any political system is inseparable from leadership as the leaders are the means to attain the objectives of a political system.

Leaders are not only helpful in achieving the objectives of a political institution; but have also many other functions to perform in a society. Leadership is a process of mutual stimulation and is based on relations between an individual and a group built around some common interest and behaves in a manner directed or determined by the leader himself.

Thus, in any society, in order to satisfy various needs of the people, there are different types of leaders—all playing important roles in their respective fields of activities.

Generally, the development and welfare personnel of our country have been seen going to the villages with pre-conceived notions about some fixed characteristics[6] of a leader, and in many cases fail to strike at the right type of leadership. As a matter of fact, there cannot be certain fixed characteristics and functions of a leader as the three factors, time, place and situation play important roles in determining them. The earlier theories of leadership may be classified into two categories, the first based on heredity and the other on "traits". Of late the modern theory is situational and an extension of it is known as situational-cum-personality theory.

Relation of leadership arises where a group follows an individual from free choice and not under command or coercion; and secondly, not in response to blind drives, but on positive and more or less rational grounds. In a leadership situation, the nature of followership is equally important. A real leader always takes the group into confidence and arouses initiative for action. It is closely related with the activities of influencing people to co-operate towards some goal which the leader considers desirable. It does not mean bossing or ruling over.

Existing Pattern of Leadership

Traditional Leaders

As noted earlier, in a tribal area for the satisfaction of various needs there have been various types of leaders and they have been enjoying authority and power and have a history behind them. In other words, they are the traditional leaders who have been operating in traditional social structure, who stand for the old ideas, values and institutions, and thus continue to satisfy the traditional needs of the people to which they are accustomed.

They are the village and regional headmen, the sacred specialists the traditional medicine man, the *shaman*, and many others who can be located very easily throughout the village or tribal institutions.

Emergent Leaders

The emergence of new trends in the formulation and implementation of the various welfare and development programmes, viz. introduction of a host of new social organisations and institutions, eg. *gram panchayat*. Youth Club, *Mahila Mandal*, co-operative, schools committee, etc., gave birth to a new set of leaders whom we call emergent leaders. Thus, they are carrying the new ideas, through the development and welfare programmes and stand for the new or emerging values and are connected with emergent institutions. Although, in some cases such emergent leaders may provide link between the old and the emerging values, they are neither the traditional leaders nor do they operate in traditional social structure. Such leaders are the *Mukhya*, the *Sarpanch*, the Chief Officer, and the number of a *gram panchayat*, and the secretary of a cooperative society, a youth club and a *Mahila Mandal*, and the school teacher and so on.

Traditional-emergent Leaders

With the emergence of the above ementioned institutions and

their leaders some of the erstwhile traditional leaders tried to swim with the new current as there was fear of being drowned in the oblivion of village masses. Some of such leaders have been very successful in the sense that they proved effective in establishing important links between the old and the new ideas, values and institutions and thus operated both the traditional as well as modern institutions and social structures. Some of them have been proved very successful in establishing a happy harmony between the old and the new and helped the people to develop along the lines of their own genius. These leaders whom we call traditional emergent are the traditional leaders with emergent roles, e.g. the traditional village or regional headman is also the *Mukhia* or *Sarpanch* of a *gram panchayat*, or the leaders of the traditional youth dormitory are also the leaders of the Youth Clubs and *Mahila Mandals*.

Application of the Knowledge

Leadership Conflict and Development

Tribal Leaders and Development :

Paharia	Murchu
Santhal	Youth Leaders
Oraon	

REFERENCES

1. Radcliffe Brown, *Structure and Function in a Primitive Society*, Cohen and West, London, 1952.
2. E.A. Hoebel, *The Law of the Primitive Man—A Study in Comparative Legal Dynamics*, Harvard University Press, 1954.
3. R. Piddington, *An Introduction to Social Anthropology*, 1952, pp. 319 and 322, Oliver and Boyd, London.
4. Sacred axe is kept with the village headman for making sacrifices on ceremonial occasions.
5. B.N. Sahay, "Changes in the Leadership Pattern among the Maler and the Santhal of Santhal Parganas, Bihar"—a doctoral thesis, Ranchi University, 1966.
6. Some leadership characteristics given by authorities on the subject have been discussed separately. Refer *Pragmatism in Development Application of Anthropology*, Bookhive, New Delhi, 110008, 1969, pp. 171-72.

TWENTY THREE

Anand Prasad Sinha

CRIME AND CUSTOM IN THE TRIBAL SOCIETY
Some Reflections

Men and the Crime

THE CRIME, the criminals and the penal law of ancient communities are better understood as the law of wrongs or the law of Torts.

The nature of crime or the type of crime amongst the tribals and their society do not at all differ from that to be found amongst non-tribals or their society. The only marked difference is the manner of commission of crime and the element of motive.

In cases of non-tribals motive plays a very important part, whereas motive is not always meaningful in the cases of tribals. Of course, motive seems to be in a few cases but by and large it cannot be said to be a condition precedent for the crime. Amongst the tribals, revenge and the element of irresistible impulses seem to be substituted for motive to be found amongst the non-tribals.

The mental condition of a criminal is extremely relevant and important both before and after commission of any crime. An important decision of the United States Courts of Appeal in the District of Columbia had laid down the rule "that an accused is not criminally responsible for his unlawful act what was the product of mental disease or the mental defect". In cases of tribals, the innocent look is by and large deceptive. The manner of crime committed may give a look of mental disorder but it completely betrays the rule of exception.

It is a socio-legal question. It is extremely important also.

A definite provision in the Indian Penal Code has been made for consideration as to whether a person at the time of the commission of the crime was suffering from such mental deficiency and did not know that what he was doing was illegal or wrong.

Crime and criminals are closely co-related with social conditions prevailing in the society. Psychology of a criminal at the time of commission of crime is also an important factor for consideration. In non-tribal society the crime doers are generally found to be having perfect normal mind, hard and stiff conscience, stout physique and extremely cruel hands. Whereas the tribal wrong doers are generally weak, simple and ignorant, exhibiting irresistible impulses and members of a well established family. In non-tribal society a community of criminals, independent of the normal established society, also exists, whereas such definite group or association forming an independent community is practically absent amongst the tribals.

A hardened non-tribal criminal is found committing crimes generally in a soft manner. Whereas a simple normal minded tribal, even accused of the first crime, is found committing dreadful acts in a very cruel manner, reflecting and exhibiting as if the act had been done by a criminal who used to do such act by deadliest weapon in the dark night, in the company of several such others.

Deep marks of repentance, sorrow and feelings of morality are, by and large, quite vivid and apparent on the face of non-tribal accused while facing trials, in the dock, inside a court room, but no such signs are visible on the tribal accused. Prisoners of the first category are always found lost in thought, whereas a tribal accused is invariably in a state of feelinglessness.

The accused of a non-tribal society exhibits signs of joy or satisfaction on their being exonerated from the charge or after their acquittal, but such feelings are always absent, in the cases of tribals. A tribal enters the dock like a statue and walks out also like the same.

The weak and ignorant tribal, committing serious and deadliest crimes betraying no element of motive is illustrated in a few cases mentioned herein under :

(i) A young but physically very weak tribal at the time of taking food had complained to his father that the cooked rice served to him was cold. The affectionate father who was also taking food had simply replied that the son should eat and should not bother about the coldness of the rice. The father had also stated that he was waiting so long for the arrival of the son and he also had not taken his food for the sake of taking it together. What an affectionate feeling and conduct is reflected in the soft words of the poor father! The son's conduct was simply shocking. He took out his *tangi* and gave a fatal blow on the head of the father. The father was no more. It is baffling. Where was the motive ? There was no case of mental defect or disease. There is no scope for irresistible impulses. Rarely, is such conduct to be found amongst the non-tribals. Of course, there are instances of patricide. But that is always on account of some deep rooted motive.

(ii) Two tribal boys aged about 18 to 20 years were tending she-goats. One of them had a flute. Both were sitting on a piece of rock. One boy requested the other to play his flute. The boy having the flute refused to oblige. Suddenly he was given a *tangi* blow by the other boy killing him instantaneously. What a dreadful act without any valid reason by a weak and ignorant Adibasi tribal boy !

(iii) A tribal man who was working in the H.E.C. had lost his son. After cremation he had called his neighbour for the ritual hair cut and other connected ceremonies as he had also gone for the cremation. The neighbour went to the tribal's place after some delay and persuasion. While the neighbour was having his hair cut, the father of the dead child suddenly gave a *tangi* blow on his head killing him on the spot.

(iv) A young man not even above twenty had killed his wife by cutting her into pieces with a *tangi* inside his bolted room at night while both had gone to sleep. The wife cut into pieces was on the cot and the

> tribal husband was sitting on it practically for the entire night. When in the morning the door had not opened people got suspicious. They had called out the accused repeatedly but there was no response. Ultimately a few villagers climbed upon the tiled roof. Tiles were removed. A hole was made and when they looked through that hole inside the room they could find the dead body of the wife on the cot and the accused sitting by her side. In spite of best persuasion the accused-tribal did not open the room and ultimately when he was threatened that he would be killed by an arrow and the arrow was aimed at him, he quietly and leisurely opened the room without any explanation or any attempt to run away in order to escape from the crime.

All through he was calm and composed in the trial and the mystery of the murder and its motive remained unexposed throughout. Really it was a dreadful act by a tribal of tender age, weak physique and having an innocent look which really betrayed the manner and nature of the crime.

A few of the instances quoted above are neither story nor fiction but realities and all the accused persons have been awarded imprisonment for life.

Neither the legal nor the psychological factor can be put forward by way of explanation for such dreadful acts committed upon such innocent and known persons.

After exhaustive reading of case records it has been found that the custom of keeping a *tangi* amongst the members of the tribal society is instrumental and responsible for the commission of dreadful crimes like murder. The *tangi* was justified several years before when it was an arm of protection and also for livelihood, in the manner that it helped in felling of the trees and thus selling the wood. Today the forest is not so dense and rarely does one require protection from animals; nor is the felling of trees permissible under the Indian Forest Act.

Therefore, if the habit of carrying a *tangi* by the tribals is discontinued the motiveless murder, murder without any purpose and abnormal murder will definitely be curtailed to a large extent.

Another important basis for crime prevailing in the tribal society is, the peculiar notion of witchcraft. This is purely on account of certain totem and taboos. If tribals are educated properly surely this evil is bound to be eradicated. Notion and belief of witchcraft mixed with liberal consumption of liquor (wine) are responsible for many murders.

It is manifest that the entire social organisation of the tribal society is linked and interlinked in the belief of totem and taboos. It is not relevant to go into such details. However, it is certain that even innocent violations of such social injunctions, at times result into dreadful acts like severe thrashing and even murder. The mode of punishment will reflect that they are severe and without any exception.

A study of crimes and criminals in tribal society will indicate that they have their roots in the concept of crime and criminals prevailing in the ancient communities during the ancient days.

The concept is based upon the theme of—"an eye for an eye and tooth for tooth".

Justice and Trial

The structure of crime and criminals and punishment prevailing in tribal society is based upon the idea of protection of the communities from disorder. The village Panch has the authority to deal with the criminal. This reflects the common will of the community which is generally represented by the village elders. The authority of the Panch is considered to be supreme. The Panch is used to assemble at the village Akhara or some other appointed place. The parties involved are called there. The accusation is made known to the wrong doer.

The Panch has the power to inflict fine and order for ex-communication. In case of witchcraft the guilty person is awarded the ordeal of thrashing and at times is even exiled from the village. At times he is beaten to death—this is also permissible. Complete revenge is in practice. A guilty man accused of causing murder, grievous hurt and the like is left at the mercy of the Khunt-brethren of the victim and consequently the wrong doer could be killed or his arm or leg be broken according to the facts and circumstances of each case.

Trial by ordeal was the only mode for judging guilt or innocence. When a person is accused of theft, boiling cow-dung water is the instrument for testing innocence or guilt. The accused has to dip one of his arms into the boiling hot liquid. It is believed that if the man is guilty his arm will get burnt. If it is not burnt, he is declared innocent. Another mode is to put small ladlefuls of burning charcoal on the palm of the accused. If the hand is burnt or if the accused throws out the burning charcoal, the moment it is placed on his hand the charge is established. The above two methods are used by the Panch which may safely be said to be the court of the entire community. It proves all acceptance.

There is also a mode and method adopted by private individuals for detecting crime and the criminal. If money or cattle or some goods are stolen the victim goes from house to house in his village with a pumkin-gourd in his hand. He will demand a little water from each neighbour's house and put it into his gourd. Thereafter the aggrieved victim will go with the gourd, a little Arwa rice and a black fowl to the village smithy and there the rice is put on the ground. The moment the fowl feeds on this rice its throat is cut with a knife. The blood of the fowl and also the water in the gourd are thrown into the blacksmith's bellows. Now as the blacksmith begins to work with his bellows, the belief is that the real culprit's belly begins to swell at the same time giving apprehension of immediate death.

Therefore, the real culprit, the moment he finds that the aggrieved victim has started this process he restores the property out of fear of death.

The system and the practice mentioned above, adopted in the tribal society can never be termed either savage or unparalleled. This can well be illustrated from crime and criminals to be found in the ancient communities prevailing in ancient English, Roman and Indian laws.

Ancient Law of Crime in England

England for more than three centuries was a part of the Roman Empire as a province. Thus it was governed by Roman

Law. The Anglo-Saxon invasion of the fifth century A.D. wiped away the system of the old legal order and replaced it by such institutions which were initially purely Germanic. The Anglo-Saxons invaded the country as a number of separate tribes. The spreading of Christianity by missionaries from the Continent infused Roman civilisation so far preserved by the Christian Church.

The law courts of the Anglo-Saxon corresponded to the territorial division of the country. The law administered by Anglo-Saxon courts was quite different from the law today as the law today plays a far more active and compelling part in social relations. In primitive times, the law court was like the Arbitrator of today who can only act when both parties submit to its jurisdiction. Self redress was a matter of rule. Any injury done, its action was confined to the injured and of his kind. It indicated that the bond of the community was weak and the bond of the family was strong. The aggrieved party was to prosecute a "blood feud" against the wrong doer till the wrong done was wiped out by retaliation. Tariff of compensation (*bot*) for injuries was fixed in proportion to the wrong done and rank of the sufferer. The laws of King Alfred indicated that if the great toe be struck off let 20 shillings be paid to him as bot, the second toe, 15 shillings, the middle most toe, 9 shillings, the 4th toe, 6 shillings and the little toe, 5 shillings.

In the laws of Ethelbert, God's property and the Churches 12-fold, a Bishop property 11-fold, a Priest property 9-fold, a Decon's property 6-fold, and a Clerk's property 3-fold.

If compensation is refused the wrong doer was declared as "out law". He could be slain by any one like a wild beast. There were certain offences which were "botless" and were punishable with death and also entailed for forfeiture of the offender's property to the King

In civil cases proof by "oath helpers" (compuragators) was in practice. The person in order to prove his cause of action must obtain certain number of persons to take oath solemnly in support of the case of the suitor.

In serious criminal charges "ordeals" were the mode of trial. The entire organisation of law of crime and criminals during the ancient English community and striking similarly with the modern state of affairs prevailing in the tribal community in which Panch and people's opinion prominently played very important roles.

System of inquisition in the criminal justice laid down in the Assize of Clarendon (1166) will be relevant to mention and is stated below :

Ancient Mode of Trial-Ordeals

(a) Ordeal of hot iron was very popular. A special ritual was prescribed. The suspected wrong doer was to carry a heated iron over a distance of 9 ft. The hand was sealed and kept under that condition for three nights. Thereafter bandages were removed. If it was clean he is not guilty. If it was unclean he was guilty.

(b) The accused was required to plunge his hand into a bowl of boiling water and take out a stone. His guilt or innocence depended upon the condition of his hand which was investigated after three days. If there was a round he was guilty. If the hand was normal he was not guilty.

(c) The two hands of the suspect used to be tied together under the bent knee. He was bound around the loins with a strong rope. A knot was made at the distance of the length of his hair. In that condition he was laid down gently into the water so as not to make a splash. If the man sank down to the knot he was to be drawn up failing which he would be declared guilty.

(d) In case of the clergy trial by ordeal was that of the cursed morsel. The accused was made to swallow a piece of food mixed with a feather or such like. If he could swallow, he was innocent. If he choked he was guilty.

The trial by battle was also very interesting. In cases of civil dispute the parties need not fight. The fight was between their respective supporters. In criminal cases battle was a serious affair. The accuser and the accused fought in person. It was deadly. In case the defeated defendant was not killed in the battle he was hanged on the gallows at once.

Law of Crime in Roman Law

The history of Rome consisted of three divisions, namely, Monarchy, the Republic and the Empire. There were further subdivisions having several periods. Roman Law is supposed to be the source of many good laws for many other countries. *Furtum* (theft) and *Injuriae* (offences relating to a person's dignity and later on understood as assault) were very common and it included practically the entire scheme of criminal jurisprudence. A difference was made between *Furtum manifestum* which meant when the culprit was caught red hunded and *furtum nec manifestum* which meant the thief was not caught red-handed. If a thief was caught while doing the act of theft and if he happened to be a free man he was scourged and "adjudged" (*Addictus*) to the complainant. It was not clear whether by this he could become a slave or was like an *adiudicatus* which meant that a person was seized by his creditor after the judgment. If the culprit was a slave he was scourged and thrown from the Tarpeian rock. When the facts disclosed *Furtum nec manifestum* the sentence was pecuniary which used to be double value of the thing stolen and that was to be paid. When there was suspicion that the stolen property was kept in the house of some one, the victim-complainant was authorised to search that house but he had to do so naked wearing only a loin-cloth (*licium*). He had to hold a platter (*lanx*) in his hand. If search made by the aggrieved person fulfilling the conditions stated above recovered the property, then the person in whose house it was found was pronounced guilty of *Furtum manifestum*. In some cases only the value of the articles found, three times, was to be paid. If a person refused the search of his house he was simply declared guilty of theft.

If the wrong doer came by night or in the day he defended himself with some weapon, the law permitted his killing without trial. However, one condition was laid down and that was that the slayer must cry loudly so that there may not be any suspicion that he was a murderer and then he tried to hide his act. Theft also included cheating.

Punishment awarded for the act of "breaking of a limb" was by talion which meant infliction of similar injuries on the wrong doer. This penalty could only be inflicted if any agreement for composition was made. In other cases compensation was awarded. The fracture of a bone could be compensated by the penalty of 300 asses, in case the victim was a free man; 150 asses in case the victim was a slave. In all other cases the penalty awarded was 25 asses.

One thing very prominent and peculiar was that an attack on a man's personality was readily punishable as the Romans of the 5th century B.C. were very susceptible to insult.

If a depositee did not return the articles deposited with him he acted like a thief and he was required to pay double the value of the article. A tutor who misappropriated the property of his ward had also to pay double the value. A case of damage caused to the crops of others by cutting down the same or allowing the cattle to graze was punished capitally. In case of breaking of limb or manifest theft the primitive law insisted on vengeance. In some cases the father or master of the wrong doer could buy off the vengeance which the wronged person had the right to take. Father or the master could purchase because neither the child nor the slave was entitled to retain any property. The primitive law laid down that a man was responsible for his act and there could be no exception and consideration of his state of mind or the element of intentional or accidental or negligent acts. However, later the act of murder was judged on the factor of intentional or unintentional killing.

During the Republic the law laid down was that if a man was found to have sold his wife he was to be sacrificed to the infernal gods. A child who struck his parents was to be "sacred" to his parent gods. A person found cutting the corn of another in the night was to be crucified as a sacrifice to Ceres.

Roman implementation of criminal justice was matter for the Magistrate and for the assemblies of the people. A death sentence awarded by the Magistrate must be confirmed by the people. Full powers were with the people and they could pardon anybody, they liked.

Therefore, it would appear that in the Roman Law also the most prominent and important tribunal was the people's court, like Panch stated and discussed in the case of tribal society.

In the very early stage of Roman history a system of

"blood-feud", existed. But the moment the State became powerful it took the punishment of murder into its hand. Even in the year 181 and 159 BC. the offences relating to bribery at election (*ambitius*) existed.

Ancient Hindu Law of Crime

In the ancient Hindu Law, award of compensation for crime was not considered complete and sufficient. The theme of justice, equity and good conscience played a very important part. It was the sacred duty of the king to impose punishment. Manu has said that a king who punishes those who are innocent and fails to punish those who deserves punishment becomes infamous and ultimately doomed to hell. Acts of theft, violence or any type of serious `injury could not be exonerated by giving compensation to the aggrieved party but it was the duty of the king to punish the culprit who had committed the crime against the law. Any crime leading to an infringement of a private right was punishable because it also involved the security and the tranquillity of the society.

Compensation generally was awarded in cases where injury to property has been caused by trespass, having been committed by domestic animals, cutting and destroying of trees and crops, conversion of another's property into one's use and stolen property when lost by the thief.

It was the duty of the king to get the stolen article restored or compensation paid to the aggrieved party and if he failed to do the same, the king was bound to compensate the aggrieved party from his treasury and he was entitled to recover the price from the village officers whose negligence was accountable for the escape of the thief.

Damages could be claimed from the person who cheated another. The amount of compensation was usually double the price of the article. The law took notice of nuisance and its removal and also due punishment.

Yajnavalkya has laid down four classes of punishment : censure, rebuke, pecuniary punishment and corporal punishment. These punishments were to be used separately or jointly according to the nature of the crimes. Pecuniary punishment included fine and forfeiture of the property. Corporal punishment included imprisonment, banishment, branding, cutting of offending limbs and lastly the death sentence. Again Yajnavalkya has stated that punishment should be awarded by the king after finding out certain relevant facts like, the nature of offence, the time and place of offence, the strength, age, evocation and wealth of the culprit. *Mitakshara* has added that, it has also to be found out, whether the wrong had been committed with or without deliberation and whether it was the first offence or a repetition of the offence at the time of awarding sentence. Also it has been stated by him that the punishment should be in proportion to the value of the article stolen, after considering the place and the time of the crime, and the strength of the accused.

In Hindu Law no one was exempted from punishment. According to Yajnavalkya no one is exempt from the punishment by the king even if the culprit be a brother, a son, an object of worship, father-in-law or a maternal uncle. According to *Manu* where an ordinary man is punishable with a fine, the king when committed the same offence should punish himself with thousand times of the amount of the fine usually awarded to an ordinary person.

Verbal abuse was punishable. It was divided into three classes—cruel, indecent and severe. Truth was no defence. For illustration if a man calls another one-eyed or lame, even it may be true, but caller is liable for fine.

In ancient Hindu Law there was a provision for giving security for good behaviour.

Personal violence again fell into three divisions—assault in the narrower sense of the term, battery and causing of wound.

If several people combined in striking another they were punished double the ordinary punishment. Also the person responsible for striking at the vital part was given the severest sentence.

Offence against female modesty were divided into three classes. Offence committed by force or fraud or mutual amorous desire. Punishment was awarded in accordance with the conduct of the wrong doer keeping in view the three divisions stated above. If a woman was found consenting she was also liable for punishment.

Theft was also divided into three classes : paltry theft, theft of ordinary magnitude and theft of precious things.

Again theft was divided into two categories open theft and concealed theft.

The term used open theft and concealed theft in Hindu Law, differed from that of manifest and unmanifest theft found in the Roman Law which have been stated and explained above. In the Roman Law distinction was based upon the place or time of arrest of the offender. The manifest thief was caught in the act or on the spot and before he could transfer that stolen article. In case of manifest thief he could be awarded death sentence while non-manifest thief was only compelled to refund the double of the value of the stolen article.

In Hindu Law concealed theft meant that the stolen property had been taken away dishonestly from the possession of the owner and without his consent by clandestine means. Open theft meant, taking away of another's property, of course, with his consent, but obtained by questionable means and it included cheating, taking of bribes and breach of trust.

The offence of trespass, public nuisance, offence against public justice, giving of false evidence, refusal to give evidence, production of fraudulent and forged documents, corruption in a Judge, taking of bribe by a Judge and neglect to bring certain offences to the notice of the king were all punishable under the scheme of criminal justice. At the same time right of private defence honestly and in good faith taking away some article in a state of dire necessity were recognised.

The aim of punishment in the Hindu Law was mainly based upon the concept of protection of the people and purification of the culprit.

Therefore, comparative study of the scheme of criminal law and justice just stated and discussed above will indicate that the administration of criminal justice found in the ancient communities of England, Rome and Indian societies do not differ much with that of tribal society even of today.

Custom

A particular practice adopted by an individual or a group of individuals, for some time will not give it, the status of a custom, validly recognised or having the force of law. Rules of conduct acquire the character of law by becoming objectively definite, uniform, and above all, compulsory. All creatures are creatures of habit but at a certain stage of his development, man, while retaining some instinctive reactions, comes to possess an increasing degree of choice in his habit and custom. Deprivation of liberty of a criminal, may not be the real punishment, but the real punishment is the stigma which society, itself, not the judge or the jailor inflicts upon a crime doer is the real punishment. Man may avoid to follow a particular line of fashion at the peril of his personal comfort but he is not prepared to face the ridicule which the society inflicts. Such is the force and effect of custom in the tribal society.

Legal custom is quite different from the custom evolved for conveniences, as the legal custom provides its sanction with certainty.

In order to give validity to a custom and having a force of law there ought to be positive proof of the fact of the existence of the custom. This element definitely lacks in the tribal society because of divergent custom on the same issue adopted by different sections of tribes.

The element of antiquity is also of little aid. In English law it is essential to fix the extent of the custom at least since A.D. 1189, the first year of the reign of Richard the First. Such an element is totally absent in the tribal society. It is essential to have this element because after all the older the practice the greater is the proof of its acceptance and existence.

Custom in order to be valid ought to be continuing and also it must indicate that it has been in peaceable enjoyment. There is no clear proof of the fact that so far the custom prevailing in the tribal society is concerned.

The element of obligatory force is far severe and strong in the tribal society because custom linked and having a colour of religion is always backed by sanction.

Custom must be certain. This is purely a rule of evidence. Certainty also lacks at times regarding the custom found in the tribal society.

Custom must be consistent with each other. One custom cannot be said to be in opposition to another, and that is the reason that reasonableness has another important factor.

In the tribal society custom is generally a product of dominating mind, nurtured in the belief of super-natural force and taboos than a source of spontaneous growth. Thus in tribal society custom followed at times are contrary to positive morality. Although custom by and large is non-litigious in character but in the case of tribal society to a great extent the starting point is conflict. In other societies, the starting point of custom is convention. The starting point of all developed society is co-operation contrary to dissension.

The custom prevailing in the tribal society is mostly based upon the totem and taboos evolved in a particular family having the force of the family law. The custom in the tribal society is much influenced by the instinct of possessive authority, the full control of the head of the family over his children similar to that of Patria Protesta, in the Roman Law which had given authority of life and death of the child by the father. The father is the king in his own house and a ruler in his own family.

A custom, in tribal society, is based upon totem and taboos and there is very little evidence to indicate that it has evolved upon the needs of the people. However, some based upon need of the people is not on account of popular majority but of a ruling minority. To illustrate slavery was a product of ruling minority and not on account of popular majority.

Custom found in the tribal society is not on the basis of sociological origin but it has been carried generation after generation as being the family law. No scientific explanations are available but if the custom is examined in detail it is found deep rooted in the element of totem and taboos. That is the reason that the majority of the customs prevailing in the tribal society could not attend the status of law and there is no legal validity excepting in the cases of inheritance and some family laws like adoption and marriages.

If the working and life of the tribal societies is minutely observed, it will be found that from morning till night, with the birth of a baby till death, agricultural operation or the mode of occupation for livelihood, all are tagged, linked and based upon certain conduct and behaviour reflecting, nearly custom and it may be said that entire tribal society is based upon the rigid rules of custom and any society still untouched by the influence of urbanisation exists in the phenomenon of religion mixed with magic—Custom.

TWENTY FOUR

Narayan Mishra

WORKING WITH THE TRIBES
Techniques and Tools

LIKE CHARITY science begins at home. And the science of anthropology, which is "the study of man and his works" despite the diversity of its interests is mainly concerned with the rounded study of man.

Every science has its scientific method of investigation and research, because scientific method is less wasteful and quicker. To discuss about the scientific methods of anthropological reseach is the main theme of the present paper.

Anthropological researches are based on the field work. The field is the laboratory of the anthropologist. To carry on his field work, he goes to the people he has elected to study, listening to their conversation, visiting their homes, attending their rites, observing their customary behaviour, questioning them about their traditions, as he probes their way of life to attain a rounded view of their culture. In this, he is the ethnographer, the collector of data.

Descriptions of actual methods used by anthropologists in the field are rare, though increasing attention is being given to the technical problems of methodology.

It is difficult to give an exclusive classified list of methods used in the social research. Most of the so-called methods are only different ways of collecting data. Research methods may roughly be classified into qualitative and quantitative methods according to the nature of data used. Qualitative method of anthropological research is much older. Under this method the collected information is in the form of qualitative description or self experience. The inferences drawn in this method are naturally based upon logical or philosophical rules rather than the facts.

A quantitative or statistical method is used where the phenomena can be expressed in the form of numerical data. Increasingly more and more use is being made of the quantitative methods and attempts have successfully been made to convert descriptive social phenomena into numerical terms.

To examine only such methods which are useful for collecting facts among the tribes is the main purpose of this paper. Let it be mentioned in the very outset that the selection of correct methods keeping an eye on the people and ecology is necessary. As we know that the literacy is comparatively low among the tribes and their life style and languages are also different, the investigator has to deploy observation, interview and genealogical method in general. Other methods like questionnaire case-study for which only educated informants are required, do not come under the purview of this paper for obvious reasons.

It is high time now to discuss some of these methods applied by the anthropologists for the collection of facts among the tribes. It will not be out of place to mention here that if the person from other disciplines like administration, planning, forest, voluntary organizations etc. are also trained in these methods and they apply them in the field situation, they can also collect many useful empirical facts to their advantage. The following are some of the popular anthropological methods used for the study of tribes :

OBSERVATION METHOD

"Observation is the examination of phenomena or a thing without altering it". Thus an observer is not in a position to impose anything on the phenomena, rather he will watch the natural movement objectively.

Observation may be regarded as the oldest method for the scientific investigation. The first knowledge of the universe around begins with observation. The little child, when he opens his eyes in this world finds himself surrounded by strange and unknown things. His curiosity is inspired, and he begins to observe them. Gradually, he is able to understand their significance and use. So the process goes on.

Observation must have definite objectives. Grouping haphazardly without a goal is worse than useless.

TYPES OF OBSERVATION

Though observation can be classified into various types according to their bases participant and non-participant observation are its two main kinds.

When the observer participates actively under study, it is known as participant observation. Thus a participant observer makes himself part of the group under study. He need not necessarily carry out all the activities as carried out by the other members of the group, but his presence as an active member of the group is necessary. A participant observer would freely mix with the social activities of the group, their normal and natural functioning, their feast and festivals, not as an outsider but as a member of the group. Again under participant observation the actual purpose of participation, which is the critical study of the problem should be concealed under the desire to learn their folklore, dance, music, customs and traditions.

Advantages of Participant Observation Method

(1) By participating in phenomena we know best about the reality. This method does not leave room for suspicion and speculation, moreover, the knowledge gained by this method is nearly perfect.

(2) Secondly, this method gives us an account of the actual behaviour in a genuine life situation as contrasted with the behaviour which an individual thinks he has performed or would perform under actual or hypothetical conditions

(3) Thirdly, this method allows objective observation by a skilled observer and is subject to checking by other observers.

(4) Again it eliminates errors arising from misunderstandings and misinterpretations of words and the bias likely to be present in a verbal report secured from a person.

(5) This is the method of physical science, and has all the advantages of accurate observation and measurement. When-

ever and wherever the nature of investigation and resources of the investigator permit, this method should be employed.

(6) The most important advantage which has made this method so popular is that the participant observer is generally more welcome to the group than a non-participant one. The people under investigation are generally very much willing to explain the significance of their various social activities to an outsider who is keen and willing to learn than to a person who has only an academic interest in them.

After seeing so many advantages of participant observation method one is seen in a hurry to generalise that this method knows no bounds but it has some limitations too. Some of these are as follows :

(i) If the investigator actually becomes a participant observer, he narrows his range of experiences. He takes on a particular position within the group, with a definite friendship circle. He learns and follows a pattern of activity which is characteristic of its members, and thus is less able to find out what fringe individuals are doing.

(ii) If he participates emotionally, he comes to lose the objectivity which is his single greatest asset. He may feel sympathy for a tragedy and may seek ego satisfaction within the group.

(iii) There is less standardization of data. Since he participates his experience becomes unique, peculiarly his own, so that a second researcher would not be able to record the same facts.

(iv) For many research situations it is almost impossible for the outsider to be a genuine participant in all ways. The anthropologist for example cannot be a criminal in order to study a crime gang.

Its limitations though many could be summarised in one sentence. Not all occurrences are open to observation, not all occurrences open to observation can be observed when the observer is at hand, not all occurrences lend themselves to study by observational technique.

It has been mentioned earlier that anthropologists use non-participant method. Here in this method an investigator watches the phenomena objectively. But in no case he participates in the phenomena. The non-participant observation continues for the time till he does not participate in the phenomena but soon as he starts participating it becomes participant observation.

Regarding the utility of non-participant observation method which are many, in short this could be said that it eliminates fallacies enter in the question-answer approach. One can have full and true information, one can get respect and co-operation from all the members of the society and it goes without saying that the "Spectators can enjoy more than the actor" proverb holds ideally here. A non-participant observer is sitting alert to observe and go deep into the matter, hence even the subtle trait does not escape his vision. Moreover, he is aloof from the community life, hence he studies peacefully far from the group struggle of the community.

But in addition to the advantages it has several limitations too, for example, a non-participant observer is supposed to be an objective observer, free from personal bias and prejudice but in execution it is very difficult. Again if an observer keeps himself aloof from the daily life of the community, he is suspected to be a man who may cause some harm to the community.

Moreover one does not like to reveal the secrets of one's life to a man whom one does not know well. Hence confidential information cannot be gathered by this method.

Thus from the perusal of the limitations of the observation method in general it is evident that there are a few phenomena whose observation is neither possible nor proper, on the other hand there are a few phenomena whose time and place of occurrence is not fixed.

Hence due to the limitations imposed on the observation method in general, the social scientists have invented another method named as Interview. In the Interview method most of the limitations of observation are eliminated.

INTERVIEW METHOD

The Interview consists of putting the relevant questions to the interviewee and recording his responses.

Thus under this method, set questions are asked and

answers are recorded in a standardised form. From data collection point of view this method is very important. As an investigator is mostly a stranger for the native situation he has to ask them about the various things he is not aware of.

There are several aspects of interview which will be discussed by and by but preparation for Interview, which is so basic and elementary for the procedure is analysed here. Preparation for Interview proceeds step by step in a chronological order and a researcher has to follow the step very cautiously. The various steps under preparation for the interview are given below.

Influencing Potential

Most research projects require the prior consent and goodwill of some authority or other. In many cases, particularly when there is possibility of a latent or open friction between the different parties to a social situation, it is necessary to explain the purpose of the project to all concerned who must be persuaded to agree on the desirability of carrying it out even though they may differ on other issues.

Adequate Knowledge about the Problem

While interviewing an investigator is expected to face different questions raised by the informants, and to give satisfactory answers to their questions it is essential for the investigator to have adequate knowledge about the problem.

Construction of Interview Guide

An investigator feels easy if he has an interview guide with him. Since the interview guide contains the broad outlines of the project and interview, he can have continuous interview with the informants. This guide is a break upon the investigator, which always checks him from crossing his jurisdiction. This reminds him of important matters to be collected by him in the field.

Selection of Informants

The key condition for the success of an interview is the selection of suitable informants. Every informant is not suitable for all sorts of information. Moreover how definitely such persons can be selected in advance depends upon how well-defined is the object of our inquiry and how completely the sources of such information are known. If we are interested in the wage scale of any industry, the responsible heads of the various establishments in this industry at once suggest themselves as persons from whom to secure this information. Sometimes the informants have to be divided into various age and sex groups. If an investigator is interested to know the history of the settlement of the village in question, the children will never be good informants for this question. On the other hand old men of the village can tell a lot on this topic. Similarly about the play activities children and young informants can be more suitable than the old one. Thus the problem of whom to interview, is a question of deciding who would yield most easily the desired information with the greatest reliability. Our familiarity with the field in which we are working will determine our ability to select suitable informants without employing trial and error method.

Prior Appointment for Interview

It is always better both for the investigator and informant to fix an appointment for interview. If informant is doing some domestic work, the arrival of any investigator does not please him. The informant may psychologically feel disturbed by the sudden arrival of the investigator. In such situations even if he answers, it is not wise to believe in such answers when he is not in a mood to answer. But if the investigator approaches him on prior appointment he gets both welcome and information.

Favourable Conditions for Interview

There are several factors which an investigator has to keep in mind during interview. Conditions for successful operation of the interview are many but a few of them are so elementary and vivid that they cannot be ignored. For example privacy may be regarded as a thing of prime importance. No informant, how so ever simple and cooperative he may be, will tell anything regarding the secrecy of his life in presence of others. Similarly all places are not favourable for putting all types of questions. For example if an investigator interviews an informant near a police station and puts questions regarding the persons responsible for a crime. Correct answers can never be expected at such a place. The informant may be afraid of telling the names of criminals near a police station.

Technique of Interview

After sufficient preparation for the interview has been done something about the technique of interview deserves mention. Now when the interview has been secured, its usefulness will depend largely on the personality and skill of the interviewer. No amount of preliminary preparation will serve as a substitute for tact and spontaneous insight in a concrete situation. It has been mentioned earlier that a thorough familiarity on the part of the interviewer with the purpose of interview is essential not only for self-education but also to know whether the informants actually get the meaning of the questions, and also to interpret their answers when they have been secured.

The type of interview and the kind of information sought will determine whether a formal schedule can be used in the interview. Another important factor whether or not an interviewer should write everything in the presence of informants. It has been seen from the experiences of the field workers to memorize both questions and answers so that writing can be dispensed with during the interview. The writing down of answers in the presence of informants may make them suspicious about the use of information, on the other hand, reliance on memory is subject to the possibility of inaccurate recollection of both questions and their answers. Thus to me this problem should be left to the investigator with the suggestion mentioned above.

APPROACH TO THE INTERVIEW

The first step under this should be to establish the rapport by winning the confidence of the informants. There are a great variety of devices for this purpose. Ordinarily the interviewer will first introduce himself and refer to the local or other backing of the investigation after friendly greetings are exchanged in accordance with the cultural pattern of the interviewee. The purpose of the interview should be explained then. Accordingly, it is well to emphasize that information alone is sought, that the informant's help is sought as an act of generosity and lastly that the information will be treated as confidential, and will never be used to the informant's disadvantage.

The Interview Proper

When all these are over the interviewer has to lead the interview. It has been reported by the experienced field workers that it is well to start with easy conventional questions which no one objects to, or with questions of special interest to the informant. To get the informant to talk at all, on any subject, is the first objective here. Once he has started answering questions, he will answer many inquiries. This stage of interview which is technically known as the "interview proper" has to be handled very cautiously both for academic gain and physical security. Therefore an interviewer should keep the following points in mind by way of prescription :

(1) Show interest in everything the interviewee wishes to tell you.
(2) Be at ease with the interviewee, thus helping him to be at ease with you.
(3) Act as to give the interviewee the feeling that you consider his situation seriously.
(4) Allow sufficient time to learn the facts which will enable you to understand the problems involved.
(5) View all the problems confronting the interviewee from his point of view.
(6) Meet the interviewee on his own terms.
(7) Gain, keep and deserve the interviewee's confidence.
(8) Gain sympathetic insight into problems confronting the interviewee.
(9) Assign social status to the interviewee
(10) Ask only questions which you would not resent answering about yourself under similar circumstances.
(11) Ask questions which can easily be understood.
(12) Ask questions which do not employ their answers.
(13) In asking questions be frank and straight forward rather than cunning.
(14) Avoid extracting information against the will or knowledge of interviewee.

(15) Allow the interviewee to tell his history in his own way and to take his time in telling it.

(16) Allow the interviewee to think for himself and give him time for it.

(17) Listen with interest the account of interviewee thought that may not be useful for you,

Though there are various types of interviews, the structured, unstructured, individual and group interviews are the main kinds popularly known to the social scientist.

In the structural interview a complete schedule may be used. The interviewer is asked to get the answer to those questions. This is why that this is also known as controlled, guided or directed interview. Contrary to this is the unstructured interview, which is also known an uncontrolled, unguided or undirected is useful for gaining the confidence of the informants in the beginning. It is generally held in the form of a free discussion. In individual interview only one individual is interviewed at a time, to collect confidential and personal information. Whereas whenever two or more informants are interviewed at a particular time that makes a group interview. This interview is useful for collecting more information for group life and has the advantage of being less expensive and less time consuming.

Genealogical Table Method

The genealogical table method has proved of such value in anthropological research that it is now taken as essential technique in cultural investigation. It is commonly found that genealogical knowledge plays an important part among non-literate people.

Thus genealogical method is used in tracing back the ancestry for several generations with the help of standardised symbols and charts. It is clear that this method has a functional value, because genealogical data are used in the regulation of marriage, inheritance of property, succession to chieftainship etc.

Regarding the Uses of Genealogy

In a small community it is often possible to take the genealogies of all the individuals of one particular village, and this census can thus form the basis not only of sociological work but also for investigation on population and migration.

The study of kinship, so necessary to social anthropology, can only be properly undertaken by means of genealogical method. On the occasions of ceremonies connected with birth, marriage and death genealogical data concerning the principal participants are invaluable.

In addition to these, popular anthropological research methods relevant for working with the tribes, in the wake of the modern inter-disciplinary approach, several methods of other social sciences particularly of sociology, psychology and statistics have widely been used by the anthropologists. Thus in anthropological researches various types of Questionnaire, Schedule, Case Study, Life history and Statistical Methods are very commonly used.

SUGGESTED READINGS

Goode and, Hatt, P.F., *Methods in Social Research*, McGraw Hill Book (W.G.) 1952.

Lundberg, A.G., *Social Research*, Longmans Green & Co., 1942.

Palmer, Vivien, *Field Studies in Sociology*, University of Chicago Press, 1928.

Paul, Benjamin D., "Interviewing Techniques and Field Relationships" in A.L. Kreber (Ed) *Anthropology To day*, University of Chicago Press, 1953.

Young, P.V., *Scientific Social Surveys and Research*, Prentice Hall, Inc. U.S.A., 1966.

TWENTY FIVE

K. N. Sahay

METHODS OF WORKING WITH TRIBALS

MY PAPER deals with general considerations mainly relating to the methods of working among the tribals, which are uppermost in my mind and it will give you a feel as to how anthropologists work in a field in tribal areas. The observations made in this paper are equally relevant for a researcher, a development worker or a tribal administrator. While doing it, illustrations have been given from my own field-work, mainly from among the tribals of Chotanagpur. While going through this paper, you may sometimes feel that what I am saying just common sense. But I would like to submit that while working in a field situation, specially with tribals, it is these small things which matter most and play a decisive role in making your mission a successful one.

What Constitutes a Tribe

When we talk about the tribals, it will not be out of place to begin with delineating the concept of a tribe. There exists a controversy as regards what really constitutes a tribe. But by and large, in its widest anthropological sense, the term denotes those traditional beliefs, arts and practices which an individual acquires as the member of a particular society. It is a homogeneous ethnic group with a specific sense of identity based on common language and culture. It is large enough to be a viable group and small enough to be mobilised for common action (Beteille, 1977: 7-14). It also implies a primitive level of technology, absence of the system of writing and lack of a highly specialised division of labour. It is generally associated with a definite territory and has a well-defined political boundary. A tribe is a group usually isolated in jungles and hills which develop in them a world view suited to that ecology. As such, it is cut off from the main stream of Indian life and to use the anthropological jargon. possesses 'local' or 'little' traditions which are generally parochial in nature.

Tribals vis-a-vis Hindus

It is to be noted that there is a difference in the manner tribals and Hindus are to be approached or adjusted with. On the other hand, these people also adjust with a stranger in two different ways. The Hindus have a caste oriented society and if you go to work among them, they would be curious to know about your caste affiliation at the earliest opportunity. And as soon they know it, you are 'socially placed' and can get more easily accommodated in the initial contact situation, which is, of course, not without significance. Besides, the Hindu community operates and is integrated in the regional and countrywide cultural milieu and as such, they can understand the purpose of your visit much better than the tribals.

As regards the tribals, they operate in a different demographic and cultural set-up, as a result of which the situation of initial contact with them is more likely to be marked by a sense of 'otherness', 'suspicion' and 'distrust'. Moreover, some tribal communities may also have historical experience of exploitation at the hands of Hindus. Against this background, any initial lapse or lack of tact on the part of the worker or investigation makes the situation all the more critical. Subsequently what one should expect from the field, largely depends as to how tactfully the worker has behaved in the initial contact situation.

Winning the Confidence in Initial Contact Situation

The situation given above, calls for winning the confidence of the people at the initial stage. The worker must be able to convince the tribals that he is a person having genuine desire to know way of their life or for their betterment whatever may be the case, and not to do any harm to the community.

But it is not so easy and requires not only skill and patience; but also a background of other's culture and appreciation of their social and cultural values. Here I am reminded of an incident which took place while working among the Malpaharia of Santhal Parganas in 1955. The Santhal Paharia Seva Mandal had set up a number of Kalyan Kendras which besides other things, imparted education to tribal children. In a village where I was putting up in one such Kalyan Kendras, I found that there were two teachers from non-tribal areas and the only thing they did for the whole day was to curse their fate for having been thrown among the 'wild people' and say all abnoxious things to the tribals. It resulted into a strained relation between the villagers and these welfare workers and thus the very purpose for which these workers were there was defeated.

What is desirable, is a thorough human approach and a philanthropic keenness to help the people. Human mind is highly sensitive and no amount of wit and sophistication on the part of investigator would convince or impress the tribals or win their heart unless the former feels a genuine love and sympathy for the people and it gets translated into real behaviour towards them. A worker with genuine love for the tribals would treat them kindly like his own people and behave with them at the level of equality.

Preparations before Leaving for Field

Proper preparation need to be made before a worker leaves for the field. Library-work is one of them. While doing library-work one has to keep in mind different categories of literature. Firstly, there is literature available on the tribal community one is going to study. Secondly, there is literature on development work, already done among the people of that area. The third category may relate to similar developmental works implemented in other communities elsewhere. Still another type of literature relates to the philosophy of change, processes of change, motivations and theoretical implications of change which will acquaint you with the effects or reactions of change you are going to introduce as a development worker or how it can be controlled so that it does not produce any adverse effect on other aspects of life of the people. Besides, a worker should also know about the various field-methods and techniques used by anthropologists in their fieldwork.

Another kind of preparation, and still more important, is the 'mental preparation' to face any kind of field situation whether good or worst. In fact, the worker is concerned with two different worlds; one of his own and the other of the tribals he is going to work with. He has to be guided by two sets of norms, values and ethics and is supposed to assume a double standard by way of mental preparation for the field. To make it more explicit, an example may be cited. The norm of our own society does not permit us to go uninvited to a wedding place, a feast, or any function of a family. But while in field, you have to do it for the sake of work.

I am reminded of an incident in this connection. When I was working in Khapiya, an Oraon village, I was informed that a *Hariari Pooja* was going to take place in a family. I was deliberately not informed as they did not want a stranger like me to meddle in their private affairs and obtain information. But as soon I came to know of it, I went to that house uninvited, and sat talking with reluctant people while they were making preparations for the *Pooja*. After some time, when the necessary preparations were made, they began to go inside the house where the *Pooja* was to be performed. I also followed them, but I was sharply opposed by the people saying that they did not allow a stranger at the place of *Pooja*. I felt thoroughly embarrassed and insulted at the behaviour of the people, but there was no way out than to swallow this dose of 'insult'. I did not allow my sentiments to be obsessed by this thought as it would have seriously affected my relations with the people and interfered with my field work. I took it that, while in the field I was nothing more than a field-worker and I must not allow the values and sentiments of my own culture to have a sway on me. Similarly, whatsoever higher may be your social status, in the field situation, you must forget it, and allow the tribals to treat you at par with them. You have to 'step down' and find pleasure in attuning yourself with the tribals' manners and etiquette which at times may seem to be just opposed to that of yours. This is the index of a successful field work.

Still another type of mental preparation may be in relation to accommodation. The tribals, usually do not have enough space of living and if you want accommodation in their village, they will not be able to provide it so easily. A field worker has very often to share his accommodation in a cattleshed or such other impoverished, dirty or exposed portions of a house.

Creating the Rapport

For effective and fruitful field-work, it is necessary that the worker should be 'accepted' by the village community; because what we aim at is not just 'information'', but 'reliable and verifiable information'. Unless the worker is accepted by the community, no real information would be forthcoming and there may be just rationalised and misleading answers. I am fond of telling my students that the role of an anthropologist and field-worker is that of an artist. Just as an artist makes a sketch from life and his merit depends on how exactly he draws the sketch to tally with the original model; if the nose is long or the eyes small, he also reproduces it exactly with meticulous care. He has no subjective choice to make and his line-work is precisely and strictly guided by the contours and other bodily features of the model. Likewise, a field worker also has no subjective choice to make, he depicts the situation *exactly* as it exists and to be exact and objective, first, the confidence of the people must be gained and their cooperation sought.

What is suggested here is that the worker should devote a reasonable time in winning confidence of the people and creating rapport. For this, it is necessary that the worker should initially mix up with as many persons, and with as many different types as possible, and explain his real purpose of visit and assure them that no harm would be done to them. It is also advisable not to take out pen and paper in the initial stage of contact, this may make the people suspicious. After the initial understanding has been reached, the best field method to begin with is village census for which you have to move from door to door and contact every family of the village.

It should be noted that while making rapport, it is necessary first to contact key persons of the village who are holding any traditional office, like secular and religious head of the village, or are otherwise important. Violation of this rule may sometimes lead a worker into trouble. I am reminded of my own experience at village Khapiya when I made this mistake. I made the first visit to that village with a letter of introduction from a teacher of that area in the name of an Oraon named Gere Lakra. I stayed at his house for two or three days after which I went to Ranchi for a brief period. When I went back to the village, things had changed in an alarming manner. As soon I had entered Gari's house, he told me point blank that I should immediately vacate the house. It was evident that after I had left, the villagers had called a *Panchayat* meeting and accused Gere Lakra for sheltering a stranger who may be a "thief or robber" and "harm the villagers". The villagers felt angry as I had not consulted their village secular or religious heads. The Panchayat further said that this stranger should be immediately turned out of his house, otherwise, in case any untoward thing took place in the village, the entire responsibility would lie on the head of Gere. It was with great difficulty that the problem could be solved, but I had to leave his house accordingly. This is one precaution, but still the problem remains and the tribals may brand you as a Government official who is there to exploit them (as goes the popular image of Government officials) or impose any exorbitant taxation. The people may also have all types of wild conjectures about you and if you are working in a minority religious group, it is not unlikely that they associate you with some anti-religious organisation. While working at Shefali, a Catholic village in 1957, I had a similar experience. Though I tried my best to convince them of my academic purpose of visit, the villagers were highly suspicious of my bona fides and had a lingering suspicious that I was connected with some anti-Christian organisation and had come in their midst to dissociate them from their Christian faith. It was not without a background and could be known that only a few years back in 1954, the Madhya Pradesh Government had set up a Niyogi Committee to look into the allegations of fraudulent means used by Christian missionaries in the conversion of local tribals. The Catholic tribals of Shefali associated me with this type of organisation and considered my presence as dangerous to their faith.

After the initial contact is established, it is useful to make participant observations. It is an important field-method in Anthropology and I not only lived in the midst of the people, but danced, ate, drank, attended their Church together and participated in their life cycle ceremonies and a series of their agricultural or other activities with a view to establish a sense of unity. It could yield rich harvest. However, this made some of them suspect that I was from the C.I.D. and had gone there to collect some secret information. Soon, the news spread in the whole area about my presence and "suspicious activities" in the village. It enraged many people from other villages too and they tried to instigate the people of Shefali to 'kick me out' of the village. In case, the latter expressed their reluctance to do it, they volunteered to help the villagers in throwing me out of Shefali. At village Gulni in Nawadah District, I had to face a similar problem when the villagers took me to be a Khasfia (C.I.D.) of the Government, having come there to find the truth behind a Hindu-Muslim quarrel which had recently taken place in the village. The whole village was initially worried and perturbed on this account and the villagers had a very cold attitude towards me. Still some other villagers mistook my door to door census for some form of excessive taxation which the Government might impose.

Initially I had to face a similar problem at village Sanwaria where some villagers suspected that I was a thief having come to steal valuables and information from among them. One of the villagers even stealthily took away my field-notes to an educated person of other neighbouring village to get them checked to see if they contained any objectionable information about the villagers. Some of the villagers believed that I had come to the village to acquire their fields for an agricultural farm as there existed such a farm in the neighbouring area for which fields were actually acquired from local tribals.

Any way, in spite of all these initial suspicions, I mixed with a maximum number of villagers and patiently went on explaining to them the genuine purpose of my visit, and that, no harm would be done to them. In due course, I was gradually accepted in the village community and the people started developing an attachment to me and took my word, though a few of them remained suspicious till the end. I had taken with me some field-reports and monographs on tribals containing pictures and I frequently showed them to the people saying that I was going to prepare a similar report on them. This convinced the tribals. It was interesting that some of those who were uncooperative and hostile in the beginning and had created hurdles, turned out to be the best and trusted informants. At the Catholic village, some of the informants even went to the extent of confessing that they had not ever seen such a generous person like me who mixed with every section of the people, whether children, young, or old, men or women, poor or well-off, with equal love and attention and my behaviour reminded them of Catholic fathers (Priests).

Sometimes while working in a faction-ridden village, people have a natural tendency to suspect that the worker might side with one of the groups. Even though he assures them of his neutrality, people may not take his words easily unless it is translated into actual behaviour towards the people. I had to face this problem while working in village Sevra of Agra district. In the beginning, they did not trust me and tried to avoid me. But when I met everybody with the same care and attention, and when they thought that I was dependable impartial and a responsible person having gone there purely with an academic interest, they poured out their heart to me.

While working with tribals, I always put up in the midst of the villagers; I preferred to stay in their out-houses and take my food with one of the families as a paying guest. It gives me an opportunity to be close to the people and observe their life intimately. However, it has its own pitfalls. While doing so, the worker must be very cautious as he is also subjecting himself to a closer scrutiny of the villagers and the slightest mistake on his part may affect his field-work. In case one is accompanied by a servant, it needs all the more care, for a servant may not be cautious or conversant with the norms and values to be observed in a field situation like you and he is most likely to commit a mistake or act irresponsibly which may spoil the field and make the people hostile. What is suggested here is to engage a local boy from the field which will also help in the creation of rapport.

While in the field, the worker has to keep a track on every thing that happens in the village. Unless one remains alert, he will miss many things. A good worker knows the things in the offing and he must get prior or first information of the events and incidents taking place in the village whether it is a Church service, or a public or private ceremony, a meeting, a life-cycle ceremony, a quarrel, a theft, hunting and fishing expeditions, dance or drink, cow-slaughter or the arrival of a guest in the village. Unless it is so, it would be difficult to cover these events and make personal observations or collect the first hand authentic data. While doing my own field work, at first, people thought that I interfered too much in their affairs and I became a laughing stock, but in course of time they were impressed with my keenness and sincerity and took me to be harmless and at the same time, as something inevitable from which it was difficult to escape. I could thus win their sympathy and affection.

Sometimes, the worker has to become so close to the people that it is not inadvisable to use some local classificatory kin-terms like *Bhabhi* (sister-in-law), *Kaki* (aunt) and *Ayo* (mother) provided it does not make this 'relationship' so awkward as to hinder the informants from passing on desired information to the worker. One has also to distribute tobacco, cigarettes, or lemon-drops to children to please the informants or make them informal. It is often the experience of an anthropologist that when he goes to the field, he goes like a stranger and suspect, but when he comes back, tears roll down the eyes of many villagers as if they were parting with their own kin. It is also an index of a good field-worker.

However, it should be borne in mind that one must not go beyond a particular limit while creating friendship as it may sometimes lead to complications. Cases have been found when some investigators worked among the tribals and identified themselves so closely with them that their sentimental attachment with informants brought subjective elements in their study, or even they refused to publish their work after completing the field-work.

Culture Shock

A worker, coming from a culture where cultural values, norms or practices are markedly different or diametrically opposed from that of the people he is studying, produces a shock in him known as culture shock. While working with tribals, one has to make oneself mentally prepared to bear such cultural shocks, if any, otherwise it will make one biased which will consequently affect rapport-making and interpretation of facts.

When I first visited a Christian village, it was the time of Easter and the tribals were heavily drunk. They would visit each others' homes with social calls and were served with drink. On my arrival in a family I was also served with rice-beverages and they did now allow me to go unless I accepted it from their hand and sipped something out of the leaf-cup offered to me. Initially, it was a great ordeal for me to taste the beverage as I could not stand even its smell, but I had to bear the situation for the sake of field work.

On the very first day of my stay in the village when I was taking a meal with a Christian family I overheard the head of the family talking with somebody that he also had been to the neighbouring forest to bring beef where a calf was killed by a tiger and he would enjoy a rich meal that night. Even though I had made myself mentally prepared for all adverse circumstances in the field, the disclosure of this fact was shocking as it had never touched my imagination. Immediately, it occurred to me that the tribals do not have any sense of pollution like Hindus and though beef was not served to me, the meal I was taking, might have been cooked in the same pot in which the beef was cooked. It filled in me a sense of aversion for the food served there and I was emotionally upset. For days together I remained upset and had to pass through a real ordeal when I went there for meals. I did not, however, disclose my reaction to anybody. In due course, I got adjusted to the situation so much so that on several festive occasions I witnessed cows or bullocks being slaughtered or cooked by Christians and myself sitting there talking with the people.

The Oraon are one of the few tribes of Chotanagpur who have been known for *Ottanga* (head-hunting). Still, it is believably practised in some pockets of Chotanagpur. Once while working in village Khapia, I had an encounter with a person who was notorious in that area for *Ottanga*, and it was my sheer wit and tact which could frighten him and save me from his clutches (Sahay, 1978 : 98-99).

In this connection I am also reminded of my 'beatings' which I got at the hands of women at the occasion of *Holi* in a Hindu village called Sevra in Agra district. There it is customary for the women folk to beat the male members with sticks and the males are supposed only to run away. Sometimes the beatings are so severe that it leads to injuries and even hospitalisation.

Ideal Field-Worker and Professional Ethics

In a field situation, the tribals have a general tendency to think that the worker is in a position to solve many of their problems and help them materially. It creates a strong tendency in some workers to tell a lie and give them false hopes just to secure their cooperation. Some category of workers, specially many foreigners, go to the field in a hurry and want to squeeze the maximum information within a short time by distributing money, gifts, or giving other material favours. Some other workers are known to be squeezing benefits from the tribals by impersonating themselves as Government official and inspiring fear, or exerting some sort of pressure. But all these go against the professional ethics of an ideal field-worker, as an ideal worker is not only he who himself collects rich data, but also sets a good example as a field-worker and sees to it that when others visit the field next time, their work also gets much facilitated. This is an ethical consideration which, if ignored, may spoil the field and make things difficult for other workers.

In this connection, I am reminded of my own experience at the Christian village Shefali. During the course of my stay there, I was so closely associated with and attached to the people, that some of them, mostly women had begun to think that 'I was getting the true light of Jesus Christ in my heart and would soon embrace their religion'. A few of them also gave indirect hints that in case I accepted Christianity, I should give first preference to their daughters if I contemplated marriage. However, I thought that it would be against the field-ethics to create a deliberate confusion on this point and I told them frankly and repeatedly that in spite of the fact that I loved many things in Christianity, I had no intention of accepting Christianity in the near future.

The tribals have a free society where sexual segregation does not exist, and by and large, they are known to be giving tacit approval to pre-marital sexual romance. A worker must be very cautious not to feel attracted by this, as besides going against the professional ethics, it will spoil the field and expose the worker to a mortal danger.

Selection of Informants

All that a person says in the field, must not be taken on its face value unless it is cross checked from three, four or more informants. Selection of informants must be very carefully made as not everybody can be a good informant.

There are certain persons who know the least about a topic on which you want information. If you are working on religion, young men or those who take least interest in it, cannot supply much or be reliable about dates. You will naturally have to ask the religious specialists or those otherwise closely associated with such activities.

There are others who are informed, but they are so biased that they have a tendency to suppress or distort the facts. Still others, cannot narrate a thing in a systematic manner and leave several gaps in their information. They neither listen to you carefully nor are they in a position to understand exactly what sort of information you want; they just go on taking whether relevant or irrelevant.

There are still some other persons who have a lingering suspicion in their minds regarding the genuineness of your work, or they speak out of fear, or under some sort of pressure. As a result, they give rationalised or misleading answers.

Under the circumstances, what is desirable is to select only such persons as informants, who understand the real purpose of your study, are cooperative and able to grasp exactly what type of, and how much information you want, who are frank and open hearted and who can precisely answer your queries. After the informant has been selected, he should be properly trained so that he could know how systematically and precisely he should answer your queries.

Again, it is necessary that one should prepare four to five such reliable informants for different topics of study and there should be one chief informant in each group who has store of reliable information, and with whom the informations could be finally checked. In a group—interview, however, information gets mutually checked and corrected.

Dearth of Informants

Sometimes a worker is faced with a dearth of informants, specially in the busy agricultural or hunting seasons. But this problem can be solved by making advance engagements or meeting them at their places of work. At times, the informants need to be contacted at odd hours such as early morning, late night or just at mid-day during summer or rainy seasons. and that too, in field, barn, jungle or some other distant places. The worker has no alternative than to interview them wherever they desire. Under the circumstances, the worker should help them in their work while taking the interview, to cause least inconvenience or disturbance to them. (Ibid, 1978 : 92-99).

Approach of Study

Towards the end, a few things may be said in relation to the approach of the study. While working with tribals, as with any other community, one should work with this awareness in mind that culture is a functional whole; different aspects of culture are closely inter-linked, they are integrated and interact upon each other. Unless one works with this awareness, he won't be able to collect relevant date which will reflect this inter-dependance, and which is necessary for a welfare oriented research.

Secondly, the study of value system of a community is of utmost importance in the study of a cultural group, specially when it is connected with development programmes and we think of bringing any type of change in their life. In fact, values are the set of preferences and motivations for certain acts or forms of behaviour which are deeply rooted, and help us to understand and interpret the culture of a given people in its correct perspective.

It is a matter of common knowledge that a number of welfare works undertaken by the Government failed in the beginning. One of the reasons attributed to it was that the Government officials tried to push a programme ignoring the fact that it can have any adverse affect on other aspects of life. A number of resettlement schemes started by the Government among the Maler of Santhal Parganas, Parhaiyas of Palamau and Uthlu Birhors of Bishunpur failed because the officials could not imagine that these tribal communities were living in the forested surroundings from time immemorial and their style of life including their religion, life cycle, rituals, folklore, belief-system and economy, were deeply attuned to that surrounding and in case they were settled in the resettlement colonies it would seriously upset other aspects of life. For instance, these tribals lived in small and impoverished huts with a small door and no windows, but the houses provided by the Government were too big for them with big doors and windows which would allow "easy entry of all types of evil spirits". Such thinking may appear ridiculous to us but it should not be ignored that their life is very much guided by such considerations and real development work must take these aspects into consideration. The tribals were asked to live in resettlement colonies but nobody cared to know how difficult it was for them to bring their gods and deities, or shift their religious shrines to these colonies as they were not transportable commodities. Similarly, their folklores was full of descriptions of jungles, animals and the vegetable world, which will lose their meaning if they came to live in colonies.

Here it would be interesting to cite an example from village Sanvaria, an Oraon village, where a much needed well when constructed by the Gram Panchayat, was completely abandoned as "the Government people did not give them money to perform marriage of the well" without which customarily, they do not drink water from a newly constructed well. It is a pity that a well costing a few thousand rupees could be dug out but the tribals could not be given a small amount for performing this ritual. Any development work must be realistic, practical and take into consideration the total cultural perspective for its effective implementation.

Another point of importance is that while initiating a development work, the insider's view, what we call the "emic approach" in anthropology, must be taken into consideration. We should shun the attitude of parentalism that we know too much about them and their problems. For a balanced approach we shoùld delve deeply into their minds and should know as to how the people would themselves like to solve their problems. In fact, learning and helping should go together.

Again, not only it is enough to have a good intention and want to help the people. It is really important as to *how* you are going to help them. Means and ends both should be viewed as interdependent.

SUGGESTED READINGS

Beteille, Andre, "The Definition of Tribe" *In Tribe, Caste and Religion in India* by Romesh Thapar (ed.), The Macmillan Company of India Limited, Meerut, 1977.

Sahay, K.N., "Culture Change in Tribal Bihar", In *Field Studies on the People of India : Methods and Perspective*, by Surajit Sinha (ed.), Indian Anthropological Society, Calcutta, 1978.

TWENTY SIX

S. N. Ratha

A NOTE ON TRIBAL EDUCATION

LIKE ALL other sectors of socio-economic life, educationally the tribals are at different levels of development. In most areas the literacy is extremely low. Formal education has made very little impact on tribal societies.

Prior to 1950 the Government of India had no direct programme for the education of tribals. With the adoption of the Constitution, the promotion of education of scheduled tribes has become a special responsibility of the central as well as of the state governments.

Since then the problems of the scheduled tribes have received the special consideration of the governments and exclusive developmental programmes were drawn up for their upliftment. In this scheme of development education came to occupy an important position.

In introducing into and promoting formal education in the tribal areas a large number of difficulties have been encountered. The general complaint is that there is large scale wastage at the primary level; and the tribal children, and particularly their parents, are least interested in education. This allegation against the tribal exposes our ignorance about the tribal way of life.

> For a tribal family, to send its grownup girl or boy to school is essentially a matter of economics; and entails dislocation in the traditional pattern of division of labour... many parents can not just afford to send their children to school.
>
> (Elwin 1963 : 84).

Some states tried to attract tribal children to school by providing mid-day meals, clothing, small amounts of pocket money, supply of free reading material. The situation, however, remains the same.

The other chronic difficulty in the way of educational progress of the tribals is the nature of their habitat. Without exception tribal villages are scattered. This entails long travels to attend schools. This acts as a great dissuading factor. For example, a primary school in Arunachal Pradesh caters to the needs of a population of 2,654 (nearly two times the national average) and covers an average area of 247.5 sq. miles (65 times more than the national average). Though the picture in all tribal areas does not seem to be as bad as that prevailing in Arunachal, they are certainly not adequately covered by schools.

The structure and the content of education also pose as dissuading factors in attracting tribal children to school. Sharma has rightly pointed out that "the urban middle class oriented educational system has got superimposed on the entire nation both in terms of its structure and content" (1976 : 2-3). Further, there are tribal areas where more than one agency of different, often, conflicting idealogies compete with each other to entice tribal children. "In one village in Manipur," Elwin wrote in 1963 (p. 89), "there are no fewer than five schools, each run by a different missionary group". The present picture along the foot hills of Arunachal is also much the same. The tribals should not be bewildered and confused by different idealogies. Sometimes violently conflicting social, religious, and political ideas are imposed on them by the schools when they are run by organizations with different ideologies.

The school building itself poses as a distracting factor in most tribal areas. Dilapidated, often roofless structures standing as lone sentinels in the midst of a featureless spot away from the village are often pointed out as schools. Most primary schools in tribal areas are single-teacher-managed whose presence in the school is more an exception than a duty.

The problem of the medium of instruction has been posing a great irritant partly because we have not understood the tribal sentiment for his own language and partly because disintegrative socio-political forces misguide the tribals in certain specific instances. The Arunachal story can again be pointed out as an example of an extreme case of a hesitant policy in this important sector of development.

Until independence Assamese was the medium of instruction at the primary level. Then it was replaced by the local tribal dialects and a large number of text books were prepared. This continued up to 1965. After 1965, as per the recommendations of the Ering committee, "instructions in all the schools of NEFA from the primary stage onwards" had to be imparted "in a recognized language of the country". The Committee also recommended uniform text books but proposed that "special chapters may be added in these text books to deal with the history, geography and the customs of the various tribes inhabiting that area" (Quoted in Roy Burman : 235). English, and one of the national languages, however, was the medium until 1975-76.

It is not clear whether in arriving at this decision the committee had the benefit of consultation with educationists who have the experience of scientific research in such matters.

It may not be out of place here to refer to a UNESCO report on the medium of instruction. It emphatically recommends that even where leaders of the tribal people do not want their language to be the medium of instruction, an attempt should be made to persuade them to change their mind. The language policy in tribal areas needs to be examined from this angle. The problem is pedagogical though a lot of sentiment is also attached to it.

With these operational difficulties in the background, the programmes should be formulated for tribal education. Some of the following points may be useful for popularising education among the tribals.

1. The schooling system in the tribal areas should be brought under one centralized control. A multiple approach to the system of education should be avoided. For all practical purposes schools and their curricula should be placed at par with any other school. In no event should a tribal child be placed in a position where he cannot procure admission in higher standards simply because he had taken his primary

education in a school of a particular type. This confusion must come to an end.

2. Under the traditional tribal set-up a child enters adulthood with confidence. He knows his environment thoroughly well, knows how to construct his own house, cultivate his field, weave his cloth; in short, he acquires all the skills to lead a reasonably comfortable life within the limitations of his culture. The simple skill of reading and writing acquired in an over-formal school is no match for this. We cannot afford to push him back to his environment naked. Therefore, a balance should be struck somewhere to evolve a system of curricula where the tribal school, in addition to being a part of the national scheme, should have a supplementary curriculum adopted to the specific local conditions.

3. The supplementary curriculum should be biased towards crafts and should inculcate a sense of the dignity of labour, qualities of cooperation and social discipline. Certain tribal activities, like agriculture as once suggested by Chattopadhyay (1953), dancing, singing, hunting, tribal games and archery must be allowed to find fullest expression in the extra curricular activities of the school thus providing some continuity of the traditional values and forms of organization (Sachchidananda, 1967).

4. A scheme is to be worked out through which the school children shall be able to link up the school and the teacher with their parents and the tribal activities. The school has to act as a centre of dispersal of simple technical know-how beyond the skills of reading and writing and become an effective agent of social change. This teacher-student-parent continuum should be able to generate a congenial atmosphere, so that the broad purpose of education, which is to enable an average citizen to comprehend the social, political, economic and other processes and forces around him, is fully served.

5. Needless to say this utopian scheme largely depends upon suitably trained and dedicated teachers.

The Dhebar Commission had rightly suggested a separate cadre of teachers for tribal areas with some additional inducements.

In case the idea of a separate cadre of teachers for tribal areas is translated into reality, we would suggest that the training centres for such teachers should be located in tribal areas so that the trainee, along with his classroom lessons, also acquires some knowledge about the tribal way of life of the area.

A bad teacher shall be a liability and may be positively dangerous.

6. Female education has not received the required attention in tribal areas. Illiteracy and ignorance gripping the female folk distort the female-role models and perpetuate ignorance and superstition. As far as possible female teachers may be appointed. If not, the Andhra government's method of employing the wives of the teachers on some honorarium to bring the girls from and reach them to their houses may be tried. The presence of a woman in the school, even if she is not a teacher adds to the confidence of the girls and their parents.

7. All tribal schools should be of the residential type with adequate hostel facilities. This will not only ensure adequate attendance and minimise wastage in education, it will also encourage the tribal children to join if they are saved from travelling long distances to attend schools. School timings and the holiday schedules should be adjusted to meet the local needs. A balance has to be maintained between the needs of education and the needs of the family.

8. The medium of instruction should be the language of the pupil. There seems to be little understanding of what his language means to a tribal. It is to him a vital element in his culture. He feels at home in it, and there is little doubt that by encouraging it, we definitely assist the process of integration. While teaching regional and national languages the most important tribal languages should not be forgotten.

The tribal love for the language can best be illustrated through a case from Mizo Hills. Because of economic constraints and low circulation the local mission stopped printing the Bible in the Lakher dialect. The Lakhers reacted sharply. Their choice was for the language rather than for Christianity.

Further, Article 350A expects every local authority to provide adequate facilities for instruction in the mother tongue at the primary stage. This solemn promise should not be flouted in any case.

9. In the successful formulation of the policy for tribal education text books assume great importance. They should include lessons depicting the life of the tribals, their folk lore, songs, history and the lives of their cultural heroes. These subjects should be woven into ordinary text books as well to enable the non-tribal and tribal people to understand each other. This will add to their regard for each other and give them added confidence that their way of life, history and culture are getting adequate support from other members of the society. (Elwin, ibid : 87).

SUGGESTED READINGS

Chattopadhyay, K.P., "Tribal Education", *Man in India*, Vol. 33, No. 1, 1953, pp. 18

Elwin, V. (ed). A *New Deal for Tribal India*, Government of India, Ministry of Home Affairs, 1963.

National Council of Educational Research and Training *Tribal Education in India*, Publication No. 20; 1969, pp. 187-195.

Roy Burman, B.K., "Demographic and Socio-economic Profiles of the Hill Areas of North East India", 1970, *Census of India*, 1961.

Sachchidananda, "Socio-Economic Aspects of Tribal Education" *Triba Education in India*. NCERT Publication No. 20 pp. 1967, 99-120.

Sharma, B.D., Planning for Educational Development in Tribal Areas, Occasional Papers on Tribal Development, Government of India, Ministry of Home Affairs, 1977.

TWENTY SEVEN

S. M. Shah

EDUCATION FOR THE SCHEDULED CASTES AND SCHEDULED TRIBES

An Evaluation of the Post-Matric Scholarship Scheme

OVER ONE-FIFTH of India's population comprises Scheduled Castes, Scheduled Tribes and other Backward Classes who, by and large, live below the poverty line. The Scheduled Castes, suffer from certain traditional social handicaps, such as, the practice of untouchability. A large majority of tribal population inhabits isolated hilly areas which are often inaccessible. For these reasons, the above sections have not been able to take fuller advantage of the planned socio-economic development of the country.

While the Constitution has prescribed certain special safeguards and protective measures for these classes, the successive Five Year Plans have regarded their amelioration as a major objective of national policy. In addition to allocations under the general sectors of development, a sum of Rs. 1006 crores has been provided in the Revised Draft Sixth Plan (1978-83) for the programmes in the backward classes sector (including special central assistance for the Tribal Sub-Plan). It is noticed that out of the total amount spent under the successive plans in the backward classes sector, over 48 per cent has been spent on the educational schemes.

In recognition of the importance of educational development of these communities in the strategy or their overall integrated development, a substantial amount in the Fifth Five Year Plan has been allocated under the backward classes sector for awarding the Post-Matric Scholarships under a Centrally Sponsored Scheme. Expenditure on this Scheme rose from

Rs. 2 crores during the First Plan period (1955-56) to about Rs. 52 crores during the Fifth Plan period (1969-73). The outlay proposed in the Annual Plan for the year 1980-81 is Rs. 21.25 crores.

The number of scholarships has also been steadily increasing over the years. During 1977-78, nearly 4.17 lakh students had received Post-Matric Scholarships. Of them 3.52 lakh were Scheduled Castes and 65 thousand Scheduled Tribes. It is estimated that there is 10 per cent increase in the number of scholarship holders every year. Based on the figures available for 1976-77, it can be said that there were about 3.87 Scheduled Castes and 1.47 Scheduled Tribes scholarship holders per thousand population—the corresponding expenditure per thousand population being Rs. 1403 and Rs. 539 respectively.

Evaluation Objectives

The study of the Post-Matric Scholarship Scheme was undertaken by the Programme Evaluation Organisation in 1972 at the instance of the Planning Commission in order to evaluate the organisational aspects of the Scheme, to assess the impact on the educational advancement of the Scheduled Castes and Scheduled Tribes and to indicate how the Scheme could be made more effective.

Coverage and Methodology

The study was conducted in 18 States, 31 districts and 175 institutions. Both qualitative and quantitative information were collected from different levels by the field teams. Besides 175 heads of the selected institutions, the sample included 839 beneficiaries of whom 569 were Scheduled Castes and 270 Scheduled Tribes (Annexure I). The number of districts selected in a state varied from one to three. The districts were selected on the basis of (a) number of scholarships awarded per lakh population of the Scheduled Castes and Scheduled Tribes; (b) proportion of the Scheduled Castes and Scheduled Tribes population; and (c) the staff availability of PEO teams. The institutions in the sample districts were selected on the basis of the largest number of scholarship holders for each of the eight selected courses, namely, (i) Arts, (ii) Science, (iii) Commerce, (iv) Medicine, (v) Engineering/Technology/Architecture, (vi) Agriculture and

Animal Husbandry, (vii) Law, and (viii) Teachers' Training and Physical Education. From each of the selected institutions, 10 per cent of the beneficiaries per course were selected at random. The field work for the study was started in April, 1972 and completed in October, 1972. Information on the general programme has been updated.

The following instruments were used for data collection; (i) Guide points for State and District Level Notes; (ii) State and District Level Schedules; (iii) Schedule for Institutions; and (iv) Schedule for Beneficiaries.

Main Findings

Profiles of the Sample Institutions and Beneficiaries

About one-fifth of the sample institutions were located in the rural areas. Half of the institutions were run by the Government and the remaining by the private bodies. Three-fourths of the institutions were coeducational. Over one-third of the institutions were offering general courses, while the rest were offering mostly the professional courses. Majority of them had graduate and post-graduate levels of education and had hostel facilities (Annexure II)

The teachers belonging to the Scheduled Castes and Scheduled Tribes in the selected institutions constituted only a small proportion—the percentage being 1.63 and 0.81 respectively.

Of the total 839 beneficiaries, about two-thirds were the Scheduled Castes and one-third Scheduled Tribes. Over two-fifths of them were studying general courses like the Arts and Science. Majority of the beneficiaries had the rural background with cultivation as the chief means of livelihood of their parents. They, however, represented the lower income group and in age were between 15 to 25 years. About 84 per cent of the beneficiaries were males and 16 per cent were females. Over twenty per cent of the beneficiaries were married (Annexure III).

Inter-State and Inter-Community Variation

Considerable disparity in the rate of expenditure was noticed among the States both for the Scheduled Castes and Scheduled

Tribes. The states which had taken greater advantage of the Scheme were Maharashtra and Gujarat. Madhya Pradesh, Orissa, and Rajasthan however, seemed to have lagged behind.

Inter-state variation in the growth of scholarships was marked. Four States (Andhra Pradesh, Gujarat, Kerala and Maharashtra) accounting for 17.4 per cent of the Scheduled Caste population, claimed one-third of the total scholarships given during the year 1970-71 whereas the states of Orissa, Rajasthan, Himachal Pradesh and Madhya Pradesh (where the Scheduled Caste population account for 19.3 per cent of the total claimed only 6.1 per cent. Even in respect of scholarships for the Scheduled Tribe students, considerable disparity in the progress in the Scheme was noticeable among the States. States in the eastern region, such as, Assam, Meghalaya, Nagaland, Manipur and Tripura, accounting for only 10 per cent of the total population were able to secure 40 per cent of the total number of scholarships, whereas the states of Bihar, Madhya Pradesh, and Orissa accounting for nearly half (49 %) of the total Scheduled Tribe population, claimed less than one-fourth of the total number of scholarships awarded during the year 1970-71.

Rate of Scholarship

In view of the rapid escalation of prices in recent years, the amount provided by way of scholarship was considered inadequate both by the awardees as well as by the heads of educational institutions who were interviewed in the course of this study. Based on this observation, the Scheme was rationalised in September 1974 by upgrading the rates of scholarship, maintenance allowance, book grants, etc.

Enrolment

In the selected institutions, the Scheduled Caste and Scheduled Tribe students constituted about one-eighth of the total students. Only a small percentage of Scheduled Castes and Scheduled Tribes (6.2% and 4%, respectively) were pursuing post-graduate studies. Girls constituted about 10 per cent of the total scholarship holders in the case of Scheduled Castes and about 20 per cent in the case of Scheduled Tribes.

A large proportion of scholarship holders were studying

Arts. Enrolment in the professional courses, such as, medicine, engineering agriculture, etc., as well as in the post-graduate education was very low.

Stagnation and Wastage

Percentage of failures for both Scheduled Castes and Scheduled Tribes was found to be substantial (37.1 and 36.8%, respectively). Majority who passed, secured only a third division or a mere pass. Figures of failure were highest (61.3%) in the case of law and lowest (13.6%) in the case of agriculture.

Some scholarship holders gave up studies as soon as they were able to secure jobs to supplement the meagre income of their families. Other reasons mentioned prominently were: family circumstances, financial difficulties, lack of interest in studies and poor academic performance.

The magnitude of the problem of wastage resulting from stagnation and drop-outs can be gauged from the fact that out of every 100 Scheduled Castes and Scheduled Tribes students joining any one of the courses, only 47 in the case of Scheduled Castes and 52 in the case of Scheduled Tribes appeared in the third year examination. Out of them, only 24 in the case of Scheduled Castes and 39 in the case of Scheduled Tribes could pass the final examination.

Delay in Disbursement

There was a considerable incidence of delay in the sanction and disbursement of scholarships, particularly in the states which had not taken measures to decentralise administrative procedures and delegate authorities at the level of the district.

Lack of Supervision

The absence of proper arrangements for supervision of the Scheme was noticed. Officer-in-Charge of the Scheme, both at the State and district levels, had visited the institutions only rarely. Generally, officers made field visits only on the receipt of complaints.

Lack of Career Planning

There appeared to be no agency for providing any guidance to students belonging to Scheduled Castes and Scheduled Tribes in the choice of courses and career-planning. There was also no link-up between this Scheme and employment opportunities available in different spheres of activities.

Main Suggestions

Based on the findings of the study, the following suggestions emerge :

(1) Steps should be taken for streamlining the procedures currently followed for sanction and disbursement of scholarships and to minimise the procedural delays at all levels. The states which have not so far adopted the Central Government's suggestions to decentralise the administration of the Scheme by delegating greater powers to the district level officers should be persuaded to do so. Ad hoc funds may be placed at the disposal of the heads of the institutions so as to enable them to make some advance payments to the eligible students, pending the receipt of formal sanction.

(2) There is scope for improvement in the administrative arrangements for supervising the operation and performance of the Scheme.

(3) The present practice of awarding scholarships to all the Scheduled Caste and Scheduled Tribe students to pursue any course irrespective of their past academic performance needs to be reviewed. Those reporting poor academic performance should be diverted to the vocational training courses. Some limit should be fixed on the award of the number of proportion of scholarships to the Arts courses.

(4) Steps should be taken to improve the performance of students through tutorials, special coaching schemes, and 'book-banks'. Special grant may be given for this purpose to the institutions.

(5) There is a need to revise the amount of scholarship on the basis of the type of course and the location of the institution (rural, town and city).

(6) The scholarships to Scheduled Castes are awarded subject to the 'means test'. But in practice, almost all

the applicants manage to get the scholarships. There is no arrangement at present to verify the income certificate, even on a sample basis. It seems desirable that a suitable mechanism should be devised for this purpose.

(7) Talented students should be identified district-wise and arrangements made to place them in good residential institutions. For this purpose, a few merit scholarships for each district may be allocated on the basis of Scheduled Caste and Scheduled Tribe population.

(8) Those who undergo vocational or technical training should be assisted to become self-employed. For this purpose, there should be a close link between vocational training, facilities for credit and subsidies, and the employment oriented programmes operating in the rural sector.

(9) Special attention should be given to the states, districts, and caste-groups, where the coverage is not satisfactory, and where glaring disparity in the availability of scholarship is noticeable.

(10) Since the proportion of girls benefited by the Scheme is very small, special incentives may have to be thought of to encourage them to pursue higher education.*

(11) In order to extend the coverage of the Scheme with the existing limited resources, the feasibility of treating a part of the scholarship amount as loan may be considered, particularly in case of those pursuing professional courses or post-graduate education.

Summing Up

It seems that at present this Scheme is being operated with the limited objective of providing economic assistance for pursuing post-matric education. As indicated, there is no link up between this Scheme and the employment opportunities available in different sphere of activities. A career-planning linked with the

*The rate of scholarship for girls has since been raised as compared to the boys by way of incentive to the tune of Rupees 10 to 15 to attract more girls.

award of post-matric scholarships to Scheduled Caste and Scheduled Tribe students may go a long way in this regard. If suitably restructured, this Scheme could not only facilitate self-employment for post-matric scholarship holders, but also help in creating infrastructure for the provision of a variety of services which may assist in the process of modernisation of agriculture and the introduction of improved technologies in various aspects of rural life.

ANNEXURE I

Details of the Sample

State	District*	Number of Institutions**	Number of Beneficiaries		
			Scheduled Castes	Scheduled Tribes	Total
1	2	3	4	5	6
1. Andhra Pradesh	East Godavari	4	25	2	27
	Guntur	6	23	4	27
2. Assam	Kamrup	7	20	24	44
3. Bihar	Patna	6	22	3	25
	Ranchi	8	12	38	50
4. Gujarat	Ahmedabad	7	29	10	39
	Surat	7	16	21	37
5. Haryana	Rohtak	4	11	—	11
6. Himachal Pradesh	Kangra	4	8	7	15
7. Jammu and Kashmir	Jammu	7	18	—	18
8. Karnataka	Mysore	7	23	1	24
	South Kanara	6	8	5	13
9. Kerala	Ernakulam	5	20	11	31
	Trivandrum	8	26	4	30
10. Madhya Pradesh	Gwalior	6	26	2	28
	Raigarh	4	6	21	27
11. Maharashtra	Chandrapur	6	16	7	23
	Nagpur	7	33	16	49
12. Meghalaya	United K & J Hills	6	3	25	28
13. Orissa	Cuttack	5	20	7	27
	Mayurbhanj	1	8	11	19
14. Punjab	Jullundur	6	16	—	16
15. Rajasthan	Alwar	3	14	10	24
	Jaipur	8	23	17	40
16. Tamil Nadu	Madurai	6	28	1	29
	Tiruchirapalli	5	20	1	21
17. Uttar Pradesh	Kanpur	6	35	—	35
	Meerut	7	22	1	23
	Pithoragarh	2	2	7	9
18. West Bengal	Darjeeling	6	14	14	28
	24 Parganas	5	22	—	22
	Total	175	569	270	839

*Selected on the basis of number of scholarships awarded per lakh, proportion of S.Cs/STs population, and availability of PEO teams.

**Selected on the basis of largest number of scholarship holders for each of the courses.

ANNEXURE II

Details of the Sample Institutions

Category	Item	No.	Percentage of the total no. of institutions
1	2	3	4
Year of inception	Before Plan	77	44.0
	First Plan	23	13.1
	Second Plan	27	15.1
	Third Plan	34	19.4
	Annual Plan (1966-69)	11	6.3
	Fourth Plan (1969-70 to 1970-71)	3	1.7
Location	Rural	32	18.3
	Urban	143	81.7
Distance from District Head-quarters	Upto 10 Kms.	118	67.1
	11 to 20 Kms.	10	5.7
	21 to 40 Kms.	12	6.9
	41 to 60 Kms.	15	8.6
	61 Kms. and above	20	11.4
Management Run by	Government	87	49.7
	Private	86	49.1
	Local Body	2	1.1
Type of Institution	For male students	33	18.9
	For female students	6	3.4
	For both male and female students	136	77.7
Distribution of institutions by Scheduled Castes and Scheduled Tribes.	Both Scheduled Caste and Scheduled Tribe students	117	66.8
	Only Scheduled Caste students	54	30.8
	Only Scheduled Tribe students	4	2.3
Type of Courses	General	66	37.7
	Professional	101	57.7
	Mixed	8	4.6
Level of Courses	Graduate	83	47.4
	Postgraduate	4	2.3
	Both Graduate & Post-graduate	60	34.3
	Diploma/Certificate courses	27	15.4
	Others	1	0.6
Hostel facilities	Men	86	49.1
	Women	7	4.0
	Both	53	30.3
	None	29	16.6
Compulsory Residence		32	21.9

ANNEXURE III

Distribution of Sample Beneficiaries

Particulars of sample Beneficiaries	Scheduled Caste No.	%	Scheduled Tribe No.	%
1	2	3	4	5
Types of Courses				
Normal day course	521	91.6	229	84.8
Morning/Evening course	48	8.4	41	15.2
Level of Course				
Under-graduate	86	15.11	47	17.41
Graduate	341	59.93	161	59.63
Post-graduate	58	10.19	23	8.52
Certificate				
Under-graduate	33	5.80	15	5.56
Diploma				
Under-graduate	43	7.56	24	8.89
Post-graduate	8	1.41		
Course Taken up				
Arts	125	21.97	63	23.33
Science	99	17.40	55	20.37
Commerce	75	13.18	32	11.85
Medicine	66	11.60	28	10.37
Engineering	59	10.37	29	10.74
Agriculture	31	5.45	14	5.18
Law	55	9.67	24	8 89
Teachers' Training	59	10.37	25	9.26
Sex				
Male	517	90.86	226	83.70
Female	52	9.14	44	16.30
Age (Years)				
15-20	252	44.29	129	47.78
20-25	241	42 36	117	43.78
25-30	56	9.84	18	6.67
Over 30	20	3.51	6	2.22
Marital Status				
Unmarried	417	73.3	227	84.1
Married	150	26.4	42	15.6
Widow/Widower/Divorced/ Separated	2	0.4	1	0.4
Place of Normal Residence in Rural Area				
Upto 10 kms.	67	11.8	25	9.3
10—15 kms.	154	27.1	60	22.2
Over 50 kms.	169	29.7	108	40.0

ANNEXURE III—contd.

1	2	3	4	5
Place of Normal Residence in Urban Area				
Upto 10 kms.	121	21.3	44	16.3
10-15 kms.	19	3.3	5	1.9
Over 50 kms.	39	6.9	28	10.4
Occupation of Parents/ Guardians				
Cultivation of land	170	29.8	149	55.2
Service in Govt./Private	141	24.8	72	26.6
Agricultural Labour	87	15.3	8	3.0
Artisan/Household Industry/ Traditional Village Service	70	12.3	15	5.6
Agricultural Labour (unskilled)	54	9.5	4	1.5
Trade, Commerce, Transport and Communication	20	5.1	13	4.8
No occupation	12	2.1	6	2.2
Others	6	1.1	3	1.1
Monthly Income of Parents/ Guardians				
No income	15	2.6	6	2.2
Upto Rs. 100	214	37.6	48	17.8
Rs. 100-200	202	35.5	88	32.6
Rs. 200-300	106	18.6	67	24.8
Rs. 300-400	21	3.7	30	11.1
Rs. 400-500	9	1.6	19	7.0
Over Rs. 500	2	0.4	12	4.5

TWENTY EIGHT

R. Gupta

IMPLEMENTATION OF TRIBAL WELFARE PROJECTS

Bidisha A Case Study

THERE ARE about 427 scheduled tribes in India now. The stress is on the word "now"; for in the earlier centuries there must have been a larger number of such tribes. The fact is that such ethnic groups have often merged with the Aryans ever since the latter spilled over into the Indian plains; often they have stopped short of completely losing their identity in the dominant ethnic and cultural situation while becoming a significant part of it. The process has been going on in this country since pre-history; the Harappan culture, archaeological evidence shows, had marks of contact with the merchants of Kulli culture (Ratha : *Caste as a Form of Acculturation* : p. 39). It is not that cultural traffic has entirely been one way; it is easy to note that the incoming cultures have absorbed much the autochthonous cultures. This is inevitable and understandable. In course of their wanderings, the Indo-Aryans for instance adopted much culturally from the life-styles of the other peoples they came in touch with in friendship or war. (In Ratha : p. 41 we come across significant parallels between details of Harappan culture and traits of contemporary Hindu culture; "contemporary" is the word used by Ratha). We cannot hold forth in Vedic culture any particular segment of it as the model; for while on the move or while settling down, the Indo-Aryans have constantly changed culturally through absorption and/or adjustment (Editorial in *Man and Life* Vol. 3, Numbers 3+4).

While such absorption and adjustment have occurred the fact remains that since its intrusion into this sub-continent the Vedic culture has remained dominant in the process. Professor Redfield has described such a situation in his *Peasant Society and Culture.* In this volume he has developed the concept of the great tradition. Many anthropologists have transposed the concept of the great tradition and the lesser tradition to the Indian anthropological scene (for one such attempt please see *Man in India,* Vol 37 No. 2—1957). Many would have preferred "dominant" tradition to "great" tradition—but these are but words. There can be no doubt that the gravitation towards the dominant Vedic culture of the many lesser autochthonic cultures has been pronounced. As it happens, until very recently the dominant culture in the country has been the caste structured Hindu culture. The ethnic groups accepting the Hindu culture have also accepted the place given to them in the hierarchy; even the hostile Islamic culture in pre- and post-partition India has been very much under the influence of caste based Hindu culture (in this connection see Rahim Mondal's illuminating article dealing with the rituals followed by the Muslims of Howrah district in matters of birth and death—*Man and Life,* Vol. 3—p. 80).

In his *Caste in Modern India and Other Essays* Srinivas has described this process as "sanskritisation". Bose has called it "Brahmanisation" in his essay "Hindu Method of Tribal Absorption" (*Culture and Society in India*). Much earlier, in 1925, Dutt referred to the process as "Aryanisation of India". All these words refer to the same social process of absorption of other cultural domains by the hierarchical Hindu culture. The controversy indicated by such differentiation of words is not useful; all these words refer to the same process. As a matter of fact Ratha in his *Caste as a Form of Acculturation* refers to this process of joining the mainstream as "accretion".

II

Our subject is "Implementation of Tribal Welfare Projects". The relevance of your long discussion of the "sanskritisation" may well be questioned. I would like to explain here why it was necessary to dilate on the point before we come to deal with the main matter. It indeed is a fact that the process of change of powerful ethnic groups by the dominant group has been going, as said earlier, since pre-history. But the process has often been cruel and painful. We find at the dawn of Vedic history in India, the autochthons were regarded as enemies; they were "beyond the limits of the Aryan social order (i.e. *avrata*, *apavrata*, and *anyavrata*)". They were the enemies, and the dasas, the slaves. In *Man and Life*, Vol. 3 Numbers 3 and 4, the editorial explains the evolution of the caste system starting from a situation of mild colour bar which we condemn in the present day South African White society (where it is not mild, however). In the more developed phase of the system the caste hierarchy was based on what has been described as the "parallelogram of pollution and purity". (Ibid., p. 5). The new arrivals in the fold, if politically weak or materially poor, as most other ethnic groups were, usually were put to perform functions which were considered impure. The latterly tribal derivatives therefore found themselves a place lower in the hierarchy, with all the associated hardships and disadvantages.

Even in the comparatively recent times the oppressive impact of "sanskritisation" has greatly disturbed scholars and social workers. Verrier Elwin's response to such situations is characteristic. In 1934 in *Modern Review* he pointed to "the appalling poverty, destitution of this heroic and fascinating people . . . . You are equally certain to be awake at night—and for many nights—haunted by the scenes of suffering you have witnessed, and wondering what judgment must be passed on the society that can calmly allow such things to continue from generation to generation . . . . ."

Archer expressed the whole situation in beautiful poetry addressed to Elwin :

Among your burning hills, the lonely jungle
Roars in the summer. The sterile land roasts;
And news comes up like the clouds
While you are active in the needs of peace
Saving the gestures of happy lovers.
The poems vivid as the tiger

Faced with the destruction from the septic plains.
And you with your love and art delay
The crawling agony and the death of tribes.

(*Man and Life*, Vol. 2, Nos. 1 & 2, p. 2)

It therefore follows that laissez faire in the process of "accretion" or "sanskritisation"—call it what you may—is unlikely to benefit the weaker sections of humanity. It calls for social engineering with practical skill and intellectual approach ; the intention is not to oppose the flow towards the mainstream but to help easy fusion and intermingling of streams. I know to say this is to take a value stance. But in India that is the only value stance possible. Over the centuries various ethnical and cultural groups have mixed with and absorbed each other; to take any other value stance is to go against Indian history. Let us recall now that before sanskritisation set in here we had (or probably had) a situation of apartheid. Such situations exist elsewhere in the world at the present moment. What should be the value stance of the anthropologist in such geo-cultural areas ? In a world where distance is being destroyed by communications, human integration of the Indian model is perhaps the best base of a world value stance—a stance which does not rule out diversity.

III

In the areas of anthropological processes we are discussing applied anthropology and action anthropology are the two better known techniques. Naturally the question arises : What is the difference between applied anthropology and action anthropology ? Dr. Sol Tax who coined the appellation "action anthropology" in 1951 has given his answer to the question (Applied Anthropology in India, 1968, p. 35) : "If applied anthropology presupposes a body of scientific knowledge—compendent empirical propositions—developed by theoretical anthropologists and awaiting application to particular situations when we are asked to do so by management, government, administrator, or organisation, then action anthropology is far different. For one thing, the action anthropologist can have no master; he works as a member of the academic community. For another, the action anthropologist realises that his problem is less the application of general propositions than the development and. . . . Classification of goods and the compromising of conflicting ends or values . . . He is and must be theoretical anthropologist, not only in background but in practice . . . . One may characterise action anthropology by saying that the community in which it works is not merely its subject of study but also its object".

Very well put. We, however, do not note any basic clash between applied anthropology and action anthropology. On the other hand we shall not be wrong in saying that action anthropology is a mode (most acceptable to the academician) of applied anthropology. After all these are words. As Sol Tax says earlier in the essay : ". . . .when I was a graduate student the great word was functionalism; people were or weren't functionalists and some who were supposed to be denied it. It turned out of course that the label covered many things. . . ." But, more than words, what may have upset Dr. Tax and his many followers is Nadel's definition ("Essay on Applied Anthropology" by S. F. Nadel, *Encyclopaedia Britannica*, 1968) : "(*Applied Anthropology*) indicated, and in a sense proclaimed, the new interest of social (or cultural) anthropologists in research meant to give practical aid in other bodies controlling public life." Many anthropologists may not agree with this definition. In fact to prevent anthropology from being used as economics is, that is a tool of government, the Society for Applied Anthropology "published in 1951 a carefully worded code of ethics. It appealed to the social conscience of the individual research worker and to his responsibility at all times to uphold the moral tenets of our civilisation." (Nadel). Speaking for myself I have a simple stand : Applied anthropology is action anthropology as Sol Tax defines the latter. There is, however, a small caveat to be entered. Nobody on earth is independent—and nor is the action anthropologist. It is important for him, even in order to follow the path charted by Sol Tax, to cooperate and be cooperated with by the communities, the state and all its organs. Our case study of Bidisha, a pathfinding effort in action anthropology will make it clear.

IV

Sol Tax publicity coined the words "action anthropology" in 1951. He first developed the theme at a symposium in Chicago in 1957 under the auspices of the American Anthropological Association; the argument was published in *Human Organisation*, Volume 17, No. 1 Spring 1958. There is a reason for recording these dates. P. K. Bhowmick on his own, and apparently without the benefit of Sol Tax's guidance. commenced his action anthropology in Bidisha in the district of Midnapore (West Bengal) as early as 1954-55. The details of the development work when we go into them later would show that Bhowmick instinctively followed the lines of action anthropology laid down by Sol Tax. You have in his field work the same framework, the same postulates and almost the same dos and donts that Dr. Tax thought of. But we shall also observe that Bhowmick had much to do with the state and other communities, sometimes with advantage and as often as not.

Before we go further with the case study of Bidisha, we have to learn a little about the Lodhas, the subject and the object of Bhowmick's action anthropology. In the work at Bidisha much of the Hindu caste hierarchy is involved; and apart from the Lodhas, other tribes like the Santals and the Mundas also figured in the action research. But Bhowmick got involved in action largely because of the Lodhas. Here was action anthropology all over again—for Bhowmick was first an academician in this matter; the Lodhas were the subject of his field research and the subsequent doctoral thesis. Hence the need for a close look at them to start with.

The Lodhas of West Bengal are known as one of the ex-criminal tribes, probably around 20,000 now in number. According to Dr. Bhowmick's survey very early in the fifties that of the known criminals of the district, about onet-hird were Lodhas—commonly accused of committing dacoity, burglary, pilferage and theft (in some recent instances in which Lodhas were involved, women have been reported to have been criminally assaulted). Bhowmick has attributed the criminality of this tribe to ecological displacement. He has argued that originally these Lodhas were a forest-dwelling tribe, living by foodgathering and hunting. But as the district got denuded of forest, the Lodhas were displaced in situ, and lost their means of livelihood. There was another aggravating factor. Early during the British administration of Bengal the forest lands were "permanently" farmed out to the zamindars. Therefore, even when the woods were there, the Lodhas living inside as forest dwellers were "trespassers". Anyway after the forests disappeared, the food gathering of this tribe by lifting a chicken or a goat of the more economically developed communities naturally became "anti-social" acts. Another consequent fact contributed to the tribe's criminality. Unskilled as they were in organised cultivation, those of them who migrated east in search of physical labour and food, often took to thievery, unable as they were to compete with more sophisticated ethnic groups for agricultural chores. The various complex situations with which the Lodhas failed to fit have been recorded by Bhowmick in his very short paper on "Ex-Criminal Tribes of India" (*Indian Museum Bulletin*, Vol. VIII, No. 1, 1978).

(1) Economic and territorial displacement, i.e. loss of livelihood which caused loss of self-confidence.

(2) Being not specialised in any profession they could not fit themselves into the existing greater economic structure.

(3) Stigma of criminality lowered their social status and prestige in the society.

(4) Subsequent police oppression, punishment and torture completely loosened their group cohesion and solidarity.

(5) Arrest and confinement in jail completely shattered familial bondage and relations, fostering atomised or individualistic mentality.

(6) Poverty exposed them to exploitation and made them surrender to many undesirable situations.

(7) Selling the stolen properties to others and having very little economic benefit out of it made them think that non-Lodha people were dishonest and tyrannical. This made them more suspicious and revengeful.

(8) Chronic poverty and a low aspiration level retarded the zeal and enthusiasm of these people, and it developed constraints in their culture, making them lazy and lethargic. These made them unresponsive to any sort of change or innovation.

(9) Constant police torture, and torture by the neighbours made them migratory. Thus they began to lose the sense of belonging.

(10) These ultimately made them isolated and retreat into the shell of their old traditions.

Thus circumstanced, the Lodhas, not having rudimentary education, no skill in crafts or arts, no land in their possession, no fixed employment as share-croppers or farm labourers or work-house workers—have developed a peculiar tendency to live far below the poverty line, and indulge in spurts of anti-social activities whenever their hunger provoked them to go against the society and the law of the land. . ."

I myself have had, both in the company of Bhowmick and on my own, opportunities to study this tribe. To what has been quoted from his writings, I would like to add that the Lodhas as a tribe are in a state of transition. One may say that their distribution in space is reflected in time; the Lodhas beyond the Subarnarekha are the archetypal and the acculturation towards the settled society gaining in pace as their eastward habitations are studied. Since the tribe was denotified several attempts have been made to absorb them in the Sanskritic culture around. It will be useful to mention them here :

(1) From the very early fifties the Bharat Sevasrama Monks have worked amongst the Lodhas, trying to educate them in letters as well as in crafts, with some success. They still have a settlement in the Jhargram Sub-division.

(2) At Kukai, in Keshiari Police Station, Prabhas Mridya, a Sarvodaya worker did some successful social work among this tribe.

(3) At Aulgeria, a social work organisation guided by the late Professor Priya Ranjan Sen tried to settle some Lodha families.

(4) But all these were social work—praiseworthy social work—but not action/applied anthropology. Only at Bidisha in the same district Bhowmick started his institutional action anthropology. His role from the very start to this date has been that of an academician; he

has applied his theories and modified his theories in perspective of application. Ordinarily an ethnographist would think of the following action plan for the Lodhas :

(a) Transition to the level of farming economy, agriculture combined with the rearing of livestock.

(b) Simultaneous transition to a cultural level approximating to the level of the communities around.

Bhowmick started more empirically. I remember travelling along with him in my jeep with shovels to cut our path through the villages of Birkanr and Daharpur. In 1955 Bhowmick started at Daharpur a night school. Then with his own money, and funds gathered through charity welfare work such as spinning, weaving of Khadi continued for a few years. In 1959 the Government appeared on the scene. With the State help (amounting to nearly Rs. 60,000 a model colony was started for 39 Lodha families. This meant roughly Rs. 1,500 per family.

But the Government did not have any follow up scheme. The state effort consisted mainly of providing funds for building houses. I noticed this trend in Aulgeria (Thargram) also; massive huts were built for the Lodha families. I questioned such state action in an essay called "Lodhas Revisited" in a 1959 issue of *Man in India*. In Bidisha also, after the houses were built, and land was bought, the State did very little to develop the colony's economy. In other words, the absorption of the Lodhas in farming economy did not take place as speedily as it should have. A cooperative was organised in the very early sixties. Through this cooperative a few cycle-rickshaws was bought. Some pump-sets were acquired, a few cycles, a clock and a sewing machine were purchased. The quantum shows that the State did not have any plan and the purchases were made merely in order to spend for the sake of spending—as required by public financial culture.

Therefore, the Government projects failed everywhere except :

(1) In Dholkat, where the monks were capable of collecting money through charity and were more determined in

such matters than the State's Tribal Welfare Department.

(2) And in Bidisha, where in 1967-68 Dr. Bhowmick liquidated the phoney co-operative assisted by the State, and struck out on his own action anthropology. Hence the need for a rider to Dr. Sol Tax's definition of action anthropology; the State's help is useful, and little can be done without co-operation from the surrounding communities.

V

The Bidisha project from now on developed around culture. Culture cannot be long sustained without economy; but in the absence of anything else a cultural equation with the surrounding castes and tribes can help. When Bhowmick first visited the area "there was not a single literate individual amongst the Lodhas." (P.K. Bhowmick on "Development Schemes as Factors of Social and Economic Changes" in the *Journal of Social Research*, Vol. XI, No. 1, 1968). He continues "In religious and recreational affairs also there are significant trends of change in this particular village (Bidisha). A few Lodhas getting better harvest and agricultural output propitiated the Goddess Lakshmi on Thursday, by blowing conch-shells. . . like any other Hindu. The sacred Basil plant has been planted in most of the courtyards on an altar. Ceremonial propitiation of Hari (Vishnu) has already been started by many and Vaishnavas come to propitiate the Deity on such occasions and consecrated 'good' is distributed by the Lodhas amongst the guests."

A large residential school in the main institution now round which all other phases of action anthropology are to be viewed. In this school there are tribal children to teenagers —Santhal, Oraon and Munda. There are hierarchical Hindus mainly of the lower castes. They read according to the syllabus laid down by the State. They sing Tagore songs, and hymns from the Vedas. They follow an academic life based on physical work.

I myself did not like this style of bringing up the young when I first came close to the institution. I even thought that the name Bidisha was sanskritically pretentious. Tagore music and Vedic hymns, I thought, were pretentious. But I have now no doubt I was wrong. There obviously was a method in what Bhowmick did—a method which we may guess from the following lines he wrote in the essay quoted earlier:

> In psycho-emotional aspect the Lodhas in general had to suffer from a complex which kept them away from the contact of other people. This was due to their suspected criminal propensity. This sort of timidity and tribal shyness forced them to maintain a spirit of isolation. . . But at present they have overcome such a feeling and no longer try to avoid a stranger. . . The Lodha boys in the hostel now participate in many functions, celebrations and cultural activities, and recite poems, sing songs and stage dramas with a feeling of assurance and forwardness.

This is a very important psychological phase in tribal development. The action anthropologists through action and research try and identify for particular ethnic groups particular times of development. What would work for the Lodha may not work for the Santal. No one would argue for forcible conversion through sanskritisation—the drab monotony of complete cultural integrity is to be avoided. In the case of the Santal for instance, while close articulation with the mainstream is desirable, and perhaps inevitable. Yet a little Santal diversity in the Indian unity is probably not merely to be wished—but perhaps can be helped. But the Lodha do not have the strong cultural position which the Santal have. Losing the forests they have lost all—and they have not yet acquired the culture of the hoe and the plough share. The caste-Hindu understands the Santal, with his attitude towards life and merriment. The Lodha to him is not a cultural entity but a social vermin. Hence Bhowmick's undisguised sanskritisation of the Lodha is understood by the other tribes and castes around and goes a long way towards his social acceptability.

The action anthropologist can appreciate the need for different approaches to different ethnic groups only through action research. And a prior hypothesis as to what should be done and should not be done may lead to the kind of error Verrier Elwin committed when he pleaded for his National

Parks. Later he understood his mistake and recanted : "But although in the earlier years I had thought in terms of preserving tribal culture, I came later to think in a less static way. . ."

Structurally there is little difference between apartheid and National Parkism or the principle behind the Amerindian Reservations. Apartheid protects the dominant minority; Reservations protect the weak ethnic groups. But neither is in the development of human race a productive or a positive stage.

VI

Bidisha is not merely a model but should also be a "starter". There should have been many more action research workers, many more Bidishas. Here we may consider the need for periodical evaluation of such projects, and the role of the state. Bhowmick himself published in *Vanyajati* of October 1975 an assessment of case histories of some social work among tribes. I think there should be institutional monitoring. The intention is not to interfere with the work of the action anthropologists. The object of such monitoring will be mainly to observe the development of the projects, and go to the aid of action research when required.

We have observed how the lack of fruitful thinking and action on the part of the State retarded the progress of development work amongst the Lodha. In Bidisha while cultural articulation of the Lodha with the other more sophisticated communities in the neighbourhood may have been established, the lack of economic development in the area may distress many observers. There is also a danger that unless the State immediately comes to the aid of the Bidisha project, its impact on the district wide problem may fade. The problem is not only that the bureaucracy is often ineffective owing to the Government financial culture. The bureaucrats themselves do not appreciate the philosophy of action anthropology. I find no solution of these problems except in employment of anthropologists to help the tribes to progress and play their role in managing national affairs.

TWENTY NINE

Abnindra Narayan Sandhwar

GLIMPSES OF PRIMITIVE ECONOMY AND APPROACHES OF DEVELOPMENT

A Case Study of Tribal Bihar

INDIA IS a land of diversity with more than sixty crores of its people at various levels of development. In its extensive territory from the Himalayas to Indian Ocean and from the Arakan hills to that of the deserts of Rajasthan, it has a number of cultural, ethnic, linguistic and political divisions. If there it the fertile land of the gangetic plain, there are also the almost uninhabited desert areas of Rajasthan and the snow clad Himalayas, densely forested territories and the sparsely populated Sunderban delta.

Demographically India presents a diverse character. In its big cities like Calcutta, Bombay and Madras, one finds thickly populated metropolis, while the hills and forests of north-east and Deccan plateau are inhabited by relatively primitive tribes. On the ethnic, linguistic and cultural groups, the tribal population of India is mainly divided into three major tribal zones or belts namely (1) the north-eastern zone, (2) central zone, and (3) the southern zone. A fourth category consists of scattered tribal pockets i.e. tribes of Andaman and Nicobar islands etc.

The north-eastern tribal zone comprises Kashmir, Himachal Pradesh, the hill districts of the Punjab, Himalayan Tarai region of Uttar Pradesh and Bihar, North Bengal, Nepal, Sikkim, Bhutan, Assam, Mizoram, Arunachal, Tripura, Nagaland and Manipur. Among the important tribes living in this zone are the Gujjari, the Gaddi, the Kinnaur, the Bhotiya, the Khasa, the Tharu, the Lepcha, the Dafla, the

Kuki, the Abar, the Mikir, the Gallong, the Mishimi, the Naga, the Khasi, the Dhongor, the Gora and the Lucai. Almost all of them stick partially to the forest economy.

The central zone begins where the Gangetic plain ends, and it extends up to 16 latitude in the south. It mainly lies in between the rivers Narbada and Godavari. The states of Madhya Pradesh, north-east Maharashtra, northern Andhra, Orissa, south-west Bengal, south Bihar and Mirzapur district of Uttar Pradesh fall under the central tribal belt of India. In this belt we find the three largest tribes of India from their numerical point of view, namely the Bhil, the Gond and the Santal. In addition to these other important tribes are the Munda, the Oraon, the Kharia, the Bhumij, the Chero, the Ho, the Kherwar, the Gond, the Helwa, the Mina etc. Besides, we have some minor tribes like the Birhor, the Korwa, the Maler, the Parahiya, the Asur, the Birjia, the Savara, the Baiga etc.

The third tribal zone of India comprises the entire Peninsular India south of 16 latitude. Ethnically the tribes dwelling in this zone are closer to that of the aborigines of Melanesia and Australia. Among them important tribes of the zone are the Chenchu, the Kadar, the Irulas, the Badega, the Kuresnoba, the Toda, the Kota, the Pulayan etc. who claim themselves as the autochthons of the area. Matriliny, the system of couvade and polyandry are some of the important institutions prevalent among these tribes. Except the Toda, the Badaga, and the Kota of Nilgiri, the economic characters of the tribes are practically the same. They are engaged in hunting and food gathering and migrate from one place to another in search of food.

In this background it would be important to give some glimpses of the primitive economy of the tribes of Bihar, in order to understand the economic problems and their development. Altogether there are 427 tribal communities all over India which constitute 38 million (380,15,162) population according to the 1971 Census. In Bihar there are thirty scheduled tribes and their total population is about 49,32,767.

The word 'tribe' generally epitomizes poverty, malnutrition, neglect, illtreatment and exploitation. Centuries of repression and other historical reasons have been responsible for separation of tribals from the mainstream of our population. Sometimes it becomes difficult for them to break through the barriers which have been created due to several factors specially to some of the isolated and economically backward communities. Several studies have been made. Different types of economic organisation have been identified. Vidyarthi has classified the tribes of Bihar into four main types[1] viz. (1) Forest hunting type, (2) Plain agriculturist type, (3) Simple artisan type, and (4) Hill cultivator type. Out of the 30 tribes in Bihar, there are a number of tribes like the Birhor (3464), the Hill Kharia (10,983), the Parahiya (14,651), the Korwa (18,717) who are hunters and food gatherers ; the Munda (7,23,166), the Santal (18,01,304), The Oraon (876,213), the Ho (5,05,172), the Kherwar (1,39,212), the Kharia (1,27,002) etc. who are plain agriculturist tribes, and are freedom-loving, politically conscious, comparatively economically well off people. Certain sections of these major tribes are in the process of urbanization, industrialisation and exploitation of minerals and some of them are heading towards an industrial style of life. The minor artisan tribes like the Chik Baraik (33,476—traditional weaver), the Karmali (26,908) and the Lohara (1,16,828—traditional ironsmiths), the Mahali (74,452—the traditional basket makers), the Nagesia Kisan (16,903—cattle herder) who are facing problem of disintegration of economic change due to the inroads of mill-made goods, and the operation of other factors in the tribal areas. Besides these there are shifting cultivator tribes like the Maler or Sauria Pahariya (59,047) of Rajmahal hills and the Asur (7,026—who were traditional iron smelters) who till recently combined a forest economy with slash and burn cultivation.

The Birhor is one of the most primitive tribes who are nomadic, hunters, food-gatherers and rope makers. They are found in the districts of Hazaribagh, Giridih and Ranchi of Chotanagpur North and South divisions. There are two types of Birhor i.e. *Uthlu* (who wander in the forest from one place to another in quest of food at short intervals of time) and *Janghi* (who are settled at one place). *Uthlu* Birhor live in a band comprising two families to 20 families. A band is called *Tanda*. They live in a small conical shaped house made of *Sal* or *Mahulain* leaves with a small opening at the bottom, which is called *Kumbha*. During dry season they mainly catch hare. It is their main source of livelihood. Almost all the members of a *Tanda* including male, female and even children above the age group of 10 years leave their camp early in the morning for the forest to collect forest edible products, *chop* fibre (bark of trees and creepers) and hunt game specially hare, and return in the evening to their temporary camp after wandering in the forest throughout the day. They may or may not get anything in their hunt and have to lead a precarious existence. They eat whatever they get. It has been found that they live at least for 2-3 days in a week without food. If they trap hare, they eat rice otherwise they go without food except some of the forest edible products. Besides hunting and food-gathering, they also prepare rope and rope made articles from *chop* fibre collected from forest. They attach a surname *Chopdar* (i.e. Biru Chopdar) perhaps associated with *Chop*. During flowering season they collect honey and sell it in the market. Only recently a few of them have started the practice of agriculture at small scale level (village Chalkari under Bishunegarh block in Hazaribagh district) after joint incentive of th Department of Anthropology and the Government of Bihar. The Birhor are almost on the verge of starvation at many places and can be understood from their daily per capita income which never exceeds 50 paise and caloric food intake is even less than 600 which is extremely low.

The Hill Kharia (Savar or Looha) are another extremely poor tribe who inhabit in the district of Singhbhum. Due to heavy cutting of forest and extraction of forest wealth by the Forest department the Hill Kharia are facing considerable difficulties and feel helpless. A large number of them were brought out of the forest in 1962-63 and were resettled in 8 villages with a view to change their eeonomy. But unfortunately according to our latest survey more than 50 per cent persons of the people either died or they again went to their original place to lead a jungle life. It is revealed from the recent study that they sometimes even eat snake to satisfy their hunger. Some Hill Kharia have become criminals under the desperate economic situation and several of them are in the jails in dacoity cases.

The Korwa are another primitive and least known tribe of Chotanagpur. A detail study has been done by Sandhwar.[2]

They are facing the problem of decreasing population. They are mainly found in the plain and hill areas of Palamau district. There are two types of the Korwa, one is *Dih Korwa* who live in the plain and practise plough cultivation and another is *Pahari* Korwa who live in the hills in the midst of the forest and presently they are basket makers and collect different types of wild edible forest minor products. The Hill Korwa, only about three decades ago were practising shifting cultivation in the *Pat* areas of Palamau district, but due to the ban on the shifting cultivation they had to adopt basket making. It is said that the Korwa were once great hunters and archers. But this skill is also vanishing due to the ban on hunting and operation of the Wild Life Act. The life of the Korwa has become precarious and they are also much under subsistence level. Even those Korwa who are practising agriculture or working as agriculture attached labourers are also poverty-striken due to lack of various agricultural and credit facilities. Many of them had to become bonded labour as they could not repay the loan to several money-lenders. A fresh spell of Christianity was introduced to them (village Nawadih in Chainpur Raj Block in Palamau District) in 1972 and many of them accepted Christianity. It appeared from their talks that proverty was one of the important factors for this conversion to Christianity as they were lured by economic aid, both in cash and kind from the Mission.

Another tribe the Maler or Saurea Paharia who inhabit the isolated hills of Raj Mahal in Santal Pargana practise shifting cultivation which is locally known as *Khallu* cultivation. In this type of cultivation they shift from one place to another in cyclic order. In this type of cultivation, the trees are cut. Big trees are removed and the rest are left there. When they get dried they are burnt and after the rains maize, *marua*, and *rahar* are simply sown in the ashes. After the harvest they leave this place and shift to another patch of land. After 4 or 5 years again they shift to the first one when the plants grow again. In this way they go on shifting from one place to another. The whole operation is associated with several religious performances of rituals.

The Birjia is another minor tribe distributed in hilly parts of Ranchi and Palamau districts of Chotanagpur division.

They are economically very poor and depressed. Previously they were also like the Korwa practising shifting cultivation, but the ban has forced them to adopt agriculture as a source of income. But due to the dearth of fertile land they have to depend mainly on food gathering and labour jobs in the Forest department. But this source of income is also very uncertain. Due to heavy exploitation of the forest they are not getting good quantity of food collection which has added much greater economic hardship to them.

The Parahiya (11,735) another little known and primitive tribe of Chotanagpur are mainly found in the forested track in Latehar Sub-division of Palamau district. One section of the tribe live in mixed Hindu villages practising agriculture whereas another live in isolation in the deep forest. The former section of the Birjia tribe is comparatively better off as they possess some agricultural land or are landless labourer. The latter section of the Birjia who were previously shifting cultivators now lead a miserable life and are getting depopulated. They also like other tribes mainly depend upon food gathering and hunting of small game. Recently they have adopted agriculture on a small scale, but it is insignificant for their livelihood.

The Asur who were a great cultural group endowed with the knowledge of iron smelting and iron tools and implements are also like other tribes today facing an economic crisis. They have adopted agriculture as a source of their livelihood along with iron-smelting and food gathering but it is not enough for their normal livelihood.

The present struggle for existence among these minor and economically backward communities has reached an alarming situation. In spite of more than twentyeight years of Community Development and Tribal Welfare Programmes most of these tribes are living below subsistence level, and are leading a miserable life in isolated parts of their country. It can be well observed that these tribes are becoming poorer and poorer because the real fruit of the welfare programmes is enjoyed by the major and advanced types of tribal and non-tribal communities in those areas. Those tribes whose economy is mainly based upon the forest are perhaps mostly affected due to heavy cutting down of the forest and its exploitation. For example we have the Birhor.[3] Their whole economy has been crippled due to this. Those who are small farmers are also not better due to small holdings, unfertile land, primitive technology, continued failures of the crops for the last couple of years and continued apathy by our plan makers and executors. It has greatly favoured the exploiters and money-lenders.

A new type of exploitation is getting momentum among the tribal communities. Large number of labourers both male and female (Reja) are being sent to different parts of the country by different *Sardars*[4] (Labour contractors). It is reported that they are subjected to various kinds of exploitation including physical torture. Once they go outside, they become helpless and they have to obey their new master. If they disobey or attempt to flee they are in many cases as reported severely beaten or given other type of mental and physical torture. In spite of this the poor people have no alternative except to fall again and again in their trap. A network of this type of organisation is operating even in the interior areas with the help of Mukhias and important persons of the village. Human exploitation and mass suffering have to be curbed at priority level.

Development and its Hazards

The need for tribal development has been well understood and well emphasised at different levels. We are completing twenty-eight years of Community Development and Tribal Welfare Programmes in India. But unfortunately they have failed terribly both at planning and implementation levels. It is reflected in the facts that even to-day the above mentioned economically backward and primitive tribes are facing starvation and some of them are facing even the problem of extinction. In most of the cases programming for them is unrealistic because these do not touch the roots of their problems. Their felt needs are not well understood, their cultural values are ignored and they are not prepared for needed and desired change. In many cases a change without creating proper atmosphere has brought different types of problems and exploitation. For example, a sudden change from barter economy to cash economy has created several new problems and has given an opportunity to exploitors. Most of the people where this type of change has been witnessed, did not know how to even count up to ten. Practically speaking, they could not differentiate between the value of Rs. ten and Rs. ten thousand. This attracted the businessmen and exploitors. From different parts of the country the businessmen brought different types of things for sale. Since in their economy money never played an important role so far for example a *Lungi* whose price could in no case more than Rs. ten was sold for Rs. fifty. For example the Heavy Engineering Corporation, at its inception paid the people a heavy amount as compensation for their land. Unless a favourable atmosphere is created and people are made conscious of accepting new change, no plan can fetch good result.

Unfortunately many good plans have failed at the implementation level, because persons concerned with implementation are generally unsympathetic to them. Some time there are many bottlenecks due to administrative flaws. There are many more hazards in their development which need to be tackled practically for real and fruitful development.

Anthropological Approaches to the Development of the Primitive Tribes

The anthropologists' approach is different from others. They first believe in creating a good rapport with the people living with them, understanding their life and culture, their cultural values, business, sentiments and conservatism, and their core of problems and felt needs. Unless these important aspects of man are well understood and well accounted at the time of planning and implementation it is believed that the programme however good and useful cannot fetch fruitful results. Hence it is essential that before planning, these important factors must be properly understood at total level and then implemented through dedicated and trained persons. Further research and action should continue during entire development programmes. An Action-Research Programme was successfully launched by the Department of Anthropology, Ranchi University, Ranchi among the Birhor of Hazaribagh District.[5]

The isolated and minor tribes have their specific problems. They are in the backwater of development. Most of them are artisan groups depending on the mercy of the dominant agricultural community. They are fruit, root gatherers and hunters enjoying barter economy. They enjoy only *Utakar* land (specially the Parahiya and the Korwa). They are ex-shifting cultivators still to be rehabilitated. They have subsistence economy. To reach them the blessings of the Plan and challenge of development cannot be tackled squarely unless special schemes for primitive tribes in their pockets and isolated areas are launched properly. Unfortunately these minor and isolated tribes could not attract the attention of policy makers and administrators till the launching of the Fifth Five Year Plan. In view of their unique economic, educational and other specific problems, community based schemes should be prepared as the basis of their felt needs and genius.[6]

While planning for development programme specially for such primitive tribes, care should be given that in no case their traditional economy is completely abolished to their detriment. Some important traditional economy should run along with new and advanced type economy till they are in a position to switch completely over to a modern one, or they can modernise their own traditional one. Their traditional skill should be encouraged and modernised. They can be developed and modernised on a pragmatic line.

The service of anthropologists should be taken significantly both at planning and implementation level. Unfortunately anthropologists are ignored by some of the administrators and planners. Of late they have started realising the important role of anthropologists, who are inducted in some study group committees and commissions appointed by the Union Home Ministry, Social Welfare Ministry and the Planning Commission.

Development schemes hitherto sanctioned by the Government by and large failed due to several factors like wrong and unrealistic planning, an apathetic bureaucracy, huge neglect of local and felt needs of the people, ignoring some of their cultural values etc. while working among a few minor tribes like the Korwa, the Maler and the Birhor, I was surprised to see the miserable human suffering, starvation, exploitation, the nauseating condition of health and hygienic and extremely tiring struggle for existence even after thirty years of independence. They need immediate development aids based on a more realistic and practical approach, culture bound and the felt-needs of the people.

REFERENCES

1. L.P. Vidyarthi, "Cultural Types in Tribal Bihar," *Journal of Social Research*, 1 (II) 75-85.
2. A.N., Sandhwar, "The Korwa of Palamau : A Study of their society and economy", *Acta Ethnologica Et Linguistica*, Wein, Austria, 1978.
3. L.P. Vidyarthi, A.N. Sandhwar and A.R.N. Srivastava, "The Birhor of Hazaribagh : An Action Research Study", *Ranchi University Research Journal*, 1979.
4. Refer Doctoral dissertation of Sushma Sahay, "Total Study of Tribal Reja (Women labourer) in and around Ranchi. Under preparation and to be submitted to Ranchi University.
5. A.N. Sandhwar, "Some Aspects of Applied and Action Anthropology with special reference to Bihar," in book *Social Anthropology in India* (ed) A.R.N. Srivastava, Books Today, Delhi, 1978, pp. 202 to 204.
6. L.P. Vidyarthi, "Future of Traditional Primitive Societies: A Strategy for their Development" paper presented in the workshop on the Marginal and Prefarming Tribes of Eastern Central India, Ranchi 1976.

INDEX